The Victorian Countryside

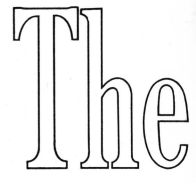

Edited by

G. E. Mingay

Professor of Agrarian History
University of Kent at Canterbury

Routledge & Kegan Paul   London, Boston and Henley

Victorian Countryside

Volume Two

First published in 1981
by Routledge & Kegan Paul Ltd
39 Store Street, London WC1E 7DD,
9 Park Street, Boston, Mass. 02108, USA and
Broadway House, Newtown Road,
Henley-on-Thames, Oxon RG9 1EN
Set in Monophoto Century Schoolbook
and printed in Great Britain by
BAS Printers Limited, Over Wallop, Hampshire
© G. E. Mingay 1981

British Library Cataloguing in Publication Data

Mingay, Gordon E.

The Victorian countryside.
1. Country life—Great Britain—1837-1901
2. Natural history—Great Britain—1837–1901
I. Title
941.08′100973′4   DA667   80-42190

ISBN 0-7100-0734-5 (Vol. 1)
ISBN 0-7100-0735-3 (Vol. 2)
ISBN 0-7100-0736-1 (The set)

Contents

Volume Two

IV Landed Society   365

27   The Landed Aristocracy   D. C. Moore   367

28   The Gentry   D. C. Moore   383

29   The Victorian Country House   Jill Franklin   399

30   The Model Village   Michael Havinden   414

31   Landlords and Tenants   T. W. Beastall   428

32   The Land Agent   Eric Richards   439

33   Landowners and the Rural Community   F. M. L. Thompson   457

34   Country Sports   Raymond Carr   475

Contents

V Labouring Life   489

35   The Workfolk   W. A. Armstrong   491

36   In the Sweat of thy Face: The Labourer and
     Work   Alun Howkins   506

37   Country Children   Pamela Horn   521

38   Country Homes   Enid Gauldie   531

39   The Country School   Roger Sellman   542

40   Country Diet   John Burnett   554

41   Rural Crime and Protest   David Jones   566

42   Labour Organizations   Pamela Horn   580

43   The Rural Poor   Anne Digby   591

44   Leisure   Robert W. Malcolmson   603

45   Rural Culture   Charles Phythian-Adams   616

46   Voices from the Past: Rural Kent at the
     Close of an Era   Michael Winstanley   626

     Bibliography   639

     Index   679

Illustrations

Volume Two

IV   *Between pages 386 and 387*

92 Charles Francis Massingberd-Mundy, D.L., J.P.
93 Colonel de Burton
94 Mrs de Burton in her Victoria
95 Family, servants and dogs at Moated Grange, Somersby
96 William Stone and a water diviner
97 Servants at Hawarden Castle about 1890
98 Servants at Poplar Farm, Hollesley, Suffolk
99 Abberley Hall, Worcestershire
100 Stoke Rochford Hall, Lincolnshire
101 The Hall in Hafodunos House, Denbighshire
102 Possingworth Manor, East Sussex
103 Bestwood Lodge, Nottingham
104 Hemsted House, Kent
105 Merrist Wood, Worplesdon, Surrey
106 Lewins, Crockham Hill, Kent
107 Avon Tyrell, Hampshire
108 Perrycroft, Colwall, Herefordshire
109 Byranston, Dorset

110 Redcourt, Haslemere, Surrey
111 Batsford Park, Gloucestershire
112 Great hall of Haddon Hall, Derbyshire
113 The dining hall at Bilton Grange, Warwickshire
114 The billiard room at Thurland Castle, Lancashire
115 The saloon at Halton House, Buckinghamshire
116 The saloon at Dobroyd Castle, West Yorkshire
117 The great hall at Rhinefeld Lodge, Hampshire
118 The entrance hall at Thurland Castle, Lancashire

Between pages 406 and 407

119 Waddesdon Manor, Buckinghamshire
120 Stoke Rochford Hall, floor plans

Between pages 418 and 419

121 The kitchen at Minley Manor, Hampshire
122 A Victorian fernery
123 Architectural gardening at Shrubland Park, Suffolk
124 Parterres at Trentham Park
125 Terraces and park at Tortworth Court, Gloucestershire
126 East Lockinge, Oxfordshire
127 (a), (b) and (c) Somerleyton, Suffolk
128 The homecoming of Lord and Lady Heneage of Hainton
129 An estate banquet at Coleorton Hall
130 A meet at Culverthorpe, near Sleaford
131 The eighth Earl of Harrington with his hounds
132 Two gentlemen with their 'bag'
133 A shooting party
134 Partridge shooting

V   *Between pages 610 and 611*

135 A downland shepherd
136 Home Farm, Newcastle on Tyne
137 Sheep-shearing at Nookton, County Durham
138 Sheep-shearing near Caistor, Lincolnshire
139 Cutting turnips for winter feed
140 Jack Balding of Swaby, Lincolnshire
141 Harvesting in the fens
142 Tree-felling in South Ormsby Park, Lincolnshire
143 Stooking corn near Spalding, Lincolnshire
144 Hop-picking at Alton, Hampshire

145 Jenny Andrew of Willoughton, Lincolnshire
146 A young labourer from Dartford, Kent
147 Children at Malmesbury, Wiltshire
148 A scene at Hill Wootton, Warwickshire
149 Children in a field gang in the 1860s
150 A village street scene
151 Model cottage plan
152 Shaldon Board School
153 Rules of Pehembury National School, Devon
154 A country arrest
155 Violence between gamekeepers and poachers
156 The armed poacher
157 A meeting during the farm labourers' strike of 1872
158 The banner of the National Agricultural Labourers' Union
159 Delegates of Joseph Arch's Agricultural Labourers' Union signing a petition
160 English Land Restoration League in group discussion on the land question
161 Joseph Arch in 1886
162 Mrs Clay of Swaby, Lincolnshire, with a load of faggots
163 A troop of elephants leads circus caravans into Spalding, Lincolnshire
164 Arrington Almshouse, Cambridgeshire
165 Itinerant Italian musicians
166 The King's Head, Horncastle
167 A village band at Waltham on the Wolds, Leicestershire
168 Rules of Louth Cricket Club
169 The Gainsborough football team in the 1890s
170 Charlie Scholes hiding in his punt
171 Ice-skating at Cowbit Wash
172 Queen Victoria's Diamond Jubilee celebrated outside the Hart Hotel,
     Spilsby, Lincolnshire

IV Landed Society

27   The Landed Aristocracy

D. C. Moore

I

Until some eighty or ninety years ago the aristocracy were the principal English elite, in significant respects the only elite. Individually, they did many things. They had many roles. But as a group they were generally conceived in terms of two roles, that which some of them enjoyed as peers, and that which almost all of them enjoyed as extensive landowners. A half-century earlier the role as landowner had taken precedence over the role as peer. The process of change was extremely important. But it had more to do with the image of the aristocracy than with their real identity, or with their claims to a monopoly of elite status. It was a means of preserving their status in a changing social and political climate. And then, in the context of a further change of climate, a rather sudden differentiation of elites occurred and the aristocracy, whether conceived as landowners or peers, lost their monopoly of elite status.

Undoubtedly in part the loss of this monopoly was the consequence of the declining actual wealth of many landowners, the declining relative wealth of many more. Certain landowners remained very rich, especially those who owned urban land or land under which minerals had been found. But from the late 1870s, when agricultural prices broke—land values had peaked a few years earlier—landowners ceased to comprise the vast majority of very rich men.[1] Increasingly, this category was filled by men who left their money where they made it, in financial and industrial enterprises, who did not invest it in land. In part, their behaviour reflected the declining importance of land as a source of income. Even more, it reflected the declining importance of landed estates as social organizing agencies. Obviously, to some extent landed estates lost their organizing functions because other institutions stole them away. At some critical point in the long-term migrations of Englishmen into the towns, and out of the towns into the suburbs, other institutions became more important as symbols of identity to larger portions of the population. But more was involved than a simple transference of organizing function. It was not so much that urban leaders replaced the rural, or that urban institutions replaced rural institutions. Obviously, for reasons which are related to the growing proportions of the population which resided in the towns and suburbs but which urbanization and suburbanization alone do not adequately explain, major changes were occurring in the structure of authority in the kingdom in the ways in which organizing functions were performed. In many cases, until the 1870s or 1880s, the different categories of influence—political economic, social, religious—had issued from the same or related hands and this in the town as well as in the countryside. The phenomenon not only strengthened the cohesion of the operative networks and communities, it also re-enforced the private authorities of the different elites. But now, in both town and countryside, the networks through which the loyalties of earlier *pays legals* had been channelled were becoming weaker. Also, many men had acquired direct political roles who could not be reached through these networks, who were not members of the relevant communities. Whatever the nature and strength of the operative communities and networks among them—and with the adoption of the secret ballot in 1872 these are effectively hidden—their acquisition of direct political roles greatly accelerated the bureaucratization of authority, both public and private, and the growth of public authority at the cost of private. Together, these developments defined the context in which new and more specialized elites emerged whose powers and status had less to do with personal than with impersonal relationships, and who were legitimized less in terms of their actual or putative roles within one or another network or community than in terms of their wealth alone, their skills, or their actual or putative roles within one or another bureaucracy. Many members of these new elites were hangovers from the old. But their new bases of power were as different from their old as the society and state were different in which these powers were exercised. An era had ended.

II

It had been a long era. For over two hundred years England had been ruled less from Whitehall and Westminster than from a multitude of country houses, less by the Crown and its agents than by individual landowners and their agents, less in officially determined areas of administration than in areas determined by the fortuities of land accumulation, the vicissitudes of family succession, and the vagaries of estate boundaries. The principal components of this system were scarcely legal in the constitutional sense. But the events were which brought it into being. Large landowners acquired their effective powers on the eve of the Civil Wars when the Court of Star Chamber, the Court of High Commission, and the various other organs of royal power were abolished which, previously, had supervised them and restrained them. Their loss of power is not datable in the same way. Like so many other important events in the nineteenth century it had less to do with law than with the kinds of thing which most of those who drafted and enacted the law tried to prevent. To some extent they lost their powers when the state returned to supervise them and restrain them. But to put it thus risks obscuring the ironical or dialectical aspects of the state's return—the degree to which the return was prompted by the concern to perpetuate their powers. Indeed, to put it thus risks attributing to the law that which, for much of the century, the law was designed to avoid, the disintegration of the world the aristocracy had ruled.

Conceived as peers the aristocracy were both few in number and precisely definable. With the exception of those peers of Scotland and Ireland who were not chosen as representatives of their orders, their names are to be found in the lists of members of the House of Lords. Indeed, in many cases it is these who are meant when reference is made to the aristocracy. Apart from the royal dukes, the bishops, and those who were chosen as representatives of the Scottish and Irish peers, they numbered 358 in Victoria's first Parliament, 517 in her last.[2]

Conceived as landowners the aristocracy were far more numerous. But exactly how much more numerous would depend upon how much land an aristocrat-as-landowner had to possess. And to this question no simple answer is possible. But there were two boundaries, in particular, which helped define the aristocrat-as-landowners, the one between them and their poorer neighbours, the other between them and the *nouveaux riches*. This latter boundary could be eroded by time. But not the former. The differences between the life styles and powers it distinguished were far too great. On the one side were those men, sometimes described as gentry, who could only afford the pleasures and activities of the countryside. On the other were those who could also afford the far more expensive pleasures and activities of the London season. Sometimes, an income from land of £10,000 a year was used to distinguish the two groups or, what was often taken as evidence of such an income, an estate of 10,000 acres. If such a measure is used, then in the early 1870s, almost exactly nine hundred men or families would have qualified. The so-called New Domesday, the census of landownership which was taken then, did not include the metropolis. But in the remainder of the kingdom—Scotland and Ireland were included—precisely 901 men or women were listed who had properties of the requisite size.[3] Presumably, wherever their properties were located—and many of them had properties in two, some in all three kingdoms—most of them spent a good deal of their money in England, particularly in London. In this sense they were members of the *English* aristocracy. But of those whose land itself was located in England only 363 would have qualified. Of these, 186 were peers, 58 were baronets, and 177 had no hereditary titles.[4]

Conceived as peers, the functions of the aristocracy were mainly ceremonial and constitutional, or ceremonial and political, and were performed, as a rule, in court, cabinet and House of Lords. Conceived as landowners, their functions were less formal rather than informal, less constitutional than social. Also, as landowners their functions were performed more in the counties in which their estates were located than in the metropolis. As peers, they owed their ranks to the political leaders who had sponsored their promotions and to the kings and queens from whom their patents of nobility derived. In a few cases, those of the barons by writ, they owed their rank to those kings who, in the far distant past, had summoned an ancestor to a Parliament, or to what was subsequently referred to as a Parliament, which summons was later construed into an hereditary right to receive such a summons.[5] As landowners they generally owed their status to the luck or ingenuity of an ancestor who had made his fortune either by state service, commercial success, or marriage with an heiress – which latter was usually the means of enjoying the inherited consequences of someone else's state service or commercial success. But however the fortune was made, until the last quarter of the nineteenth century its investment in rural land was an all but essential step in the social transformation of the fortune-maker and his heirs into members of that aristocracy-as-landowners from which, in the course of a few generations, promotion into the aristocracy-as-peerage might be had. From Victoria's accession until the 1880s the vast majority of new peerages were granted either to existing peers—they were promotions within the peerage—or to members of long-established landed families. Only about an eighth went to persons in neither category. Then a major change occurred: the proportion granted to these persons rose to roughly 40 per cent of the total. Industrialists without land were ennobled. Also a poet, a scientist, a physician, and even an artist.[6] The practice not only reflected the abstraction of formal status and honour from political and social functions; it also reflected a fundamental change in the relationship between landownership and power which, previously, had defined the aristocracy. It was this relationship to which Meredith Townsend, editor of the *Spectator*, implicitly referred in the mid-1860s when he explained:

> The English 'aristocracy' is . . . only another word for the greater owners of
> land. It has little to do with office. . . . Still less . . . with pedigree. . . .
> Historical associations convey influence, but they cling to the property
> rather than the race, and the 'aristocratic element' of the English
> constitution is, in fact, simply the class which owns the soil.[7]

And if, in fact, he was genuinely surprised that the criterion he used to identify the aristocracy excluded all but those who had seats in the House of Lords[8] this would only testify to the completeness of that shift of emphasis and image from the aristocracy-as-peer to the aristocracy-as-landowner which was fairly complete by the time Victoria ascended the throne.

Presumably, this shift was facilitated by those peculiarities of the peerage which distinguished it from most continental nobilities. In most parts of the continent, at least until the end of the eighteenth century, members of the nobility enjoyed significant legal privileges. Also, all legitimate children of a nobleman inherited his noble rank. In these circumstances the size of the nobility grew with the simple growth of population. Endogamy, strongly encouraged by the concern to preserve privileges which marrying out might jeopardize, was not impractical. The nobility comprised a 'class'. But in Britain the peerage were distinguished not by their privileges but their constitutional role. Apart from a seat in the House of Lords the formal legal privileges which a peer enjoyed were insignificant. And their constitutional role also limited their numbers. A given peerage could not be held by more than one person at a time. Thus, whereas on the continent the passing of generations was the means of increasing the size of the nobility, in Britain it could only decrease the number of peers. Indeed, had there been no new creations, in time, the British peerage would have all but disappeared. Most peerages were held by letters patent which specified their modes of descent—as a rule to heirs male of the body legally conceived. When a peer died who had no appropriate heir the peerage simply expired. But his property passed as testamentary settlement provided. Presumably, peers and heirs apparent to peers found their spouses among the daughters of peers rather more often than did their siblings. But average endogamy rates among the children of peers were fairly low. Nor did they rise as the number of peers increased. Rather, they declined. From the early eighteenth century until the mid-nineteenth, roughly a quarter of the sons of peers found their spouses among the daughters of peers. By the end of the nineteenth century the proportion was down to an eighth.[9] In all probability, whether heirs apparent or not, most children of peers found their spouses among the children of aristocrats-as-landowners.[10] And, until the final years of the century, the status of extensive landowner was an all but essential prerequisite for promotion into the peerage. In effect, until then those who comprised the relevant 'class' were the 'greater owners of land'.

But the dynamics of the shift of emphasis from the aristocrat-as-peer to the aristocrat-as-landowner—the dynamics of the change of image—lay elsewhere, not in the recognition of the exigencies of 'class': this was minor. Rather, they lay in the working-out of that crisis of the early 1830s when the two aristocracies, or conceptions of aristocracy, confronted one another. The one was symbolized by that majority of the House of Lords whose titles dated from *after* 1783—Pitt's Peers, they were sometimes called, who identified their interests with the close or rotten boroughs, and who, presumably, would have subscribed to Wellington's description of these boroughs as the 'true protectors of the landed interest'.[11] The other was symbolized by that majority of the House of Lords whose titles dated from *before* 1783, who supported the Reform Bill as a means of abolishing the close or rotten boroughs, and who, presumably, would have regarded themselves as members of that aristocracy whose 'real interests', as Grey put it, were favoured by the Bill.[12] In various respects this crisis was extremely complex. Before it ran its course many alliances and changes of alliance had occurred. But in one respect it was extremely simple. It concerned two rival definitions of 'legitimate' political influence or power, the one essentially legal and constitutional, the other essentially social; the one identified with the aristocracy-as-peers, the other with the aristocracy-as-landowners. By and large, M.P.s were not philosophers. They used descriptions to explain what they meant, not abstractions. Russell's statements are a case in point when he explained the crisis in terms of the differences between the two aristocracies, the one which lived on their estates, 'receiving large incomes, performing important duties, relieving the poor by charity, and evincing private worth and public virtue' the other which '[did not] live among the people, . . . [which knew] nothing of the people, and . . . [which] care[d] nothing for them'. Concerning the one, he said, 'it is not in human nature that they should not possess a great influence upon public opinion'. As for the other, 'the sooner its influence is carried away with the corruption on which it had thriven, the better for the country'.[13]

The reformers could scarcely extirpate that influence which derived from property alone, that which they generally described as 'illegitimate'. But they could abolish the rotten boroughs, the main institutional symbols of this influence. Also, by franchise and boundaries, they could fashion the residual constituencies and the new constituencies so that these would provide more appropriate arenas for the exercise of the so-called 'legitimate' influences of the different local elites, the rural elites especially. In effect, they could adapt the political system to the circumstances of the aristocracy-as-landowners. The point is not unimportant that many of the men who lost powers or influence in the guise of peer retained or acquired them in the guise of landowner. But the change itself was no less real.[14] As Townsend observed some years later, the 'great governing families' had been deprived of their 'legal autocracy' but not their 'influence'.[15]

III

Each of the thirty-one families whose history was related in Townsend's book was represented at least once in the House of Lords, some more than once. But the measure of their continuing influence lay elsewhere. In particular, it lay in their presence in the House of Commons. According to Townsend's calculations, in the session of 1864 the House of Commons contained 110 representatives of these families. And, he went on, if the families of the great Scottish and Irish landowners were added to them it would be found that 'sixty families supply . . . one third of the House.'[16] Townsend's explanation of this was somewhat complex. In part, he attributed it to their wealth and the consequent advantage they enjoyed of being able to launch themselves in politics when they were twenty years younger than their possible rivals. In part, he attributed it to the charisma of their names. But even more significantly he attributed it to the 'instinct of control given to able individuals of all classes . . . [which] they alone have as a class' and, further, to 'the ability . . . [which they had] always displayed . . . to take the lead in all productive enterprise; they reformed agriculture, opened mines, built great harbours, planted forests, cut canals, accepted and profited by the railway system, and built the faubourgs of the great cities'.[17] Clearly, from Townsend's point of view it was important that the influence of the aristocracy be a measure of their personal qualities, not of the roles which institutions allowed them to perform; also, that they be involved in the various activities he specified in direct decision-making capacities, not merely as the owners of the land on which, in consequence of others' decisions, these activities were carried out. But whatever the personal qualities of individuals, institutions were crucial. Also, in most cases it was not as individual decision-makers but either as the employers of such decision-makers or as receivers of rent that they were involved. Aristocrats-as-entrepreneurs were relatively few. They became fewer as the century progressed. But Townsend's explanation is no less important for all that. While it distorts the aristocracy's real role and thus obscures much of the grounds of their continuing influence, it reveals the grounds on which, in his eyes, their continuing influence could be acknowledged.

Until fairly recently little attention has been paid to the ostensible role of the aristocracy in promoting economic growth. Indeed, they have been generally described as the inhibitors of economic growth, not its promoters: Townsend's description was rather unusual. But, essentially, the logic of the usual description was political. Both during the nineteenth century and for some years after, economic growth was generally associated with those political decisions which majorities of the aristocracy, whether conceived as peers or landowners, opposed. In particular, growth was associated with the adoption of free trade, with the repeal of the Corn Laws—and there were few policies which more members of the aristocracy opposed more strenuously. For many years the ultimate failure of their opposition and the dramatic nature of the contemporaneous economic growth seemed to provide a clear answer to the question concerning the aristocracy's general economic role: only when they had been politically beaten did real growth occur. But recently, reflecting the recognition of both the complexities of economic growth in general and the social and cultural components of the contemporary arguments about the Corn Laws, considerable doubt has been cast upon the adequacy of this answer. In consequence, questions concerning the economic role of the aristocracy have been reopened—by some, essentially, as means of studying the process of economic growth in general; by others, essentially, as means of clearing the aristocracy of the charges which previously had seemed proved against them. The logic of the one is direct and obvious. The logic of the other is less direct and less obvious. In fact, the charges derive from those utilitarian values which Townsend implicitly invoked while trying to explain the continuing influence of the aristocracy. But while the substitution of the image of the entrepreneur for that of the semi-feudal magnate may have made it easier for Townsend to acknowledge the continuing influence of the aristocracy, this substitution explains neither their behaviour nor the real sources of their influence.

In the late eighteenth and early nineteenth centuries many landowners and their agents did much to develop their properties directly. The third Duke of Bridgewater and James Brindley played important entrepreneurial roles in developing Bridgewater's Worsley mines and the canal by which his coal could be carried to

Manchester.[18] In the northern coalfield the third Marquess of Londonderry and John Buddle, and the first Earl of Durham and Henry Morton, played analogous roles.[19] And, as Professor Spring observed some years ago, 'from coal it was but a short step to railroads'.[20] In the mid-nineteenth century, on his estates in Barrow, the second Earl of Burlington, later the seventh Duke of Devonshire, was directly involved in a number of mining, railway, and industrial enterprises. On his estates in Eastbourne he was somewhat less directly involved in the building of a seaside resort.[21] In particular, wealth accrued to those families whose properties allowed them to profit most from industrialization, population growth, and the increasing concentration of population in the towns. Over the long term, until the late 1870s, agricultural rents rose—and, in part, for reasons other than those which David Ricardo had described: not only because of the simple growth of population but also because of increments of productivity. But the increased value of agricultural land was as nothing compared with the increased value of urban land or—in consequence of the statute of 1 William III which settled the question that all subsoil minerals with the exception of gold and silver belonged to the surface landowner—the increased value of land under which coal or other minerals were found.[22] Recent studies of local economic growth and recent economic studies of particular estates have shown that early in the nineteenth century the owners and agents of a fair number of estates were actively engaged as entrepreneurs. But these studies have also shown that in most cases the role of entrepreneur was abandoned as the century wore on; the seventh Duke of Devonshire was somewhat exceptional. Often at the loss of considerable actual or potential income, landowners withdrew from the role of entrepreneur to the more familiar role of *rentier*.[23] In this role they could enjoy increments of value which others produced with minimum risk and expense to themselves and minimum jeopardy to their status; also— but the advantages of this were somewhat contingent—with minimum social involvement. The question remains to what extent this tendency left later generations of James Brindleys, John Buddles, and Henry Mortons without clear institutional outlets for their energies and ambitions until the latter years of the century when joint-stock companies became numerous. But this much seems certain: at the middle of the century the assets of many estates which were comparable to those which joint-stock companies later controlled were deflected from direct productive investment. For members of the aristocracy it was essential to be rich: but to be rich in those somewhat special circumstances which rural landownership allowed, those in which wealth was both directly and 'legitimately' convertible into social control. It was this aspect of the matter which Townsend ignored. But this aspect helps to explain their fairly strong preference for their agricultural rather than their non-agricultural properties, the differences of relationship which obtained in these different categories of property, and the changes of relationship by which they tended to distance themselves from their non-agricultural properties while increasing the organizational intimacy of their agricultural properties. And, presumably, this aspect also helps to explain why for so many years the purchase of a landed estate was the symbol of success, and why, again, when the aura of landownership and the real powers which landownership conveyed were somewhat tarnished and curtailed, an increasing proportion of peers was recruited from non-landed families.

In the mid-1860s the Grosvenor family, Marquess of Westminster since 1831, Dukes of Westminster from 1874, were reputed to be the richest family in Europe.[24] There were two foundations to their wealth. The one was property in London which an ancestor had acquired by a fortunate marriage in the late seventeenth century— most of Belgravia, Mayfair, and Pimlico. The other was the building lease. Such a lease was the means by which, ultimately, a lessor could take possession of buildings which a builder had put up at his own cost. During the term, usually between eighty and ninety-nine years, the lessor enjoyed the relatively small ground rents which reflected the value of the land alone. The lessee enjoyed the other and larger rents which reflected the value of the buildings. But when the lease expired the lessor received the rents for the buildings as well.[25] The report in the mid-1860s that the Grosvenors' London properties would be worth £1 million a year when the existing leases fell in was a gross exaggeration.[26] However, while the reality of £250,000 a year[27] sufficed to set the family in an income category of their own, the family were much more affectively involved in their far less valuable properties outside of London. In the 1870s these properties amounted to under 20,000 acres, worth less than £40,000 a year.[28] But they provided nexuses which, apparently, were totally lacking with respect to the others. In 1846 when the future duke came of age, and in 1852 when he was married, there were extensive celebrations on the family's rural estates. But, apparently, none on their London estates. The Cheshire gentry and the various categories of agricultural tenant were appropriately entertained. But, apparently, not the London tenants.[29] To note that different varieties of property gave rise to different varieties of relationship is not to dispel the significance of the consequent differences in behaviour. Rather, it is to explain these differences.

The wealth of the Russell family, Dukes of Bedford since 1694, had a similar basis— building leases and mining leases applied to properties acquired by several marriages and several stints of state service. Their agricultural properties were larger than those of the Grosvenors. But their most valuable properties were located in the centre of London, in Bloomsbury and St Pancras, Covent Garden and St Martin's. In the 1880s, when various building leases fell in, these properties became worth more than £100,000 a year.[30] But a generation earlier the possible anticipation of such income had not deterred the seventh Duke, an enthusiastic agriculturist, from horrifying his agent by suggesting they be sold.[31] Nor did the differences between the incomes from agricultural and mineral exploitation tilt his preference away from the former. It was a source of considerable profit to him that the operators of one of the largest copper mines in the world were his lessees. As was the custom, these paid a fixed minimum rent designed to secure the working of the mine and royalties which varied according to the quantity and value of the minerals raised.[32] But he deplored the speculative fervour which mining encouraged and, as Professor Spring has noted, 'when ironstone was found on his Midland estates, ... [he] refused to allow it to be mined because it would disfigure the countryside'.[33]

In the eighteenth century the Gower family, Marquesses of Stafford from 1785, Dukes of Sutherland from 1833, were directly involved in numerous mining and industrial ventures in Staffordshire and Shropshire. Indeed, the first Marquess, like his brother-in-law, the third Duke of Bridgewater, was a prototypical entrepreneur who might have provided Townsend's model. But from early in the nineteenth century, in the context of mounting problems of trade fluctuation and labour relations and competition with neighbouring producers, his heirs, at considerable loss of actual and potential income, retired to *rentier* roles.[34]

Presumably, the strong preferences which many landowners expressed for their agricultural as compared with their non-agricultural properties were neither testimonies to their dislike of money nor simple bucolic affectations, but measures of their realization that relationships having to do with agricultural property could be the source of power in ways in which relationships having to do with non-agricultural property could never be. Contemporaneous changes of relationship underline the point. While the Gower family and numerous others were substituting leases for direct exploitation of their non-agricultural properties many landowners were reinforcing the nexus which their agricultural properties provided by substituting tenancies-at-will for leases. In part, the merit of a tenancy-at-will was its flexibility. A lease specified the rent to be paid over many years. A tenancy-at-will was available for re-negotiation each year. As such it was more appropriate to the circumstances of significant price fluctuation. But in all probability tenancies-at-will were substituted for leases less for economic than for social reasons. A tenant-at-will was structurally dependent in a way a leaseholder was not: he could be evicted at six months' notice. In one respect the political importance of his precarious status was often exaggerated. Notwithstanding the allegations of various mid-century Radicals, the county voters who qualified as £50 tenants-at-will, the so-called Chandos clause voters, did not manifest any greater political agreement with their landlords than did other categories of county voter. Where such agreement obtained it was manifest by all categories. In effect, such agreement was not the consequence of the specific legal position of the individual tenant-at-will. Rather, it was a measure of the ramifications of the estate itself.[35] However, while wrong on the details of their case, the Radicals were right in the larger context. Within this context leases were symbols of tenant independence, tenancies-at-will of estate cohesion. They expressed that concept of territory implicit in the suggestion, in the early years of the century, that the owner of a great house emblazon the surrounding milestones with his coat of arms.[36] Also they expressed those concepts of status and discipline which were implicit in the description, some years later, of the sheriff, attended by forty or fifty liveried tenants on horseback, all waiting on the road some distance outside the county town for the arrival of the circuit judge. By the nineteenth century there was no longer any real power attached to the office of sheriff. It was almost purely honorary, held for a year by prominent county landowners in succession. Indeed, as the description of the waiting sheriff and his liveried tenants suggests, what made the office worthwhile was the opportunity it provided to display the symbols of personal status. The judge, when he finally arrived, moved from his own to the sheriff's carriage and the troop then proceeded into town, trumpeters going before.[37]

IV

In the mid-1830s, using a variation of Russell's argument about the two sections of the aristocracy, Archibald Alison, the Tory writer, claimed that the aristocracy had brought the reform crisis upon themselves. In part his variation took the form of describing as sequential what Russell described as contemporaneous. 'Formerly,' he declared,

> the great families lived for the greater part of the year upon their estates, and opened their magnificent mansions to all their neighbours; . . . The young men of talent in their vicinity looked to these palaces as the centre of their promotion, . . . and the families in the county were linked to them, not merely by similarity of feeling and principle, but the recollection of happiness, experience, and favour conferred . . . under their roof. It was this mysterious compound of gratitude, admiration, and flattered ambition, which produced the influence of the great families.

But now all this was changed. The aristocracy had cut themselves off from 'their natural supporters and friends in their own counties and vicinity'. Not only did they spend more time in London, they brought their London ways back to the countryside. When the season was over and those rounds of rural entertaining were begun which took them from one great house to another, they still consorted only with themselves. In consequence, they knew 'as little of the people, whose support is necessary to preserve their own estates or honours from the clutches of the Radicals as they . . . [did] of the Kalmucs or Hindoos'. Nor did their neighbours know them 'even . . . by sight'. But, Alison went on, it was not too late for them to restore their influence. Indeed, as he described it, the very 'hatred at the Aristocracy' was a measure of their potential influence once they had mended their ways. For what the hatred expressed was that disappointment and anger which they could readily soothe by abandoning their 'exclusive system', by reopening 'their magnificent mansions to all their neighbours'.[38]

That the aristocracy restored their influence during the middle years of the century is beyond question. Presumably, in part, they did so by restoring the various nexuses which the 'exclusive system' had weakened. But the question cannot be answered whether they restored these nexuses for instrumental reasons of the sort which Alison described, or to accommodate themselves to the circumstances which the first Reform Act created, or because they came to share those corporate and hierarchical values which Russell attributed to that section of the aristocracy which 'evince[d] private worth and public virtue'. And, principally, the question cannot be answered because the three alternatives explain much the same behaviour. Fundamentally, the influence of the aristocracy, like that of the various other nineteenth-century elites, derived from those differentials of personal power and wealth which, until the state intruded to set the limits of contractual agreement, made one man dependent on another. The consequent networks of debt, loyalty, and animosity were the fabric of which the society was woven. They defined obligations and the limits of obligation. They provided the rationalizations of status and the grounds on which both the status and the rationalizations were criticized. And they explain the intimate connection between social relations and political action: in many cases these networks served as mechanisms of electoral recruitment. In their most dramatic form, perhaps, these mechanisms were reflected in the widespread patterns of local electoral agreement in the counties. Such agreement was most apparent on the larger aristocratic estates. But it was not limited to them. Nor were networks of debt and loyalty limited to the countryside. They existed in many boroughs, where their political impact was considerable.[39] During the middle years of the century, however, the clearest networks were those which centred on the larger landed estates; the clearest symbols of status and power were rural. As Sir Gilbert Scott, the architect, explained in the late 1850s while discussing the message which a great house was supposed to convey,

> Wealth must always bring its responsibility, but a landed proprietor is especially in a responsible position. He is the natural head of his parish or district—in which he should be looked up to as the bond of union between the classes. To him the poor man should look up for protection; those in doubt or difficulty for advice; the ill disposed for reproof or punishment; the deserving, of all classes, for consideration and hospitality; and *all* for a dignified, honourable and Christian example. . . . He has been blessed with wealth, and he need not shirk from using it in its proper degree. He has been placed by Providence in a position of authority and dignity, and no false modesty should deter him from expressing this, quietly and gravely, in the character of his house.[40]

Presumably, Scott's argument not only gratified the existing owners of great houses but those others as well who were approaching the point where they might reasonably hope to convert their own enterprise into authority. That such a conversion was considered natural is suggested by the refusal, in 1868, of the tenants on a recently sold mid-Cheshire estate to respond to election canvassers until they had received their new landlord's licence to do so.[41]

Authority was the principal adjunct of wealth and, during the middle years of the century, land was the principal symbol of authority. Presumably it was this rather than any anticipation of significant increments of rent which explains why both the prices of rural land and the numbers of great houses being built or remodelled rose into the early 1870s.[42] And presumably, too, what put a stop to these rising prices and this increased construction and remodelling some years before rents peaked in the late 1870s was the weakening of the conceptual distinction between the towns as seas of social turmoil and the countryside as a haven of calm, the tarnishing of the image of authority and dignity which the aristocracy had managed to preserve—and, it would seem, to preserve not because of their entrepreneurial roles but precisely because so many of them had withdrawn from such roles. The question remains, which was more important: the insubordination of those tenants who protested the 'unfairness' of the usual estate arrangements—those by which their landlords determined the tenants' and the landlords' rights—or that of the agricultural labourers who joined Joseph Arch's National Agricultural Labourers' Union? As an American observed at the time, the rapid spread of unionism in the countryside in the early 1870s was traumatic. For a while it was feared that 'the helots . . . [would] rise'.[43] They did not do so. Indeed, their behaviour was quite moderate. But together with that of the tenants, many of whom were demanding that their landlords' powers of determining rights be transferred to the state, it added an important condition to the message which Scott had described: there was no guarantee that what had been inherited, bought or built as an agency of social control and personal aggrandizement might not turn out to be a bad investment. The relationship between landownership and power was, in fact, contingent.

During the middle years of the century this contingency had been obscured. As long as the ultimate sources of political power were those personal networks of debt and loyalty which explain why open voting remained possible, land was the pre-eminent symbol of authority. The rituals and displays often associated with it were impressive. But these were epiphenomena—the great houses remodelled to accommodate the increased numbers of servants which custom required;[44] the *ancien régime* liveries; the practice of hiring footmen by the size of their calves, which these liveries undoubtedly encouraged;[45] even that exalted concern for precedence which was such an important social and cultural preoccupation.[46] What was crucial were the realities of relationship to which Viscount Royston implicitly referred when he observed in 1868 that his father, the Earl of Hardwicke, and the Duke of Rutland, both 'greater owners of land' in Cambridgeshire, 'were not such bigoted donkeys as to suppose they could return whom they thought proper; at the same time, they had undoubtedly the right to nominate such persons to represent the county whom they thought would be most acceptable to the constituents'.[47] According to the logic of the argument, those whom the constituents found 'most acceptable' were Hardwicke's and Rutland's relatives. One or another member of Hardwicke's family filled one of the three county seats in every Parliament between 1832 and 1879. A member of Rutland's family filled another of these seats in a sizeable number of these Parliaments. Presumably, the 'right' to which Royston referred derived in part from that combination of wealth and status which Hardwicke and Rutland both possessed in the county. It was such a combination which the editor of the North Lincolnshire poll book for 1852 recognized when he observed that 'a nobleman or gentleman representing a powerful party, and possessing the confidence of that party . . . exercises only the legitimate sway of property and character combined . . . [when he selects] a particular candidate'. But the 'constitutional power to nominate' was perverted into an 'unconstitutional power to dominate' when the necessary 'confidence' was lacking.[48] Nor was the distinction he made quite as difficult to apply as it might seem. Within limits the measure of constitutionality was political success.

To a large extent what preserved these networks were the political functions they performed—or, to put it differently, the political system in which these functions could be performed. As Alison described the first Reform Act, it was far less a threat to the powers of the aristocracy than it was to their way of life—their 'exclusive system,' he called it. Whatever the degree to which this 'system' was abandoned after 1832, at least in terms of images and the related concepts of legitimacy, power in society and state was enjoyed by those who behaved as Alison said they should. The conditions which made this possible were quite specific. Essentially they had to do with the continuing importance of patronage in all manner of activities public and private, the limited role of the state in these circumstances, and the continuing possibility of geographically separating the different gross categories of network—what was done by the constituency boundary commissioners in 1832 and what was attempted by them in 1868, by which time the earlier arrangements had lost their relevance.[49] Indeed, as the efforts and implied needs of 1868 suggest, the significance of these boundaries could no more be preserved indefinitely than the networks could be preserved whose strength depended in part upon them.

By the mid-1880s, in just about every constituency in the kingdom, the right to nominate had been transferred from the hands of the various elites who enjoyed their powers in respect of their 'property and character' into the hands of committees most of which were formally elected. In some cases the members of these committees were hangovers from the earlier dispensation. In others the very establishment of an elected committee was the means of transferring power out of the hands of such men. But whichever the case, the formation of such committees and the related emergence of mass membership political parties reflected crucial changes in the nature and locus of authority in society and state. The effective agencies of social organization and social control were no longer those which the earlier networks and the 'confidence' which derived from them had served to mobilize. A generation later, when the Parliament Act was passed, the formal constitutional implications of this were recognized. It was only possible to maintain the co-ordinate powers of the House of Lords and the House of Commons as long as the members of the one enjoyed a significant influence in the other.

These changes involved far more than the substitution of urban for rural leaders and networks. The processes are apparent in town as well as in the country-side. Many old networks of debt and loyalty were replaced by new ones. But the more important changes had to do with the replacement of hierarchical discretion by standardized wisdom and bureaucratic procedure. Within this new system many members of the aristocracy continued to claim elite status. But increasingly, those whose claims were honoured based their claims less upon their roles as landowners than upon their wealth alone or their participation in those new agencies of social control which were located in Whitehall and, in particular, in the City. And in both places, as the growing numbers of endogenous peers suggests, the role as peer enjoyed a fresh importance.

Notes

1 Rubinstein, 1977, 103.
2 *Hansard* 3rd series, XXXIX (1837); *Hansard* 4th series, LXXXVIII (1900).
3 Bateman, 1971, 495.
4 F. M. L. Thompson, 1963, 28–9.
5 Pine, 1961.
6 Pumphrey, 1934, ch. 5; Pumphrey, 1959, 9; Alfred Tennyson as Baron Tennyson, Sir William Thomson as Baron Kelvin, Sir Joseph Lister as Baron Lister and Sir Frederick Leighton as Baron Leighton.
7 Sanford and Townsend, 1865, I, 9–10.
8 *Ibid.*, I, 11.
9 Hollingsworth, 1965, 8–9.
10 F. M. L. Thompson, 1977, 44, footnote 26.
11 *Hansard* 3rd series, VII (4 October 1831), 1193–4.
12 Quoted in Butler, 1914, 255.
13 *Hansard* 3rd series, II (1 March 1831), 225.
14 Moore, 1976, especially chs 5 and 6.
15 Sanford and Townsend, 1865, I, 14.
16 *Ibid.*, I, 15.
17 *Ibid.*, I, 14.
18 Malet, 1961.
19 Spring, 1963, *passim*.
20 Spring, 1951, 6.
21 Cannadine, 1977, *passim*.
22 Stone, 1965, 338–9.
23 F. M. L. Thompson, 1963, 264–8; Ward, 1971, 72; Richards, 1974, *passim*.
24 Sanford and Townsend, 1865, I, 112.
25 Jenks, 1899, 84–5.
26 Taine, 1957, 181.
27 Girouard, 1971, 1.
28 Bateman, 1971, 472.
29 Huxley, 1967, 18, 66.
30 Spring, 1971, 41.
31 Spring, 1963, 43.
32 Jenks, 1899, 85; Spring, 1963, 43.
33 Spring, 1963, 43.
34 Richards, 1974b, *passim*.
35 Olney, 1973, 138; Moore, 1976, 50 ff.
36 Stroud, 1962, 13.
37 Howitt, 1840, 83–4.
38 Alison, 1834, *passim*.
39 Joyce, 1975, *passim*.
40 Quoted in Girouard, 1971, 2.
41 BPP 1868–9 VIII, Q. 6,427.
42 F. M. L. Thompson, 1957, 294; Girouard, 1971, 6.

43 Badeau, 1886, 288.
44 Franklin, 1975, *passim.*
45 Badeau, 1886, 20; Taine, 1957, 40.
46 Badeau, 1886, 52.
47 *Cambridge Independent Press*, 25 January 1868.
48 North Lincolnshire Poll Book, 1852, xii.
49 Moore, 1976, ch. 9.

28 The Gentry

D. C. Moore

I

In the 1830s when John Burke began publishing the directory now known as Burke's *Landed Gentry*, the word 'gentry' was not included in the title. What he published was *A Genealogical and Heraldic History of the Commoners of Great Britain and Ireland, Enjoying Territorial Possessions or High Official Rank; but Uninvested with Heritable Honours.* A decade later 'gentry' replaced 'commoners'. Whatever the specific reasons for this it is symptomatic of an important process of social redefinition and political consolidation. The conceptual boundaries surrounding the nobility were being reduced and replaced by new boundaries surrounding an enlarged aristocracy to which the gentry belonged but to which commoners did not belong.

Conceptual boundaries are important. They set limits. They imply roles. They reflect fantasies. To some extent they mirror reality and condition reality. Several generations earlier Samuel Johnson had defined a gentleman as 'a man of birth; a man of extraction, though', he added, thereby dividing the sheep from the goats, 'not noble'. His two boundaries were applied to the gentry by various nineteenth-century lexicographers. In *The Imperial Dictionary* of 1850, for example, John Ogilvie explained that the gentry were 'the classes of people between the nobility and the vulgar'. But in the eyes of John Burke, of his son, collaborator and successor, John Bernard Burke; and of numerous others, the social world was differently divided. In particular, their vision is revealed in the 'Essay on the Position of the British Gentry' by the Reverend John Hamilton Gray which appeared as a preface to the fourth edition of *Landed Gentry* published in 1862. According to Gray the restriction of the epithet 'noble' to members of the peerage was 'an abuse of terms'. The real denizens of England understood the truth, that 'the well-born English gentleman was in fact a nobleman', even though, having no title, he might call himself a commoner. But, Gray observed—and, presumably, his observation helps to explain Burke's substitution of gentry for commoner—most foreigners and many natives tended to regard all those who called themselves commoners as members of 'the "Bourgeoisie," the "Roture"'.[1] From this point of view this was an error.

To correct the error Gray described boundaries which reflect social and provincial, instead of legal and constitutional, criteria. The House of Lords scarcely figured, nor the roles of the men who received individual summons to advise the monarch; rather 'the constant marrying and giving in marriage between . . . [the gentry] and the peerage'; not the laws of succession to peerages which distinguished a single heir but the relations among the siblings from whom the heir was chosen. Time was important: the length of a pedigree. And since the length of a pedigree was really a measure of the length of time a family had owned significant amounts of land, land was important. Indeed, for the *echt* aristocracy whose definition was essential to his definition of the gentry, time and land took precedence over any other claims. As he explained,

> an immense majority of the existing peers are mere mushrooms when compared with a large proportion of our country gentry, who are much better entitled to be considered noble, because their families were established as a county aristocracy at a date when their lordships' ancestors did not possess an acre of land.[2]

As he noted, however, with obvious chagrin, what made these mushrooms less than oaks applied to the gentry as well. He admitted the point even though it 'tended greatly to complicate [his] . . . position . . . : men who have risen from humble rank to wealth [have tended] to consolidate that wealth on landed possessions'. As such, whether or not they ultimately managed 'to establish themselves among the territorial aristocracy of the country',[3] they were engaged in a process whose very recognition eroded the boundaries he emphasized. Obviously, those who claimed the pedigrees which elicited the contempt of Edward A. Freeman and J. Horace Round[4] were trying to strengthen these boundaries. Possibly Freeman was right in saying that the needs they felt 'to have come in with the Conqueror or else to be older than the conquest sap[ped] every principle of truth'.[5] But sometimes the sort of truth to which he referred is less significant than the needs which, prompting its violation, illustrate another truth.

The consolidation of wealth on land was an old practice. It was the price men paid for the status of gentleman; also, for a share of the power landowners enjoyed. Gray's insistence on distinguishing the gentry from the commoners, his refusal to recognize any distinction between the gentry and the nobility, were his contributions to the preservation of the world in which landowners retained land and power. That others contributed as well is apparent, among other things, from the fact that they continued to consolidate wealth on land. Whether they did so in spite of the accelerating growth of commercial and industrial wealth and power or because of it—whether traditional symbols were compelling because they were traditional or because the others contained too many reminders of the market place—there was no urban patrician class to speak of in Britain in the mid-nineteenth century. Possibly, for a time, the leaders of the Anti-Corn Law League threatened to create an alternative hierarchy. But this was only temporary. During most of the century real status was only available within a traditional rural context. The yearning for this status, which helped to preserve its locus and the locus of power with which it was associated, was an important political, social and cultural fact.

At one level of ambition or attainment this yearning is apparent in the observation that 'a citizen engaged in business [in a town]' would not want to build a villa from which the town could be seen.[6] At another level it is apparent in the increase in the numbers of licences issued to display a coat of arms on writing paper or cutlery. In 1830 there were roughly 7,000 or these; in 1855, 25,000; in 1868, 43,000. This was a peak, somewhat above the plateau which obtained for the rest of the century.[7] Fewer men were involved at those higher levels of which Gray spoke. The question remains how inclusion in Burke's *History of the Commoners* or his *Dictionary of the Landed Gentry* or, later, his son's *History of the Landed Gentry*, was determined. But the first contained genealogies of fewer than two thousand families. By the 1860s the son's *History* contained genealogies of more than four thousand. Whatever the real enlargement this represents—the number includes many younger sons—further enlargements were inhibited by the insistence that landownership was, as the editors of *Landed Gentry* put it in 1894, the principal 'test of rank and position'.[8] And when, on the eve of the First World War, they modified their criteria for inclusion it was not really to change these criteria. As the editors of *Landed Gentry* explained in 1914, they had abandoned their former policy of deleting families which had 'severed their connections with their ancestral homes' because of 'the vicious and crushing burden of taxation dictated by the hatred of the landowner . . . [and] the nightmare of the Death duties [which] converted . . . land from an investment into a luxury to be maintained from extraneous sources'.[9] Indeed, in the circumstances they described, to have continued their earlier policy would have been tantamount to disloyalty. Nor was much change to be anticipated immediately from their other decision, to assimilate the imperial consuls by according gentry status to those men 'who have never owned land, but have won their way to distinction and position in the service of the King and in other ways'.[10] Whatever was meant by 'other ways', many of the men who served the king were recruited from gentry families. Ultimately, the impact of these new criteria might be important, but less so than those which Edward Walford had described some years earlier. Indeed, in his *County Families*, first published in 1860, Walford suggested elite boundaries which did less to resist the changing distributions of wealth and power in the nineteenth century than to accommodate them. He not only included 'the titled and untitled aristocracy' in a single list, he claimed as a point of national pride that each edition of his manual would be somewhat out of date by the time it appeared. 'In a country like our own', he explained, 'mainly owing to the influence of trade and commerce, . . . [there would always be a] constant addition of fresh families.'[11] He was as eager to include these as the editors of *Landed Gentry* were reluctant. In 1860 many of his families had not yet bought land. Presumably some never bought any. Gray's stumblings among the ironies of mobility and status reveal the ambiguities of the criteria which he, the editors of *Landed Gentry* and numerous others tried to perpetuate. Whether Walford's criteria are really any less ambiguous in an ultimate sense, they have much to say about the social systems which were coming into being towards the end of Victoria's reign just as the others have much to say about those they were replacing, those which the first Reform Act reflected and reinforced.

II

The Reform Act was crucial in the history of the class Gray defined. Not only did it abolish the rotten boroughs, those symbols of aristocratic and 'illegitimate' power—the power of property abstracted from a social context—but in so far as possible it isolated rural from urban Britain, the counties from the towns. It provided the urban elites with constituencies of their own—in such a way as provided the rural elites with a respite from the political effects which the growth of towns had been having on the counties.[12] Status and class were fundamental to its formula—but these as defined in the light of rural criteria. The principal reformers' model was the landed estate, their goal the reinforcement and generalization of this model. As Lord John Russell had explained some time before, once the unrepresented towns were enfranchised the local elites would be encouraged to exercise an 'authority' within them to which their otherwise restless neighbours 'could conform'.[13]

The assumptions underlying Russell's statement acquired their logic from that society in which power was more a function of status than of money, and status was more a function of landownership than of position in court or government; from that state in which, as James Anthony Froude observed some year later, 'private ownership in land is permitted because Government cannot be omnipresent'.[14] To many men who deplored the 'illegitimate' powers of the rotten borough patrons and who feared the seemingly ungovernable multitudes of the burgeoning towns, landed estates represented symbols of 'legitimate' power and havens of social stability. Whatever the cogency of the notion that a constitutional reformation could be based on the landed estate model, Lytton Bulwer implicitly explained the notion when, in the early 1830s, he explained why many country gentlemen, when seen in London, were 'fussy, conceited . . . and pompous', who, when seen at home, were 'easy, dignified and natural'. In London the evidence of their status was lacking. But on their own estates and, by extension, in their own counties, it was not.[15] The point is

92 *right* Charles Francis Massingberd-Mundy, D.L., J.P. (1839–1913), photographed at South Ormsby Hall, 1900. He came from a long line of Lincolnshire landowners noted for their work in the agricultural improvement of the wolds (Hallgarth Collection)

93 *below left* Colonel de Burton in uniform at Buckminster Hall, Billingborough, Lincolnshire (Hallgarth Collection)

94 *below right* Mrs de Burton in her Victoria at the main door of Buckminster Hall about 1898. She died in 1905 from an accident while driving in this carriage (Hallgarth Collection)

95 *above* Family, servants and
dogs at Moated Grange, Somersby,
east of Horncastle, Lincs
(Hallgarth Collection)

96 *above right* Conversation piece
at Old Bolingbroke, near Spilsby,
Lincolnshire: on the left is William
Stone, the squire of the village; the
flamboyant figure on the right,
somewhat reminiscent of Theodore
Roosevelt, is a water diviner
(Hallgarth Collection)

97 *right* Hawarden Castle about
1890: servants pose with the
implements appropriate to their
work (Clwyd Record Office)

98 *above* The well-to-do farmer's domestic staff: servants at Poplar Farm, Hollesley, Suffolk, pose with the tools of their trade (Suffolk Photographic Survey)

99 *above right* Abberley Hall, Worcestershire. An Italianite house by Samuel Daukes, built *c.* 1846 with an asymmetrically placed tower (From a sale catalogue, BM Maps 137b 11 (16))

100 *right* Stoke Rochford Hall, Lincolnshire, built 1841–5 by William Burn in typically early Victorian Elizabethan (National Monument Record)

101 *above*   The Hall in Hafodunos House, Denbighshire, built by C. G. Scott, 1861–6: church detail in a domestic setting (National Monument Record of Wales)

102 *below*   Possingworth Manor, East Sussex, by M. D. Wyatt, 1865–70: high Victorian verticality at its most extreme (*Builder*, 1868, XXVI, 713)

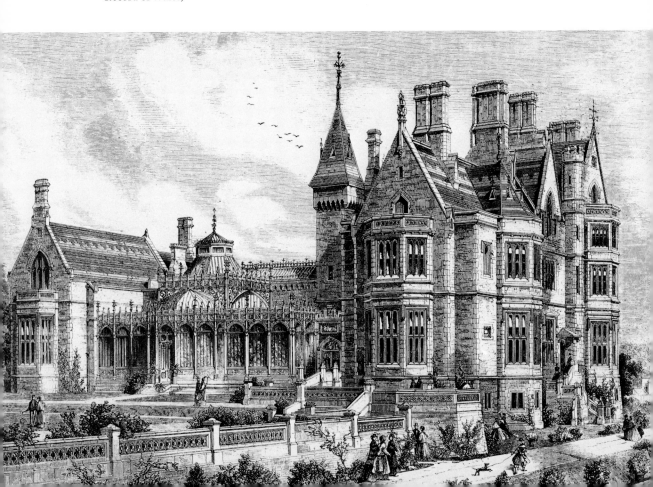

103 *above*   Bestwood Lodge near Nottingham by
S. S. Teulon, 1862: asymmetry, broken outline, much
structural decoration. The 'chapel' on the left was the
servants' hall (*Builder*, 1863, XXI, 639)

104 *below*   Hemsted House, Kent, by David Brandon,
1859–62: Jacobean asymmetry plus a high French roof
over the tower and a diagonal staircase window. Now
Benenden School and considerably altered (*Builder*,
1862, XX, 243)

LEWINS·KENT
South East Prospect
J·M·Brydon·Architect

105 *above left* Merrist Wood, Worplesdon, Surrey, by Norman Shaw, 1875–7: stone, half-timbering, brick and tile hanging, brilliantly combined (Photo: National Monument Record: copyright: Batsford)

106 *left* Lewins, Crockham Hill, Kent by J. M. Brydon, 1876–83: the same ingredients as at Merrist Wood, used on a larger and taller house (*Building News*, 1883, XLIV, 750)

107 *above* Avon Tyrell, Hampshire, by W. R. Lethaby, 1891–2: a late Victorian, free adaptation of Tudor (*Country Life*)

108 *above* Perrycroft, Colwall,
Herefordshire, by C. F. A. Voysey,
1893–4. The slate roof, roughcast
walls and strange chimneys are
right outside the country house
tradition (*British Architect*, 1895,
XLIV, 437)

109 *left* Bryanston, Dorset, by
Norman Shaw, 1889–94: English
baroque revived for the last Whig
palace

110 *above*   Redcourt, Haslemere, Surrey, by Ernest Newton, 1893–4: the beginning of Edwardian neo-Georgian, still with gables and some arts and crafts detail (National Monument Record)

111 *right*   Batsford Park, Gloucestershire, by Ernest George and Peto, 1887–93. A correct Tudor design showing the late Victorian return to horizontality and almost complete symmetry (National Monument Record)

112 *above* An early Victorian version of a celebration in the mediaeval great hall of Haddon Hall (Joseph Nash, *The Mansions of England in the Olden Time*, 1838, new edition 1869, plate XXV)

113 *left* The dining hall at Bilton Grange, Warwickshire, by A. W. N. Pugin, 1841–6: an early Victorian great hall with open timber roof (*Illustrated London News* 1855, XXVI, 93)

114 The billiard room at Thurland Castle, Lancashire, by Paley & Austin, 1879–95, fitted out in a very masculine style with leather chairs and stuffed shooting trophies (National Monument Record. A Bedford Lemere photograph)

115 *above* Halton House, Buckinghamshire,
probably by W. R. Rogers, 1882–8. A classical,
top-lit saloon, planned in a similar way to that
at Dobroyd Castle, but now used as the
principal living room (National Monument
Record. A Bedford Lemere photograph)

116 *left* A classical top-lit saloon at Dobroyd
Catle, West Yorkshire, by John Gibson, 1865–9.
Carpeted and with seats, this hall is still not
really a living room. The upper galleries give
access to the bedrooms (*Builder*, 1875, XXXIII,
953)

117 Rhinefeld Lodge, Hampshire, by Romaine Walker, 1888–90: a great hall in late Tudor style with hammerbeam roof. It includes a screens passage and minstrels gallery, but the small oriel window on the left opens out of the boudoir, where chaperones could sit comfortably and keep an eye on the party below (National Monument Record. A Bedfore Lemere photograph)

118   The entrance hall at Thurland Castle: a single-storey hall used as sitting room (National Monument Record. A Bedford Lemere photograph)

important not only because a good disposition is important but also because it describes the context of satisfaction of the men who were principally responsible for the legal basis of the socio-political system which came into being after 1832. Nor is it altogether surprising that most members of the real nobility were in a position to enjoy these satisfactions even more than they. Rather, it helps to explain the conceptual assimilation which Gray described. What they had in common were landed estates.

Estates were sources of wealth. Even more important, they were means of organizing and controlling large portions of the population at a time when rival agencies of organization and control simply did not exist and when government was constrained from interfering with landowners' powers both by appropriate doctrine and by the presence of many members of the aristocracy and gentry within it. As late as the mid-1880s the editor of the *Fortnightly Review* could observe, not wholly inaccurately, that 'the great landlords of England are really the rulers of principalities'.[16] A decade earlier Froude called them 'petty monarchs'.[17] Earlier still, Disraeli declared that government could not be carried on without the 'united aid and agency' of various institutions, among them 'the hereditary tenure of land'.[18] His explanation was absurdly dramatic, that 'in hours of peril and perplexity, external and domestic, landed estates offer something around which men may rally and save the State'. But the point is no less important. Landed estates were major foci of loyalty.

Alexander had noted this point in the early years of the century. As he observed, the next best thing to being Tsar of Russia was to be an English country gentleman.[19] Within the law the powers of these men on their own estates were almost absolute. They set the conditions on which others led their lives. Also, they determined who would lead these lives, who they would allow to remain upon their estates, who they would send away. Ultimately, the powers of these men were limited. But the processes by which these limitations were effected suggest that limitation was not intentional.

The man Froude cited in the 1870s to show 'the uses of a landed gentry' was a Benthamite named Smith who had taken a long lease on Crown property in the Scilly Isles. Thus, technically, in that part of the world where Froude described his activities he was not a landowner. But for the period of the lease the powers of the one were comparable to the powers of the other and, ostensibly, Smith used his powers as Froude believed he should. When he acquired his lease the islands were 'a rabbit warren of paupers'. When he died they were 'a thriving community of industrious men and women'. All this, ostensibly, because he had combined small holdings into large, had provided alternative work for those thus deprived of their 'potato patches', had built schools and chapels, had stopped drunkenness with a 'high hand', and with an equally high hand had decided who might remain on the islands, who might not. Presumably, those who remained enjoyed the conditions he set and benefited from them. Nor should the point be ignored that even though at his death the value of the islands was much greater than when he took the lease, his own profits from the enterprise had been less than his expenses. The difference was the price of that *noblesse oblige* which, from Froude's point of view, provided the gentry's essential rationale. To those who did not subscribe to the gentry ideal as Froude described it, the observation was clearly provocative: 'paternal government may be detestable when you have the wrong sort of father'.[20] Nor would they have agreed with his implication that one of the essential functions of law was to control such 'wrong fathers'.

The complete gentry role required participation in formal as well as informal government and, if possible, on the formal level in the national as well as the local arena. Thus it was only available to a few, those with large rent rolls whose debts, whether inherited or self-incurred, did not seriously limit their expenditures, and those who somehow managed to win election to Parliament. The season in their own houses in London, the rest of the year on their own estates—for this some £10,000 a year might be necessary, signifying an agricultural estate of very considerable size, or considerable income from such non-agricultural sources as urban ground rents or mineral royalties. Until the later decades of the century relatively few landowners had significant incomes from other varieties of non-agricultural source and few men other than landowners had such incomes.[21] Most of those who had such incomes were peers. But many on the fringe were not. Together, these comprised the national elite. Until 1905 members of this elite filled most of the cabinet offices; until 1888 they had an effective legal monopoly of county government; until 1880 those of them who were not peers filled most of the seats in Parliament for all but the newer boroughs, and even for some of those. Writing in the 1850s, Walter Bagehot attributed their continued political predominance to the fact that land was still almost the only investment 'not requiring sedulous personal attention, and not liable to be affected by political vicissitudes'. In consequence, he declared, 'all opulence gravitates towards the land. Political opulence does so particularly.'[22]

The point is not to be denied. But it explains rather less than it describes. Most political money was *rentier* money not because most would-be politicians became *rentiers*—although that was the case—but rather because the paths to power of many *rentiers* were smoothed both by their recognition of one another as participants in a common culture and, even more, by the willingness of others, their various dependants in particular, to acknowledge their leadership. Hence the importance of the communities in which these dependancy relationships obtained. Hence, too, the importance of the efforts to preserve these communities against the rising tide of that cosmopolitanism which, as Gray implied, was eroding the social foundations of the understanding that 'the well-born English gentleman was in fact a nobleman'. As participants in a common culture these men endured the same education, were satiated by the same recreations, worshipped in the same churches, married one another's daughters, and transmitted property by the same devices. Once the rotten boroughs were abolished they enjoyed political powers which, however these might differ in degree, tended to rise from the same ultimate source, their roles as 'petty monarchs'. In no county was it possible for an individual 'monarch' to determine the outcome of a parliamentary contest; it was possible in only a few of the boroughs. But in many counties their alliances and coalitions were crucial. In many boroughs the pattern was somewhat replicated, thus the taste developed for the enjoyment of that power which landownership itself provided. And in 1867–8 and, again, in 1884–5 efforts were made to preserve the contexts in which such powers obtained wherever it was possible to do so against the tides of social change and population movement.[23]

Obviously, the wish to play the role of petty monarch helps to explain the prices sometimes paid for rural land in the 1860s and early 1870s, thirty and even forty years' purchase of the rental value[24]—far beyond anything which rational economics might explain. Obviously, too, criticism of the way the role was sometimes played helps to explain the mounting chorus of urban complaint about the continuing influence of the aristocracy and gentry. But the real issues did not concern the behaviour of individuals. They concerned the powers of a class. The fact that many of the critics had a sneaking admiration for the class—indeed, that in some respects their criticisms were the expression of their unrealized fantasies—rendered their attacks peculiarly moderate. But they were no less clear. The class they criticized was open. But few gained admission. It was not a caste. But the admission fee was high—and high, in part, because the pressure for admission helped to drive up the price of rural land. The critics understood the social and political importance of estates. But many of them tended to regard estates more as agencies of coercion than as socio-economic communities. By the same token, they tended to attribute the aggregations of land which these estates represented rather more to the law than to the desires of those who used the law—rather more to the constraints the law imposed in cases of intestacy, when it directed the transmission of landed property to a single male heir, or, somewhat more reasonably, to the constraints the law allowed each landowner to impose upon his heirs, than to the decisions of individuals to consolidate their wealth on land or to retain such consolidations. Furthermore, they tended to claim that many estates were uneconomically large—that they were owned by men who lacked the capital necessary to enable their tenants to maximize production. In consequence—so their arguments ran—as population grew the balance of trade was adversely affected. Money was exported to pay for food which, otherwise, would have been produced domestically. Furthermore, serious problems arose as men congregated in the towns who had neither a future in the countryside nor, indeed, in the towns themselves—the one because land was inaccessible, the other because the capital was being exported to pay for food which should have provided them with jobs.[25]

In the early 1870s, in the hope that these criticisms would stop if evidence were educed to show that landownership was far more widely diffused than the critics contended, a national survey of landownership was undertaken.[26] However the folly be explained which this hope serves to illustrate, the resulting evidence scarcely proved the case it was supposed to prove. It showed that slightly more than half of England was contained in estates of more than 1,000 acres, a size often used to distinguish gentry estates from those owned by men of lesser status. Roughly 400 peers and peeresses owned estates in England and Wales which averaged somewhat over 14,000 acres; roughly 1,300 'great landowners' who were not peers owned estates which averaged somewhat less than 7,000 acres; roughly 2,500 squires or lesser gentry owned estates which averaged somewhat over 1,700 acres.[27] Most of the larger estates were some distance from London. Indeed, half of Northumberland and more than half of Rutland were contained in estates of over 10,000 acres. Estates of over 3,000 acres covered almost three-quarters of these counties and more than half of Nottinghamshire, Dorset, Wiltshire, Shropshire and Cheshire. But such estates covered less than a third of Essex and Surrey, and only 15 per cent of Middlesex. Estates of between 1,000 and 3,000 acres were somewhat more evenly distributed. But those of between 300 and 1,000 acres were less so. While covering roughly 20 per cent of Surrey, Essex and Kent, and slightly less of Middlesex, they covered only 5 per cent of Rutland and 7 per cent of Northumberland.[28]

In the 1873 edition of *Landed Gentry* families 'established' in the eighteenth and early nineteenth centuries constitute some three-quarters of the listings for Essex, but only two fifths of those for Shropshire.[29] Obviously, the home counties had become something of a dormitory area for those who hoped to achieve gentry status long before railways made such an area a real possibility. When the possibility was fully realized the rate of turnover of estates in the London area increased sharply, especially the rate of turnover of the smaller estates. Ostensibly, in the middle years of the century, in a region some fifteen miles from London, the average time an estate remained in the same family was only twenty years.[30] By and large, however, such were the smaller estates. The larger estates were rarely sold.[31] In effect, while the smaller estates, especially in the London area, changed hands in ways which undoubtedly detracted from their non-economic attributes, the larger estates tended to pass from generation to generation within a family in ways which undoubtedly reinforced the family's local associations and influence. These were the families which defined the gentry image. Those others which tried to share this image had come and gone in the past at something approximating the rate which caused so much grief to the editors of *Landed Gentry* when they surveyed the damage effected by the agricultural depression at the end of the century.[32]

But the reduced powers of the gentry in the later decades of the century were scarcely the consequence of political action. The evidence educed in the early 1870s did not intensify the criticism it was supposed to have silenced. Not that reason prevailed. When land was so largely valued for the status and power it conveyed it seems unlikely that the concentrations of landownership would have been reduced by facilitating land sales; indeed, possibly the very reverse. Nor was Britain's urban proletariat or her growing dependence on foreign food to be affected by restoring those somewhat mythical yeomen. In most cases the ability of gentry families to retain or enlarge their estates had more to do with the proportions of males among their offspring and the shortness of life of their widows than with the laws of primogeniture and settlement. A son brought home a dower; daughters took them away; and widows who survived for long to continue spending their jointures might so deplete a son's or grandson's income as to prompt him to build an increasingly precarious tower of debt.[33] Many townsmen remained convinced that if land settlement were forbidden and all landowners were free to dispose of their land at any time the concentrations of landownership would be reduced and production would be increased. But the powers of the gentry were not reduced in this way. Rather, their powers were reduced by factors which neither they nor their critics could control.

III

What is principally important in the history of the gentry is the usefulness of landownership as a test of status, the role of land in the rubrics of power. Others might acquire the cultural attributes whether in schools, universities or government departments,[34] thereby preserving the 'gentlemanly' idea and the concept of *noblesse oblige*, which provides such as effective means of rationalizing power. But their essence was not in these. It lay in the close historical relationship between land and power.

In part the weakening of this relationship was the consequence of the growing power which derived from other sources. Symptomatic of this process was the pride which Edward Walford expressed in 1860, that there would always be a 'constant addition of fresh families' in his manual, and the decision of the editors of *Landed Gentry*, in 1914, to accord gentry status to men 'who have never owned land, but have won their way to distinction and position in the service of the King and in other ways'. In part its weakening was the consequence of the agricultural depression, which reduced the incomes of many landowners from the peaks that were reached in the early and middle 1870s to the levels that obtained some years earlier and, in doing so, made life particularly difficult for those landowners whose indebtedness had been allowed to rise with rising rents. In part, as well, its weakening was the consequence of the changing organizational role of the landed estate, of the changing role of traditional status relationships in politics and government, and of the accelerating rural exodus and the concomitant growth of towns which, in the last half of the century, reduced the rural population of the kingdom from roughly half the total population to less than a quarter. There were, of course, political reforms. As with the first Reform Act, however, so with the second and third: these did as much if not more to shore up the powers of the existing elites in changing circumstances—the powers of the rural elites in particular—than to undermine them. Indeed, it was not so much legislation which affected the powers of these men as it was the growing omnipresence of government and the various changes of social relationship.

The organizational importance of the landed estate was not constant. It was considerably enhanced by land enclosure; also, in the context of declining prices in the immediate post-Napoleonic period, by the tendency to substitute tenancies-at-will, renewable from year to year, for leases which guaranteed many years' tenancy; and again, some years later, during what has been called the second agricultural revolution,[35] by the use of estate mechanisms to direct the application of the new techniques which the revolution comprised. Undoubtedly, many farmers initially welcomed tenancies-at-will. Whatever their loss of independence, such tenancies facilitated those adjustments of rent which, with fluctuating prices, allowed tenant and landlord to receive the proportionate incomes regarded as their due. But many farmers were less enthusiastic about the use that was made of estate mechanisms to encourage high farming. Possibly the growing sophistication of these mechanisms owed more to their economic rationale[36] than to their role in aggrandizing the powers of the 'petty monarchs'. But, whichever the case, these powers were increasingly at issue in consequence of their use in altering time-honoured procedures. As an estate agent explained in the early 1840s when pressed by tenants eager for the freedom which leases symbolized, once upon a time he, too, had been in favour of leases. But the price fluctuations of the 1820s had changed his mind. And now, when there were more questions than answers about what constituted good farming, he would only be willing 'to remove the screw if he knew his man and what he was doing'.[37]

After corn law repeal the problems of landlord–tenant relations were considerably aggravated: the issue was gone on which most landlords and farmers had been agreed, that which generally sweetened the principle that an estate should speak with one political voice. With the issue gone the disciplinary aspect of the principle became clearer. Possibly, with the increased emphasis upon production the disciplinary aspect became greater. When tenants were pressed to embark ever larger amounts of capital in the exploitation of their farms and rents were raised on the consequent increments of productivity,[38] the doctrine of mutual benefit was severely taxed. Similarly when tenants' crops were injured by game kept for their landlord's pleasure or, as the renting of shooting rights became more general, for the pleasure of those who rented these rights. Few landlords permitted their tenants to shoot. Thus, as guns became more accurate, permitting larger kills and encouraging more preservation, the game problem could become seriously divisive.

In large measure it was because tenants' grievances changed and estate mechanisms ceased to provide adequate means of redressing them that tenants increasingly appealed to the state. Understandably, such appeals prompted the pious observation on the part of various landowners, that 'life would be intolerable in any profession if men were obliged to be looking at everything in a barely legal or barely pecuniary point of view'.[39] But in the circumstances of the 1870s a rival source of intolerability was the reiteration of the principle that tenants had no rights other than those their landlords gave them.[40] A few years later, in the context of declining prices, many men insisted that the tenants' 'wrong fathers' were being adequately coerced by circumstance and need not be additionally coerced by legislation: to keep their land in cultivation they were now willing to accept almost any terms a tenant or prospective tenant might offer.[41] The view adds a dimension to Froude's argument concerning the role of law. But it was unavailing as a means of preserving the formal powers of the 'petty monarchs' or the quasi-legal integrity of the domains in which these powers were exercised. The Ground Game Act of 1880 gave tenants a legal right to kill hares and rabbits on their farms; the Agricultural Holdings Act of 1883 secured their ownership of the unexhausted value of their improvements. According to the editor of the *Fortnightly Review* such legislation would scarcely affect the largest estates. On these, he observed, 'custom will always assert its authority before that of positive law'.[42] But however long these estates retained their extra-territorial status, many of the others had already ceased to be foci of loyalty. They had become mere places of work and residence. They were still private property. Increasingly, however, government intruded to sort out the relationships between landowners and those who were no longer their dependants.

IV

However, the growing omnipresence of government was more clearly manifest in the roles of the various commissioners, assistant commissioners and inspectors who from the 1830s were increasingly active in advising and ultimately directing the operations of local authorities. For centuries such authorities in the counties had been the unpaid justices of the peace. Qualifying for their administrative and judicial roles in respect of their property and status, these men symbolized the very essence of the gentry ideal. But there lay the source of a major administrative, judicial and social problem. It was essential that these men perform their roles and perform them efficiently. But the very nature of the gentry ideal made it impossible to coerce them and difficult to guide them. Whatever the number who satisfied the principal legal qualification—ownership of land worth £100 a year, or ownership of a reversion to land worth £300 a year—and whatever the number who had been nominated by the various lords lieutenant, in 1851 there were almost 21,000 whose names had been placed on the Commissions of the Peace for the different counties of England and Wales. But in the kingdom as a whole fewer than 40 per cent of these had taken the trouble to qualify themselves so that they might act. And many of those who had did nothing more.[43] Early in the century in many counties such behaviour among the laity had resulted in magistrates' benches largely composed of clergy. Around the time of the first Reform Act the laity began returning to the bench.[44] The very need that they do so not only conditioned the discussion of their tasks but to some extent conditioned the tasks themselves. As the chairman of the Warwickshire magistrates explained in 1837 while opposing the suggestion that the magistrate's administrative responsibilities be assigned to elective boards, it was hard enough already to get sufficient magistrates to participate at the trials of prisoners at quarter sessions. They attended the meetings, usually scheduled during the first few days of the sessions, when administrative matters were dealt with which concerned them directly. Then they left. Thus, inevitably, if the magistrates were deprived of their administrative functions a total reorganization of the judicial system would be required as well.[45] Many M.P.s rose to protest against this slur upon the magistrates' much advertised devotion to duty. But in fact, while the presence of the magistrates *qua* magistrates was essential as a means of preserving the gentry ideal, their judicial functions were already performed by clerks and others, some of them magistrates themselves, who knew the law and whose roles were formalized during the course of the century by various court reforms. Indeed, in all probability the most important duty of those magistrates who did not know the law was that which the Warwickshire chairman said it was, 'their residence in the various places in the county where they lived, and where they were enabled to act as friends of the poor, and heal disputes as arbitrators and referees'.[46] Obviously what he had in mind, apart from their role in administering their own estates, was their role in administering the poor law. But in many cases, in consequence of the Poor law Amendment Act, these two roles had become one.

In the long term the creation in 1834 of a central commission to supervise poor law administration throughout the kingdom was a means of destroying the magistrates' autonomy. But in the short term it was a means of enhancing the powers of the 'petty monarchs'. How the one became the other provides an important part of the answer to the question why landownership became less useful as a test of status as the century wore on. Among the problems associated with the old poor law few were more troublesome than those which derived from the right of any magistrate to review the decisions of any overseer in his county. In part these problems were solved by depriving the magistrates of their powers of review. But such was done only to incorporate magistrates and landowners more directly into local poor law administration. Magistrates were made *ex officio* members of the new boards of guardians which succeeded to the overseers' roles. As landowners they had multiple votes in choosing the elected members of these boards. And, whenever possible, it was the principal local landowner whom the commissioners invited to serve as chairman. Since the boundaries of the poor law unions, the new units of poor law administration, were—again whenever possible—made to coincide with the boundaries of particular estates,[47] in many cases in the counties poor law administration became a simple adjunct of estate management.

But in time the commissioners and assistant commissioners who helped to achieve this end tended to circumscribe the areas of independent local judgment. Whatever their reasons for doing so—whether they were prompted more by their concern to protect the gentry from the results of their own eccentricities or were simply responding to their bureaucratic role—the consequences were the same. And other agents of the state behaved much as they behaved. Indeed, no sooner were the measures passed by which the gentry tried to shore up their own authority in state and society than the general responsibilities for keeping the peace of the county which the magistrate's commission placed upon them began to be defined, narrowed and vastly multiplied by the many new statutory responsibilities they were required to exercise, often under the eyes of inspectors. Furthermore, the question whether crime and social unrest were more effectively controlled through mechanisms of social network or through those symbolized by an impersonal police was increasingly answered in favour of the police.[48] And the irony at the core of the nineteenth-century revolution in government lies in the fact that many of the Members of Parliament who supported an impersonal police force, and many of those who voted to impose new statutory responsibilities upon the magistrates, and many of the inspectors under whose eyes these responsibilities were exercised, were themselves members of the gentry. Whatever their awareness of what they were doing, they were creating an impossible situation. Some men suggested that the magistrates' autonomy and status be restored by providing them with constituents for whom they could speak both to Parliament and to the small but growing bureaucracy.[49] From the other end of the political spectrum the suggestion was made that their autonomy and status be destroyed by extending representative arrangements beyond the borough boundaries. The concerns were very different: the legislative implications were the same. Whatever the relative importance of the different concerns, in 1888 most of the magistrates' administrative and supervisory responsibilities were transferred to new elected county councils, and their powers of supervision of the police to joint committees of magistrates and county councillors.

The government which drafted this measure was heir to the so-called party of the landed gentry. But, as the measure itself suggests, a significant mutation had occurred. Twenty years earlier Disraeli's assumptions concerning the crucial political role of the loyalties associated with such institutions as the landed estate had been widely shared among the leaders of the party. Indeed, they were widely shared among the leaders of both parties. But they were so no longer. Within the Liberal party their displacement was symbolized by the establishment of so-called representative organizations in the different constituencies, organizations which most of the remaining Whigs in the party refused to join—thus organizations which achieved the goal of the Radicals who established them, that of driving most of these remaining Whigs out of the party. Among the Conservatives the displacement of these assumptions was somewhat less traumatic. By and large, in the last decades of the century the Conservative leaders were drawn from the same families as before. But their powers in party, society and state derived less from extrapolations of those gentry relationships which Gray emphasized than from their roles in Whitehall, Westminster and the City. As W. H. Smith explained to Salisbury in the early 1880s, expressing the exasperation of the organization man for those whose lassitude was born of status, gentry relationships had ceased to be a source of strength to the party. Those who enjoyed them 'only want to be let alone to enjoy what they have: and [they] think they are so secure they will make no sacrifice of time or of pleasure to prepare against attack or to resist it'.[50] He was not alone in his analysis. Many of those who knew these men better than he confirmed his description even when they did not share his sentiments. It was Henry Chaplin, owner of 20,000 acres in Lincolnshire, who protested that while many country gentlemen were willing to assume arduous administrative burdens they might not be so willing if their right to do so had to be constantly vindicated. As he put it, explaining his concern that elected county councils might drive the gentry out of local government, '[they] might not care to undergo the intolerable annoyance of a contested election every three years with something in the nature of a continual canvass during the period intervening'.[51]

In fact, a sizeable number of gentry were elected to seats on county councils.[52] But while Chaplin's apprehensions were exaggerated, his observation helps to explain why the gentry as Gray defined them lost their positions of political predominance so rapidly in the 1870s and 1880s. When their leadership roles were challenged many of them simply left the game. Essentially, what prompted their behaviour was pride. They refused to play except according to those rules which recognized landownership as the principal claim to power. In many parts of the kingdom, however, the rules had been changed.

What determined the new rules, what prompted the challenges which marked their adoption, are extremely complex questions. But it is a useful shorthand to reduce these questions to those having to do with the weakening of the relationships on which landowners' powers were based, the erosion of the communities in which these relationships obtained, and the development of new institutions of politics, business and government which took the place of landed estates in organizing and controlling large portions of the population, in particular, the burgeoning urban population. The role of political reform in all this is somewhat ambiguous. The effects of the crises in which the reforms were enacted must be distinguished from the effects of the reforms themselves. Also, whatever the reformers' rhetoric, much reform legislation was designed to limit the political impact of social and economic change and population movement, in effect to preserve the context in which the old rules would obtain. But even when these impacts were limited the changes and movements could not be undone. And the crises themselves did much to change the context. What is striking is not the ultimate loss of power of the gentry, or the declining usefulness of landownership as a test of status, but the enduring usefulness of this test and the concomitantly enduring presence of the gentry in Westminster.

In the 1830s and 1840s significant landowners composed roughly three-quarters of the House of Commons. In the 1850s and 1860s they composed roughly two-thirds. Then, at just about the time when rural land prices reached their zenith, while rural rents were still rising to a peak in the mid-1870s, the sharp decline began in the proportions of landowner M.P.s. Between 1885 and 1905 the proportion was stabilized at roughly a third of the House. After the Liberal landslide in 1906 it dropped to a fifth. In 1910 it rose to a quarter.[53] The wrong things should not be read into those figures. That landowners continued to comprise the majority of M.P.s at such late dates has less to say about the chronology of economic change than about the ambiguities of response to such change, the importance of traditional social symbols and the stable nature of power relationships. In the 1830s and 1840s many landowners had interests besides their land.[54] By 1914, as the editors of *Landed Gentry* were forced to note, land was often 'a luxury to be maintained from extraneous sources'. And, in many cases, these other sources not only provided more money, they also provided more direct access to what were now the more effective mechanisms of social organization and social control. On the eve of the First World War some landowners owed their seats to the residual conditions their fathers had enjoyed: they sat for certain of those county constituencies whose continued isolation had been made possible by the adoption in

1885 of a single member constituency system. But in the larger world from which these constituencies were isolated landownership was no longer an important source of power or the principal criterion by which the powerful recognized one another. Into the new world of company directorships and formal organizations many peers and richer gentry made their way with considerable ease—but a smaller proportion of the lesser gentry. The conceptual boundaries had been eroded which the first Reform Act reflected and, for some time, reinforced.

Notes

1   Gray, 1862, ii.
2   *Ibid.*, v.
3   *Ibid.*, ii.
4   Freeman, 1877, *passim*; Round, 1901, *passim*.
5   Freeman, 1877, 41.
6   Loudon, 1846, 766.
7   F. M. L. Thompson, 1977, 31.
8   Burke, 1894, Preface.
9   Burke, 1914, Preface.
10   *Ibid.*
11   Walford, 1871, extract from the preface to the first edition.
12   These arguments are developed more fully in Moore, 1976.
13   *Hansard* NS V (9 May 1821), 615.
14   Froude, 1872, I, 130–1.
15   Bulwer, 1970, 91–2.
16   Escott, 1885, 26.
17   Froude, 1876, 677.
18   Reported in the *Standard* (London), 27 June 1863.
19   Reported in Howitt, 1840, 11.
20   Froude, 1876, 674.
21   Rubinstein, 1977, 120 and *passim*.
22   Bagehot, 1859, 233.
23   Moore, 1976, especially ch. 9; Chadwick, 1976.
24   F. M. L. Thompson, 1957, 294.
25   Such arguments lie at the core of Fawcett, 1865, and Kay, 1879.
26   *Hansard*, 3rd series, CCIX (19 February 1872), 639–41; the survey was reported in BPP 1874 LXXXII, pts 1 and 2; the evidence is most readily available in Bateman, 1883.
27   Brodrick, 1881, 187.
28   F. M. L. Thompson, 1963, 32 and 114.
29   *Ibid.*, 124.
30   Froude, 1876, 677.
31   Stone and Stone, 1972, 87.
32   Burke, 1914, Preface.
33   Clay, 1968; Mingay, 1963; Mingay, 1976a, 115.

34 Wilkinson, 1964.

35 F. M. L. Thompson, 1968b.

36 Such is an important argument in Spring, 1963.

37 Reported in *Farmer's Magazine*, 2nd ser., V, 1 (1842), 3.

38 For example, the cases mentioned in Arnold, 1877, 465.

39 Argyll, 1876, 498.

40 Reported in *Chambers of Agriculture Journal and Farmers' Chronicle*, 19 April 1875.

41 *Annual Register*, 1883, 114.

42 Escott, 1885, 34.

43 BPP 1851 XLVII 418 ff.; 1852–3 LXVIII 329 ff.; 1856 L 161 ff.

44 Quinault, 1974, 189.

45 *Hansard*, 3rd series, XXXVI (10 February 1837), 418–19.

46 *Ibid*.

47 Brundage, 1978, especially 105–44; Lewis, 1957, 254.

48 Silver, 1967.

49 For example, *Hansard*, 3rd series, CCXXXII (9 March 1877), 1653–63.

50 Smith to Salisbury, 14 August 1883, Salisbury Papers, Christ Church, Oxford.

51 *Hansard*, 3rd series, CCCXXIV (16 April 1888), 1371.

52 Dunbabin, 1965, 358.

53 Thomas, 1939; 1958.

54 Aydelotte, 1962.

29 The Victorian Country House

Jill Franklin

I

Victorian country houses are little known or visited, though well over a thousand are documented,[1] perhaps twice as many were built, and a very large number of them survive. They are extraordinarily varied in appearance, yet all of them make use to a greater or lesser extent of architectural elements borrowed from an earlier period, just as Georgian country houses had done. Fashion in historical style changed far more rapidly in the nineteenth century than it had done in the eighteenth, moving in sixty years from Italianate classical or Tudor and Jacobean to various kinds of Gothic, then on to English vernacular and finally round again to the classical English baroque. None of the new fashions completely ousted the previous ones, so that belated Italianate overlapped with the earliest neo-Georgian, while Elizabethan remained popular throughout the reign and after.

The great variety of styles in use at one time—and by no means all of them have been named—suggests that none was as universally satisfactory as Palladian had once been. Rapid social change had left country house owners as a class uncertain and divided over the image their houses should present, and in a single decade they could house themselves like feudal, Christian lords of the manor, classic squires, French renaissance monarchs or yeoman farmers. Yet although period styles were sometimes copied so faithfully that it can be quite difficult to distinguish fifteenth- from nineteenth-century work, more often the total effect is as unmistakably Victorian as that of Rossetti's paintings after Dante or Tennyson's *Morte D'Arthur*.

The early Victorian house, whatever its style, normally had a rectangular main block two or three stories high, with a low even roof or identical Elizabethan gables, beneath which were regularly spaced rows of large sash windows. The elevations might be symmetrical or asymmetrical, but in any case were built up on a system of balancing horizontals and verticals, often with a single tower offsetting the low bulk of the house. Abberley Hall (*c.* 1846) (Plate 99) and Stoke Rochford Hall (1841–5) (Plate 100) are in different styles, yet still have much in common. Ashlared stone was still the favourite building material, external colour was uniform and decorative trim thin and rather meagre. With certain exceptions, such as Anthony Salvin's Peckforton Castle or Sir Charles Barry's Cliveden,[2] houses of this period have a slightly tentative air despite their size, as though their designers had lost momentum in the gap between the fading of classical ideals and the arrival of Gothic ones.

By the 1860s, more than half of all new country houses were being built in a Gothic style,[3] but it was different from the early Victorian variety for it was no longer chiefly surface decoration but had become to many architects the only possible means of expression. Yet Gothic architects faced the major difficulty in designing country houses that little medieval domestic architecture of any kind survived and even less could serve as a direct model, so that everything had to be adapted for modern use, and even then much had to be borrowed from ecclesiastical buildings. However, conviction prevailed over common sense, and neither architects nor owners saw anything incongruous in furnishing the hall with a portion of thirteenth-century nave arcade, as at the Hall in Scott's Hafodunos House (Plate 101), or in lighting the gentlemen's cloakroom with a lancet window, as was done at G. Somers Clarke's Milton Hall in Kent.[4] It was no odder, they might have said, than living behind the front of a classical temple.

The real force of Victorian Gothic came not from its church detail but from characteristics that it shared in varying degrees with other current styles. The most striking of these was a tremendous emphasis on height and a consequent narrowing and constriction of all proportions. It was accompanied by marked asymmetry and broken outline, as well as by what was called 'truth', which meant giving full expression on the outside to the function of the rooms inside. Consequently country houses were no longer four-square and spreading, but piled up and aspiring. Roofs became higher and more steeply pitched, the skyline more romantic than ever before in England. Fantastic spires and tourelles, wedges, pyramids and hipped gables might be clustered together in one house over an equally varied façade, whose many kinds of windows were composed in asymmetric diagonals and triangles and in many different planes. The front door was no longer in the centre, and instead of windows matching left and right an oriel might be answered by a chimney breast or even by blank wall; sometimes the base of the staircase window rose diagonally. 'Truth' also affected the attitude to materials. Stucco was a sham and rough-textured stone often thought preferable to ashlar because of the 'interesting variety' it could give.[5] Exposed brick was now seen as honest and might be handled with considerable virtuosity. Decoration had to be 'structural', that is, differently coloured, and sometimes aggressively contrasting building materials could be used to form stripes, diapers and banded window heads. The Gothic country house looks tense and often restless; it lacks either classical magnificence or comfortable domesticity, but it has a powerful and dramatic quality all its own (Plates 102, 103 and 104).

Gothic for country houses held first place for little more than twenty years. By the 1870s owners were beginning to want to incorporate a suggestion of comfort and cosiness. Norman Shaw, the greatest of Victorian country house architects, was the key figure in evolving out of Gothic a new style to answer this need.[6] It was called 'Old English'[7] and took its motifs from the cottages and farmhouses of the home counties, exploiting tile-hanging, half-timbering, casement windows with small leaded panes and tall Tudor chimneys; or red brick might be set in friendly contrast to newly rediscovered white paint. All this variety would be assembled into a deceptively casual-looking asymmetry, as though the house had grown up at random over the years. Roofs were still broken up, windows were of all shapes and sizes but the ensemble was more informal, spread out and welcoming than in Gothic (Plates 105 and 106). It was also more bourgeois, so that those who chiefly wanted to look imposing still opted for stone-built Tudor.

Old English could be delightful, especially for houses that were not too big, but after a while there was a reaction in favour of a more unified, coherent look. It could be expressed in two ways. Some architects continued to use Tudor or vernacular motifs, though with less emphasis on correct period detail, building free and asymmetric compositions that were less cluttered and more abstract than those of the previous generation. Many of Edwin Lutyens's early country houses were designed in this so-called 'free' style (Plate 107). However, clients who liked the style mostly wanted small to medium-sized houses: C. A. Voysey and Baillie Scott, who each developed a personal version of it, were never commissioned to design a really big house (Plate 108). Where formality or grandeur was required, architects and their clients, feeling the need for strict symmetry and classical discipline, turned to the English baroque of Wren and the early eighteenth century. Norman Shaw's flamboyant Bryanston (Plate 109) of 1889–94 and Chesters of 1890–4 were influential in setting country house fashion in this direction. Ernest Newton, Shaw's pupil, preferred a rather quieter Georgian or Queen Anne (Plate 110), and Lutyens, too, added English classical to his repertoire. At the same time, Tudor and Jacobean houses became correctly symmetrical again (Plate 111). So what with the various free styles, the ever-popular Tudor, and once again classical, the client of 1900 had as wide a choice for the style of his house as had his predecessor in 1837.

II

All Victorian country houses were planned in two virtually separate parts, the main or family block and the service wing. Each part occupied much the same ground area, but while the main block was designed to be conspicuous and elaborate, the service

401

wing had to be 'invisible' like the servants themselves. For the sake of convenience the Victorians invariably put all the 'offices' on one side, where they might be screened off by bushes or banks of earth and were usually hidden from the principal garden. Complete concealment of the service wing was often impossible on the entrance front, in which case it was considered essential to be able to see instantly 'the one part of the edifice as superior and the other inferior'.[8] So the service wing was normally lower than the main block, often brick-built where the house was stone, and with all its detailing faithfully reflecting the social gradings within (Plates 104, 109 and 111).[9]

Coming inside the early Victorian country house, the caller would find himself in a formal entrance hall, possibly top-lit and with a first-floor gallery giving access to the bedrooms. Several large and high reception rooms, all simply shaped, well-lit and of classical proportions, would open off it on a clear and axially arranged plan. One of them would almost certainly be a billiard room, virtually a standard feature by the 1850s. Smoking in the main body of the house was still out of the question, and though a few early smoking rooms date from the later 1840s[10] they were well-secluded, probably in the tower, for no taint of smoke must reach the principal rooms. The main innovation of the time, pioneered by Edward Blore, Anthony Salvin and A. W. N. Pugin, was the revival of the medieval great hall, which was usually fitted up in Gothic, but could be Jacobean.[11] At first owners were a little uncertain how it should be used, so that in some houses it became the main hall, in others the dining room or a free-standing room kept for entertaining and various social functions.[12] Initially, it did not matter if the great hall had no very obvious function: at a time of social tension it evoked a comforting if unreal vision of feudal order, the lord and his docile peasantry carousing in harmony together (Plates 112 and 113).

By the 1860s the country house interior had altered. The plan became non-axial and a great deal more complicated; routes were more confusing; corridors had more turnings and rooms now included a variety of oddly-shaped bays and were apt to be darker and gloomier than before. Whereas in the eighteenth and early nineteenth centuries saloons and suites might be included purely for display, each Victorian reception room was planned for a single precise function. The living areas for the different sexes and groups in the house were systematically sorted, and segregated accommodation was provided for each.

On the ground floor a masculine suite developed as a counterpart to the drawing room, which had always been feminine territory. Each sex might use the rooms in the other domain, but it was on sufferance rather than by right. The male suite developed round the library, which had been common ground in Regency days but gradually grew more masculine in furnishing and atmosphere, so that ladies seemed less in place there.[13] Then the billiard room, which in the 1830s and 1840s was often linked to the drawing room, as at Osborne, came to be regularly placed next to the library, even though in some social circles ladies were always free to play (Plate 114).[14] These two rooms, along with a gentlemen's cloakroom and a separate entrance, formed the nucleus of the suite, and the owner's study might also be included in it. By the late

1860s, when smoking in the main house had become more acceptable, the smoking room normally adjoined the billiard room. Finally, the gun room, a typical example of Victorian specialization, appeared about this time and often, though not invariably, formed part of the suite.

Between the gentlemen's rooms on one side and the ladies' rooms on the other, lay the neutral territory of the hall. At the beginning of the period it was still the little used, formal entrance; by the 1850s it had begun a remarkable transformation into the favourite family living room; Mentmore was one of the first houses whose hall was planned as a living room from the start.[15] By the 1870s many new country houses had an adaptation of a medieval great hall or classical saloon as their principal, most used reception room (Plates 115–118). To us these halls feel too high and usually too public to make acceptable sitting rooms; to the Victorians they had the over-riding advantage of being the only place in the house that was open-plan and available at any time of day for use by members of either sex, by family or guests, dogs, even children (Plate 119).

According to Robert Kerr, author of a weighty book of 1864 on house planning, the Victorian gentleman's first requirement at home, which easily outweighed elegance, importance or ornament, was 'quiet comfort for his family and guests'.[16] By 1900 it was easy for him to be very comfortable indeed, far more so than in 1837.

The most important single element in country house comfort was warmth, which was achieved by a mixture of traditional and new methods. English rooms had always been warmed by individual open fires and continued to be so throughout this period. Consequently every living room and every bedroom had its separate fireplace, whose grate had to be cleaned, its fire laid and lit daily, its coals carried and put on at frequent intervals. The Victorians loved their cheerful, glowing fires and saw no reason to economize either on fuel or labour; but even from their point of view the system had the great drawback of leaving the corridors and outlying corners unheated. The hall, too, was often difficult to keep warm: Mrs Charlton of Hesleyside, for instance, described her downstairs as 'a cavern of icy blasts'.[17]

This changed with the gradual introduction of central heating, starting with a few installations at the end of the eighteenth century. Hot air, hot water, and steam systems were all tried, but without any pumps to aid circulation it was necessary to rely on convection, so the pipes had to be two or three inches in diameter and the radiators or grilles of immense size. Controlling the boiler and maintaining an even temperature was extremely difficult and demanded considerable intelligence and skill. Central heating remained rare in the early nineteenth century, but despite the technical difficulties it was increasingly often included in new houses from the 1840s on, though at that time it was almost always confined to the hall and corridors. However, as more of the problems were solved principal rooms, too, were provided with radiators to supplement the fires, until by the end of the century heating could be taken for granted in a new house, though certainly not in an old one. The combination of central heating and open fires was, of course, hugely extravagant, but without doubt it was luxuriously comfortable too.

Heating problems were closely allied to those of ventilation. The Victorians were newly and fully aware of the importance of fresh air; they considered that breathing 'vitiated' air was dangerous to health, even to life, and one of their objections to full central heating was that it made the air unpleasant and stuffy.[18] But they were in a dilemma since they also hated draughts. So first they made doors and windows as tight-fitting and draught-proof as possible and reinforced them with screens and thick, heavy curtain materials, but then they had to reintroduce fresh air, not only for health but even more importantly to prevent the horrible discomfort of smoking chimneys: even the best-designed chimney will smoke if the only outside source of air is down the flue. So an enormous number of patent grates came on the market, designed to draw in air and consume smoke in a great variety of ways. None was ideally satisfactory. At the same time several systems of ventilation independent of the heating systems were invented. These often involved air ducts hidden in the walls or set in free-standing pipes; open grilles in cornice or ceiling, acting as outlets for vitiated air, were common.

Owners were probably wise to be cautious over central heating in its early days. They were less conservative about new forms of lighting. In 1837 country houses were still lit by a combination of candles and oil lamps, and many continued to be so. Gas light was already available, but it was far from satisfactory. Each country house had to manufacture its own gas in its own gas house and the resulting product was so dirty, hot and smelly that it was unacceptable in the family rooms. However, it was considered good enough for the servants and was installed in service wings and corridors at least from the early 1840s.[19] Various experiments and improvements culminated in the invention of the gas mantle in 1886, by which time a high proportion of new houses had at least partial gas lighting; but by then it was really too late, for electric light had become practicable for domestic use in 1879 and was already being used in a few country houses by the 1880s.[20] Ten years later it was still far from reliable and extremely expensive to run, but when working it clearly outmatched all older forms of lighting in brilliance, cleanliness and convenience.

Plumbing arrangements also improved markedly during this period. Every Victorian country house had its own, usually abundant, water supply, and this was piped right round the house, but at first with only a few outlets apart from the w.c.s and the housemaids' closets. The gentlemen's cloakroom probably had a basin with a cold tap, but there were no other plumbed-in washbasins anywhere. The bathroom was reserved for the master and mistress, with perhaps a second one for the nurseries. Guest bathrooms did not exist, and a guest washed with jug and basin and slop-pail in the bedroom or dressing room, and bathed in a hip bath in front of the fire. Every drop of hot water had to be carried up the back stairs from the kitchen, and one manservant remembered carrying forty cans night and morning.[21] Piped hot water in the country house is not recorded in the architectural press until the later 1860s, and although there are probably instances of its being installed earlier it did not become standard even in new houses until the late 1870s or early 1880s.[22] Once piped hot water had arrived a few more bathrooms were usually, though not invariably, provided. Guests could now expect one to every two or three bedrooms, though only exceptionally one to every suite. Even the men and maidservants would have one apiece.[23] Plumbed-in washbasins never reached the bedrooms; it was felt that sleeping in a room with a plug-hole connected to the drains was an unacceptable risk to health.

The Victorians had become very conscious of the connection between health and sanitation and gave much thought to the w.c.s which were provided in generous numbers. They invariably had an outside window and usually a connecting lobby. Nor were the servants stinted, though as a precaution against smells in the house, they often had to make do with closets outside the main body of the house.[24] Drains and sewerage, too, received a great deal of attention. Glazed and impermeable drain pipes, pioneered by Henry Doulton, were obviously less hazardous to health, and there were advances, too, in the design of valves, traps and devices for eliminating 'effluvia' or dangerous smells.[25]

III

Victorian country houses were built to last. They were intended as permanent family possessions and represented a long-term investment: part of the return was to be a conspicuous and powerful position in county society, in the future if not immediately. So they were constructed as solidly as possible; building methods were sound and careful, materials durable, nothing was shoddy or sham.

Costs varied enormously, naturally. As was only fitting, the Duke of Westminster spent the most: Waterhouse's remodelling of Eaton Hall cost over £600,000; but the Duke of Northumberland paid £250,000 for Salvin's remodelling of Alnwick Castle, Earl Manvers £170,000 for his new Thoresby Hall, also by Salvin, and Viscount Portman at least £200,000 and probably much more for Bryanston.[26] Several commoners' houses also cost huge sums. R. S. Holford's Westonbirt, built by Lewis Vulliamy, cost over £125,000, and John Walter's Bearwood by Robert Kerr over £120,000.[27] Lynford Hall by William Burn for Lyne Stephen, said to be the 'richest commoner in England', was reported, when up for sale in the 1890s, to have cost £145,000 to build, and the figure is by no means unlikely.[28] Others that must have cost as much or more include Waddesdon and Rhinefield Lodge.[29]

At the other end of the scale it seems to have been impossible to build what the neighbours would have recognized as a country house for less than £6,000 or £7,000. A farmer in Hertfordshire became suddenly and unexpectedly richer when his land was found to yield coprolites or fossilized dung, used as a fertilizer. He decided to build a country house, Pirton Hall, for £5,000. 'I must beg to disabuse you of the notion of a *Mansion*', wrote his architect. For that price he would simply supply 'a good Country gentleman's house, plain and unpretending'. The final total was nearer £10,000, including stables, lodge and kitchen gardens.[30] S. S. Teulon's Enbrook, near Hythe, which was only just large enough to be reckoned as a country house at that date (1853–5), cost about £7,300 for the house alone.[31]

With such a price range no single house can be taken as entirely typical, but David Brandon's Hemsted House in Kent (Plate 104) can stand for many. The owner, Gathorne Hardy, later Earl of Cranbrook, bought the estate of just over 5,000 acres for £124,000 with money he inherited from his father's Staffordshire ironworks. The accepted tender for the house was £18,000, the final cost £23,000, but that sum did not include such items as the gasworks, grates and furniture, which brought the complete bill to almost £33,000.[32]

Few really detailed sets of building accounts survive, but both at Westonbirt and Bearwood a little over half the building money went on wages, the balance on materials and transport. Wages ranged from £2. 12s. 6d. per week for the most highly skilled men to 10s. per week for labourers; but since the building process was hardly more mechanized than in the Middle Ages and very few items were prefabricated, huge numbers of men were needed on the site. Well over 400 men were employed at various times on Westonbirt, and 110 men sat down to the 'roofing supper' at Hemsted.[33] The size of the house was only one of the factors affecting the final price. Stone naturally cost more than brick, and stone itself varied in price according to quality; Chilmark was more expensive than Bath stone, for instance.[34] Bearwood, which was brick-built with lavish decorative trim in stone, can suggest relative costs. Some 4,250,000 bricks were made on the estate at a cost of £6,400 and the total bricklaying bill was just over £17,000. The stone, Mansfield for trim and York for paved floors, was just over £17,000, plus £850 for cartage, and the complete stonemasonry bill was over £26,000. Country houses needed huge amounts of timber, and at Bearwood the total figure for joinery work was over £40,000, nearly as much as the brick and stone together. Ironwork cost £9,000, including £4,000 on rolled iron joists, £4,600 went on plumbing and leadwork, £6,000 on the stoves and heating apparatus. Painting, glazing and gilding came to only £7,000 together and plastering the same. The architect's commission was the standard 5 per cent of the cost of the house, plus travelling expenses.[35]

Most houses bear witness to the Victorian preference for durable materials. Many have no external paintwork at all: Mentmore had copper window frames, other houses had unpainted oak or teak. Indoors the servants' wing would have its walls plastered and painted, but in the reception rooms wood panelling or tooled leather hangings were often preferred (Plates 113, 117 and 118). Consequently far less maintenance was necessary than in the days of stucco outside and lavish paintwork inside.

After an owner had decided how much to spend on building his new house, he next had to work out the maximum number of servants he could afford to keep. The plan of the house was geared to this figure. Of course servants were essential to domestic comfort, but above a certain size of household, say fifteen indoor servants, the precise number made little difference to the family's standard of living, though a considerable one to its status. Thus livery servants, who for much of the time were of little practical use, had a function merely in being conspicuously on view. Such an attitude to domestic service was possible and even made sense because throughout the nineteenth century domestic servants, women especially, were cheap and available in huge numbers; and of all the domestic jobs to be had those in the country house were among the most sought-after.[36]

Consequently, although a great deal of thought was given to the smooth running of the house, good planning had absolutely no connection with labour saving, at least until towards the end of the period. Running hot water in the bathroom was a success not because it saved the servants carrying the cans but because it saved the guests having to wait for them. A well-planned house was one where the work could be reasonably shared out between a fixed number of servants, and so organized that each servant could carry out his duties without getting in another's way. To achieve this the Victorians classified the various jobs, providing a separate and appropriate place in which each was to be carried out. In earlier times the brushing of the family's clothes had been done in the servants' hall; a Victorian house had a separate brushing room.

One aim of the planning was to ensure that men and women servants had no unnecessary contact with each other, not only in the sleeping quarters but also in the course of their work: segregation would promote efficiency and propriety at one and the same time. It was equally important that the servants should not disturb the family's illusion of privacy, even though everyone knew they were there and that it was impossible to keep secrets from them.[37] Separate entrances, staircases and corridors brought home who was who and prevented unnecessary contact. The architect of Rhinefield Lodge noted that 'an important feature of the planning of this house is that no servant's room or office, with the exception of the attic dormers, can overlook the grounds at any point'.[38]

The work of the country house was organized, as in the eighteenth century, into three departments, headed by the cook, the butler or steward and the housekeeper. These three, and personal servants such as the ladies' maids, were known as 'upper servants' and were sharply differentiated in duties and status from the under servants, who did the really hard and menial work. Demarcation lines were rigid and no servant, even the lowliest, could be asked to do the work of another.[39] Also, in any large house much of the servants' time was spent in waiting on each other. T. F. Buxton, the owner of Easneye, near Ware, had twenty-three servants and reckoned that fifteen waited on the family and eight on the fifteen.[40] It is no wonder that from 1830 to 1870 or later the service wing grew more elaborate and occupied more space in relation to the main house than ever before.

One early Victorian house can give an idea of the general principles of layout. Stoke Rochford Hall in Lincolnshire (Plate 100) was built in 1841–5 at a cost of some £60,000 for Christopher Turnor, a hereditary landowner.[41] His architect was William Burn, famous for his skilful planning.[42] Each household department had its own cluster of rooms. The butler, who had five menservants under him in 1871, had his section in the basement under the main house.[43] This arrangement gave the footmen easy access to the hall and front door, though the basement bedrooms for the menservants were much disliked.[44] Next came the housekeeper's section, placed beneath the exclusively family part of the house, known as the 'private wing', so that the housekeeper had easy communication with her mistress in the boudoir overhead. The housekeeper's room was used as her office and sitting room, and often as a dining room by the upper servants. In 1871 the housekeeper had under her four housemaids, two still-room maids and three laundry maids. Further on came the kitchen department, staffed by the cook, two kitchenmaids, a scullery maid and a dairymaid. It was arranged round a kitchen court, one side of which held the servants' hall, the only room where the under servants could legitimately spend any time in the company of the opposite sex. The laundry and the brewhouse were the furthest from the main house because of the smell and steam.

Perhaps the most remarkable feature of the plan to modern eyes is the distance from kitchen to dining room, some 40 metres. This was no lapse on the architect's part but rather an instance of good planning, since the Victorians were terrified of kitchen smells, cabbage water above all.[45] Far better for the footman to walk the length of two cricket pitches than risk tainting the dining room. Then each staircase has its meaning and function. Only guests and adult members of the family might use the principal staircase from the hall to the first floor; housemaids, footmen and children were relegated to different and minor backstairs. A little later houses could have a staircase reserved for visiting bachelors, a nursery stair, a young ladies' stair.[46] All this multiplication made still more work. It was only towards the end of the century that planning sometimes became a little simpler: the kitchen could be a little closer to the dining room, the service wing contracted slightly, staircases were fewer. But where comfort was concerned labour saving meant nothing.

IV

Before he reached the comforts of the house the visitor had to pass the lodge, whose style would warn him what to expect of the mansion, then drive through the park or grounds. Few of the landscaped parks surrounding the Victorian country house were entirely of Victorian creation. So much landscaping had been done in the eighteenth century that after 1840 comparatively few large new estates were assembled from untouched or agricultural land. Among the exceptions to this are Bylaugh Hall, Norfolk, a house of 1849–52, built in the middle of turnip fields and landscaped by W. A. Nesfield, the best-known landscape designer of the time; Waddesdon Manor, where the planting of well-grown trees created an instant park out of an outlying portion of the Stowe estate; and Cragside, where William Armstrong made a romantic Rhineland forest grow on a bare Northumberland hillside.[47] But Aldermaston Court, Tortworth Court and Bearwood were more typical (Plate 124): each replaced an earlier house whose park had been landscaped in the eighteenth or early nineteenth century, leaving the Victorians to make only comparatively minor alterations.[48]

In any case, whether it was an entirely new creation or not, the Victorian park would have startled an eighteenth-century gentleman a good deal less than its mansion. It was likely to reflect the ideas and practice of Humphry Repton and the effect aimed at in the wider landscape was still one of heightened naturalness. The free outlines of the planting emphasized the contours of the slopes and opened up views to the distant horizon, suggesting or exaggerating the extent of the estate. If nature permitted, a river or stream was dammed to form a sinuous lake in the middle distance, its banks partly shaded by trees and shrubs.

The Victorians liked to use a great variety of species in their planting and were particularly fond of conifers and plants with dark shiny leaves, such as laurels and rhododendrons. Many new species from all round the world became available in the early Victorian period, including hollies, weeping trees, conifers, bamboos; monkey-puzzles were in plentiful supply from 1843, Wellingtonias from 1853.[49] Their novelty of form or exotic colour were always eagerly welcomed, but plants were now juxtaposed with a botanist's eye rather than a painter's. J. C. Loudon thought Kent and Repton had 'indiscriminately mixed and crowded together' their bushes and trees, and that it was better to arrange them by species according 'to their kinds and forms' in the way that would 'best display the natural form and habit of each'. He called this the 'Gardenesque' style, and it led on to the fashion for specimen gardens and the planting of specimen trees (Plate 122).[50] The Victorians also liked strong colour contrasts and a romantic overall effect. The eighteenth-century grounds of Stourhead were designed to be neat, trim and idyllic. By the nineteenth the outlines were blurred, the planting was lusher and denser, and far more dark-leaved plants were used; the rhododendrons were Regency but the peak years for conifer planting were the early 1850s.[51]

The treatment of the approach altered too. The Victorian country house was not for public viewing, as the eighteenth-century one had been. Privacy was now much more important than grand initial display, and in order to keep the park and the garden front of the house secluded the Victorians made the carriage drive wind round the edge of the park, so that the visitor caught his first sight of the gardens, lake and main prospect only after passing through the house. Many older houses, Hatfield among them, had their main entrance moved round to what had once been the back.

The immediate surroundings of the house altered much more than the outer park. Repton had often used terraces and flower gardens as a transition between the man-made bulk of the house and the apparently natural park, but now a formally planned, carefully detailed, small-scale foreground became one of the most characteristic, if impermanent, features of early and mid-Victorian grounds. Sir Charles Barry gave many of his houses a setting or intermediate zone of Italianate terraces bounded by stone balustrades at different levels, often linked by formal stairways and punctuated by urns and possibly statuary. He called it 'architectural gardening'[52] (Plate 123). The terraces themselves were laid out with elaborate and symmetrically designed parterres, edged with box, and filled with coloured stones or tightly packed, highly coloured bedding plants. Beyond the parterres would be shrubberies, rose gardens and specimen gardens, until finally the park proper was reached.

In the later part of the century bedding-out became rather less popular, and the parterres were often replaced by borders that were still formally and symmetrically laid out but were now planted with what were referred to as 'old-fashioned flowers', hardy if humble perennials, freely arranged as in a cottage herbaceous border.[53] William Robinson and Gertrude Jekyll were the principal propagandists for such planting, advocating softer and subtler colour schemes and stressing the importance of attractive foliage and good ground cover.[54] Architectural features such as pergolas, stone-bordered pools and garden pavilions were often included, and as the zones were no longer so rigidly demarcated the flower garden took on some of the manufactured naturalness of the park. At the very end of the century another reaction brought a revival of formal and symmetrical gardening in keeping with the new symmetry in architecture.[55] Both kinds of garden design flourished until the Great War.

V

By 1900 there was little demand for landscaping on the grand scale. The number of houses built, like Hemsted, as the centre of a landed estate had reached its peak in the 1870s, and it dropped continuously from then on.[56] The agricultural depression and the competition of cheap foreign food had caused a considerable fall in rents and the sale value of land, especially in arable country. Many owners of large estates who were dependent on their rents had to cut expenditure; others were forced to try and sell out altogether. The result was something of a glut of country house estates on the market.[57] By the 1890s it was easy and far cheaper than formerly to buy or rent a period house. Such famous houses as Houghton Hall, Hesleyside and Apthorpe were up for sale in the 1880s and remained on the market for years.[58] This naturally made it even harder to sell modern country houses. Octavius Coope, M.P., the brewer, paid £120,000 for his estate in 1878 and spent £30,000 on building his house, Berechurch Hall; but when he put the estate up for sale ten years later the best offer (not accepted) was £80,000, and in 1894 he had still not disposed of it.[59] In these circumstances the idea of building a new country house inevitably lost much of its glamour.

At the beginning of the reign hereditary landowners had built three times as many houses as the *nouveaux riches*. By the 1880s they were building only half as many, and by the 1890s fewer than a fifth.[60] Those of them who could still commission large houses almost certainly had non-agricultural money, like Lord Portman, paying for Bryanston with his London rents. New men were still building very large country houses, though fewer than before, but towards the end of the century their money probably came from different sources too. They were now more likely to be in biscuits, general groceries or soap, like G. W. Palmer of Huntley & Palmer and Marlstone House, Berkshire, Hudson Kearley (later Lord Devonport) of International Stores and Wittington House, Buckinghamshire, and his neighbour, Robert Hudson of

Hudson's soap and Danesfield. South African gold paid for Cavenham Hall in Suffolk and for Tylney Hall in Hampshire. Shiplake Court was built by a stockbroker, Wightwick Manor for an ink and paint manufacturer. And, as before, bankers, shipowners and brewers all built country houses.

It was nothing new for rich and successful members of the middle classes to move into the country, but now, instead of transforming themselves into landed gentry with country houses surrounded by estates of hundreds if not thousands of acres, they often preferred a medium-sized house with grounds of tens of acres, grounds which in all probability had originally belonged to some great landowner forced to sell off outlying parcels of land in order to keep going.

Professional men, as well as business men of all kinds, now commissioned these houses in the country. Much of Norman Shaw's work in the home counties was for successful Royal Academicians, Philip Webb's last house, Standen, was for a solicitor, Leonard Stokes's Thirteover for a barrister, Voysey's Greyfriars for the writer, Julian Sturgis. Although Shaw and Lord Portman ensured that no one could make a mistake about Bryanston, the look and style of a house in the country such as Redcourt (Plate 110) was often indistinguishable from that of a newly built, modest country house with a proper estate. True, the grounds were small and the owner could not hope to move in county society, but still his house was a well-built and valuable piece of property and he could live in it in the greatest comfort without having to worry about tenants and rents. No wonder that by 1900 many owners preferred the appearance of a country house to the reality.

Notes

1   Principally in the architectural journals: *Civil Engineer and Architects' Journal*, 1837–67; *Builder*, 1843–; *Building News*, 1855–; *Architect*, 1869–; *British Architect*, 1874–; *Academy Architecture*, 1889–; *Studio*, 1893–; *Builders' Journal*, 1895– ; *Architectural Review*, 1896– ; *Country Life*, 1897– ; and in Pevsner, 1951–74.

2   Peckforton Castle: British Architectural Library, Drawings Coll., W8/12 (1–15); *Country Life*, 1965, CXXXVIII, 284–7, 336–9; Girouard, 1971, 73–7. Cliveden: *Builder*, 1850, VIII, 318; Barry, 1867, 119–22.

3   Franklin, 1973, 15, 19.

4   *Building News*, 1874, XXVII, 254.

5   *Civil Engineer* 1860, XXIII, 129.

6   Girouard, 1971, 44–9, 141–6, 158–60; Saint, 1976, 24–53.

7   Eastlake, 1872, 110, 131, 135, 339.

8   Kerr, 1864, 226.

9   Scott, 1857, 157; Stevenson, 1880, II, 142; *Civil Engineer*, 1864, XXVII, 181.

10 Osborne House, 1845: Girouard, 1971, 25; Abberley Hall, *c.* 1846: sale catalogue, BM Maps, 137b, 11 (16); Bricklehampton Hall, 1848: sale catalogue, BM Maps 137b 11 (17); Mentmore Towers, 1850–5: *Builder*, 1857, XV, 738–40.

11 Blore: Goodrich Court, 1828–41, V & A Drawings 87430, 1–40; Nash, 1845, 12. Moreton
    Hall, 1841–3, BM Add. mss 42027, vol. 28, 15–17. Salvin: Harlaxton Manor, 1828–38,
    Country Life, 1906, XX, 522–32; 1957, CXXI, 704–7; Hussey, 1958, 239–48; Pevsner,
    Lincolnshire, 1964, 561–5; Pugin: Scarisbrick Hall, 1837–45, Pevsner, *North Lancashire*,
    1961, 218–23; Stanton, 1971, 28–33; Girouard, 1971, 60–4. Bilton Grange, 1841–6,
    Stanton, 1971, 176, 200.

12 Dining room at Great Moreton Hall and Bilton Grange, free-standing at Bayons Manor
    and Hall, Barnstaple (see Pevsner, *North Devon*, 1952, 92).

13 Loudon, 1833, 796; Gore, 1849, I, 288; Kerr, 1864, 129; cf. Eliot, 1876, Bk 5, ch. 6.

14 Fullerton, 1847, I, 9; Ticknor, 1864, 358; Yonge, 1853, 35; Cavendish, 1927, I, 145;
    Knightley, 1915, 226.

15 Disraeli, 1938, 159; *Builder*, 1857, XV, 738–40.

16 Kerr, 1864, 73.

17 Charlton, 1949, 176.

18 *Builder*, 1854, XII, 288; Stevenson, 1880, II, 221.

19 For instance at Worsley Hall, Lancashire: British Architectural Library, Drawings Coll.,
    Worsley Account Book, 12–23 October 1843.

20 Girouard, 1971, 17.

21 Lanceley, 1925, 177.

22 Didsbury Towers, 1865: *Builder*, 1873, XXXI, 222, 722. Crown Point, Norwich, 1865: 1872
    sale catalogue, Norwich Public Library. Bayham Abbey, 1869–72: *Builder*, 1871, XXIX,
    985–7. Wykehurst Park, 1871–4: *Builder*, 1872, XXX, 565–7; Murphy, 1883, 90.

23 Stevenson, 1880, II, 75; Muthesius, II, 56.

24 For instance at Clouds, plans British Architectural Library, Drawings Coll., V14
    (11–216). Cf. Westonbirt, British Architectural Library, Drawings Coll., R.S. Holford,
    letter 16 November 1865.

25 Stevenson, 1880, II, 265–74; Saint, 1976, 180–4.

26 Eaton: Smith, 1971, II, 387–99. Alnwick: Pevsner, *Northumberland*, 1957, 69. Thoresby:
    Thoresby Account Book, Nottingham University Library. Bryanston: Saint, 1976, 432.

27 Bearwood: Berks. RO: Walter Papers, Building Accounts, 1864–70. Westonbirt:
    Westonbirt Papers and Fortnightly Returns, 1864–71, British Architectural Library,
    Drawings Coll.

28 *Estates Gazette*, 31 December 1898.

29 Waddesdon: Fowler, 1894, 171–2. Rhinefield: *Builder*, 1889, LV, 121–2.

30 Herts. RO: Pirton Papers, 71830–72035; Hanscomb, 1967, 159.

31 *Builder*, 1854, XII, 486–7.

32 *Builder*, 1862, XX, 242–3, 259; first Earl of Cranbrook, *Private Diaries*, and Hemsted
    Account Book, East Suffolk RO: HA 43/T501/286–306 and 178.

33 Westonbirt computed from Fortnightly Returns, see note 27; Hemsted: Cranbrook
    Diaries, 28 October 1860, see note 32.

34 Estimates and correspondence for Pangbourne Tower owned by Mr J. V. Hamilton.

35 Kerr, 1864, 223; *Builder*, 1884, LXVIII, 549; F. M. L. Thompson, 1963, 187.

36 Franklin, 1975, 221.

37 Disraeli, 1845, 157; Trollope, 1869, II, ch. 51; Kerr, 1864, 75; Lethaby, 1935, 99.

38 *Builder*, 1889, LV, 122.

39 Dana, 1921, 40.

40 Information from his grandson, Mr J. Buxton.

41 Pevsner, *Lincolnshire*, 1964, 644.

42 Kerr, 1864, 476; *RIBA Transactions*, 1869–70, series 1, XX, 121–4.

43 1871 census, PRO: RG 10/3357. (In the 1851 census, the jobs of the menservants are not given, and in 1861 the family and many of the servants were away.)

44 Horne, 1930, 236.

45 *Builder*, 1886, L, 87; Cholmondeley, 1897, 52.

46 Early bachelor stairs at Bearwood: Kerr, 1864, 3rd edn, 1871, plates 35, 36; Westonbirt: British Architectural Library, Drawings Coll., V7/3 (1–17); nursery stair at Highclere Castle (Sir Charles Barry): plans at house; young ladies' stair, Bearwood.

47 Bylaugh Hall: *Builder*, 1852, X, 517–9; *Building News*, 1869, XVI, 272 ff.: Waddesdon Manor: Fowler, 1894, 171–2; *Gazette des Beaux Arts*, 1959, series 6, LIV, 13–16: Cragside: Girouard, 1971, 143–4, 293–9; *Country Life*, 1969, CXLVI, 1640–3.

48 Aldermaston Court: *Country Life*, 1899, VI, 240–2; 1907, XXII, 54–9. Tortworth Court: *Country Life*, 1899, V, 592–6: Bearwood: *Country Life*, 1969, CXLIV, 964–7.

49 Hadfield, 1960, 314, 322–3.

50 Loudon, 1840, VIII.

51 Woodbridge, 1971, 14–18, 28–30.

52 Barry, 1867, 113–19.

53 Girouard, 1977, 152–8.

54 Jekyll, 1899; 1900; Jekyll and Weaver, 1912; Robinson, 1883; Clifford, 1962, 206–11.

55 Blomfield and Thomas, 1892.

56 Girouard, 1971, 6.

57 *Estates Gazette*, 8 January 1881, 14 October 1882, 14 July 1883, 6 February 1892, 4 January 1896.

58 *Estates Gazette*, 31 October 1885, 15 October 1887, 7 January 1888, 7 January 1893.

59 *Estates Gazette*, 7 January 1888, 6 January 1894.

60 Girouard, 1971, 6.

30 The Model Village

Michael Havinden

In discussing model villages it is as well to be clear at the outset what we are talking about since the term can be used to describe a wide variety of settlements. Probably the most generally recognized would be a planned village, such as Nuneham Courtney in Oxfordshire or Milton Abbas in Dorset. These were completely new villages, established on fresh sites because a landowner wished to remove an older village which had become an unsightly impediment to the development of his garden or park. These might perhaps be regarded as the ideal types, but they are not typical model villages. The typical model village would be more like East Lockinge in Berkshire (now Oxfordshire), which was an ancient historic village dating back to Saxon times; but which was partly resited and subjected to large-scale redevelopment, modernization and 'prettification' by its owners, Lord and Lady Wantage, in the mid-nineteenth century.[1] The motives were partly aesthetic, partly philanthropic, and also practical—the belief that a well-housed and contented labour force would be more stable and more efficient than a miserable and discontented one.

However, although the typical Victorian model village was probably the handiwork of a paternalistic landlord, there were also other important types. These included co-operative settlement schemes inspired by people like Robert Owen and even Tolstoy; and the settlements established (albeit briefly) by the Chartists around the mid-century. There was also another type of growing importance: the model industrial village (of which Owen's New Lanark was perhaps the archetype) later developed in the direction of garden suburbs, such as Bourneville, near Birmingham; New Earswick, near York; and Port Sunlight, near Birkenhead. The term 'industrial'

414

may also be understood quite broadly; it comprised villages devoted to mining and railways and also newly established small ports. Finally there were the seaside resort villages, of which Thorpeness in Suffolk was a representative type.[2]

If there was such a wide variety of model villages it is not surprising that the motivations and inspirations behind them should also have been many and varied. Before looking at these in more detail the chronological question should be briefly disposed of. Strictly speaking, a Victorian model village should be one built between 1837 and 1901; but these dates have no significance for the subject. The inspiration for builders often lay in changes of taste which occurred in the late eighteenth century (especially the rise of Romanticism and the passion for the picturesque); whereas motivations like the desire to improve living standards, which were powerful in the late nineteenth century, continued on beyond 1901 without any break. So for purposes of convenience we shall take the century of peace between 1815 and 1914 as our time period. Although it was a period which witnessed more rapid and more profound changes than at any preceding time in British history, it was at least unified by one important influence which did not greatly change: namely the economic, political and social ascendency of large (and frequently titled) landlords throughout the countryside.[3]

I

As we have seen, eighteenth-century model villages like Nuneham Courtney, Milton Abbas, and New Houghton, Norfolk, were really by-products of the landscaping activities of people like 'Capability' Brown and Nathaniel Kent. They excited no particular interest in themselves, and no powerful social, humanitarian or aesthetic interests were involved in their construction. But by the nineteenth century this attitude was beginning to change. The villages were becoming objects of interest in themselves, although the aesthetic pleasure they were intended to give their owners was still a very much more powerful motive than any desire to improve the comfort or the well-being of their inhabitants: that was to come later.

It was the rise of the 'picturesque' movement in aesthetic fashion, and particularly the new interest in cottages as a specially important symbol, which seems to have been the initial inspiration for the early nineteenth-century model village. Many artistic trends, like the poetry of Byron and Wordsworth, and the landscapes of Constable, no doubt contributed to the generalized development of the mood, but it seems to have been the specific influence of two theorists which gave the movement its real driving force. These were William Gilpin and Sir Uvedale Price. Gilpin made tours in the latter part of the eighteenth century to encourage people to visit romantic and remote areas, such as Wales or north Devon, where wild and picturesque elements of an older age still survived. The enthusiasm of Wordsworth and Coleridge for Lynmouth gorge, and later the Lake District, were part of this development. Gilpin was bored by the classical regularity of a village like Nuneham

Courtney, which, although he admitted its superior convenience, seemed to him to lack the charm of the picturesque village. This charm was essentially based on a variety of styles in cottage building.

> When all these little habitations happen to unite harmoniously and to be connected with the proper appendages of a village—the winding road, a number of spreading trees, a rivulet and a bridge and a spire to bring the whole to an apex—the village is compleat.[4]

Sir Uvedale Price elaborated these sentiments in his *Essay on the Picturesque* (1794) where he encouraged landlords to remodel their estate villages along these lines, saying,

> there is, indeed, no scene where such a variety of forms and embellishments may be introduced at so small an expense, and without anything fantastic or unnatural, as that of a village; none where the lover of painting, and the lover of humanity, may find so many sources of amusement and interest.

Price's vision of the ideal village is well illustrated by his later comments on some cottages painted by van Ostade:

> Their outline against the sky is generally composed of forms of unequal heights, thrown into many different degrees of perspective; the sides are varied by projecting windows and doors . . . [and they demonstrate] what still may be shown in the playful variety and intricacy of buildings and their appendages, where space, elegance and grandeur are unthought of.[5]

It was not long before this alluring seed bore fruit, and strangely it was one of the masters of classical architecture, no less a person than John Nash himself, who designed the prototype for all later picturesque villages—Blaise Hamlet. The site was a few miles to the north-west of Bristol in the parish of Henbury, outside Blaise Castle, the mansion and park of the patron, the wealthy Bristol Quaker banker, J. S. Harford. Fortunately the nine ornate cottages built by Nash round a green in 1810–11 now belong to the National Trust, which has saved them from becoming totally engulfed in the surrounding suburbs of Bristol. Each cottage was built to a separate design and every device of the picturesque was employed to maximum effect—steeply pitched thatched roofs, dormer windows, rustic porches and luxuriant creepers abounded; but Nash's greatest pride was in the lofty and elaborately ornate brick chimneys. Yet although Harford prided himself on his humanitarian interests (and campaigned against the slave trade) the accommodation offered in these cottages was extremely meagre. Admittedly they were intended for elderly people, but one small, dark living room downstairs and a couple of bedrooms in the eaves were all they provided—plus exterior wash-houses and privies tucked away at the back. Clearly, aesthetic interests had triumphed over the residents' convenience, and this unfortunate example remained powerful throughout the nineteenth century.[6]

However, its influence declined from the 1840s when awareness of the appallingly bad housing conditions prevailing in so many rural areas became more widespread, and the desire to improve standards began to prevail over purely aesthetic considerations—although it was still hoped to combine the two. A leader in the movement for better standards of convenience and hygiene in cottages was Prince Albert, who became the active patron of the Society for Improving the Condition of the Labouring Classes, established in 1848. The society circulated plans for model cottages (see Plate 151) and, using the Prince Consort's example of improvements on the Crown estates, inspired landowners to rebuild cottages and remodel villages. The prince was responsible for improved cottages at Windsor, and for model villages at West Newton (Sandringham estate, Norfolk) and Whippingham (Osborne estate, Isle of Wight). Soon some of the wealthiest landowners, like the dukes of Bedford, Devonshire and Northumberland, were following the prince's example and setting a fashion which others were eager to emulate.[7]

There were, however, a number of problems which could easily deter all but the very wealthiest enthusiasts. The first was economic: cottages were a bad investment. Some figures from the Duke of Bedford's estates in the 1890s, relating to fifty-two cottages, show that the average cost of construction was £296. It was generally believed at the time that the gross rent should be about 10 per cent of the capital to cover rates, repairs and incidentals, and allow some measure of profit on the investment. This would imply a yearly rent of £29.60. In fact the duke drew between £2.60 and £5.20 a year from these cottages, depending on their size. If we regard £4 a year as an average rent, the return on the investment was only about 1.3 per cent.[8]

This economic problem was compounded by the fact that the inhabitants of model cottages, or model villages, were frequently not the employees of landlords but of tenant-farmers. Hence the landlord had no direct interest in subsidizing their wages. Where the model village was built primarily for domestic servants or estate employees, as at Edensor on the Duke of Devonshire's Chatsworth estate, this problem was minimized; but it must generally have acted as a deterrent. Another linked factor was the fear of erecting cottages whose occupants might become unemployed and hence fall on the poor rates. Indeed, so great was this fear that many landlords were more concerned with pulling down cottages than with erecting them. Villages of this type were known as 'close' villages, and a vigorous controversy raged on their relative merits and demerits as compared with 'open villages', which became correspondingly overcrowded and insanitary.[9] In fact, in view of the strength and pervasiveness of the deterring factors, it is surprising that so many model villages were built.

The desire to retreat to a self-sufficient, co-operative rural settlement is very ancient. No doubt it embodies a faint folk memory of ancient village communities, as well as a reaction against the pressures and tensions of city life (which were reinforced in the nineteenth century by the dirt, disease, noise and squalor of so many new industrial towns). Robert Owen was an early enthusiast, though most of his attempts to found rural settlements, both in England and America, were disastrous failures. One of his dissident disciples, William Allen, had better fortune though with Lindfield in Sussex, founded in 1831, and successfully based on smallholdings.[10] Fergus O'Connor tried to lead the Chartists in the same direction in 1848 after the failure of their mammoth petitions demanding the suffrage; but the few settlements which were established, like Charterville in Oxfordshire, Great Dodford, Worcestershire, and Snigs End, Gloucestershire, soon failed as social experiments, though they struggled on as centres for a few smallholders.[11]

Finally, there were the quite different motivations which inspired the builders of industrial villages. Their problem was usually to provide accommodation for a workforce which had to be attracted to a new site convenient for the mill—whether it was water or steam. Some of the early industrial villages like Turton and Egerton, Lancashire, which were built by the Ashworths for their employees, were relatively utilitarian,[12] but if the manufacturer were very successful, elements both of philanthropy and desire to make a mark entered his motivation, as can be seen with Sir Titus Salt's Saltaire (1850s) near Bradford,[13] and Lord Leverhulme's Port Sunlight (1890s) near Birkenhead.[14]

II

As we have seen, the 'picturesque' style reigned almost unchallenged in the early nineteenth century, and only gave way slowly, and in scattered places, to rival styles. Some notable picturesque villages after Blaise Hamlet were Somerleyton in Suffolk, Ilam in Staffordshire and Old Warden in Bedfordshire. Somerleyton, near Aldburgh in east Suffolk, was built for the great railway contractor, Sir Morton Peto, and was largely designed by the architect, John Thomas, in the 1850s. It is described by Gillian Darley as perhaps the most successful functioning picturesque village today.[15] Another good example is Ilam, set magnificently on a site in the Pennine dale country of north Staffordshire. It was designed by George Gilbert Scott in 1854 for a wealthy manufacturer, Jesse Watts Russell. Its garishly coloured tile-hanging is quite out of character with the vernacular architecture of the area, but gives the village an unmistakably 'picturesque' stamp.[16] Old Warden, Bedfordshire, built for the Ongley family around the middle of the century is another example well worth a visit, with much pretty thatch and elegant decorations.

One of the first rivals of the picturesque was eclecticism, which by its very nature can hardly be regarded as a style, and has, inevitably, produced some of the most extraordinary and eccentric of all the model villages. The picturesque style emphasized variety, but variety within the confines of a certain unity of approach and treatment. Eclecticism took this variety to its logical conclusion and removed all restraints. The best example is probably to be seen at Edensor, by Chatsworth, where the Duke of Devonshire built a remarkable collection of cottages in contrasting

418

119 Masons at work on the construction of Waddesdon (*Gazette des Beaux Arts*, 1959, series 6, LIV, 15)

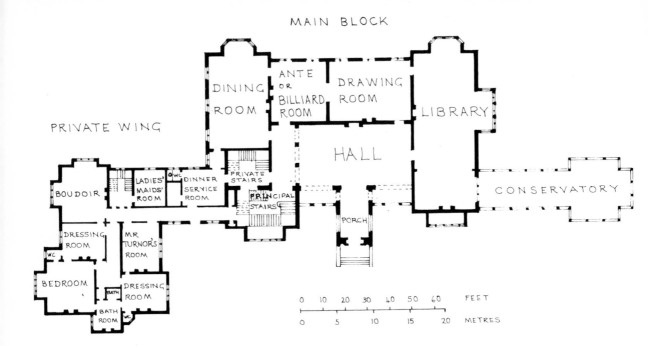

MAIN BLOCK

PRIVATE WING

DINING ROOM

ANTE or BILLIARD ROOM

DRAWING ROOM

LIBRARY

HALL

CONSERVATORY

BOUDOIR

LADIES' MAIDS' ROOM

WC

DINNER SERVICE ROOM

PRIVATE STAIRS

PRINCIPAL STAIRS

PORCH

DRESSING ROOM

WC

MR TURNOR'S ROOM

BEDROOM

BATH

DRESSING ROOM

BATH ROOM

WC

0 10 20 30 40 50 60   FEET

0   5   10   15   20   METRES

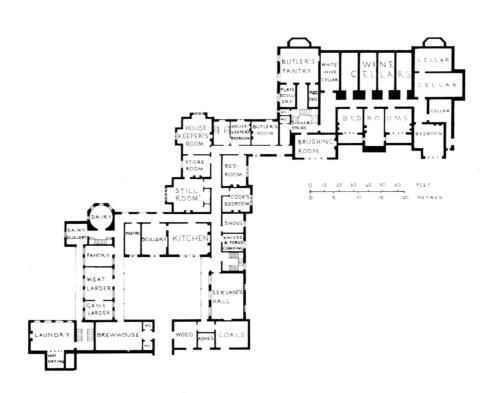

BUTLER'S PANTRY

WHITE WINE CELLAR

WINE CELLARS

CELLAR

CELLAR

PLATE SCULLERY

PLATE SAFE

WC

WC

DINNER STAIRS

CELLAR

BEDROOMS

BEDROOM

HOUSE-KEEPER'S ROOM

HOUSE-KEEPER'S BEDROOM

BUTLER'S ROOM

BRUSHING ROOM

STORE ROOM

BED-ROOM

STILL ROOM

COOK'S BEDROOM

0 10 20 30 40 50 60   FEET

0   5   10   15   20   METRES

DAIRY

DAIRY SCULLERY

PANTRY

SCULLERY

KITCHEN

SHOES

KNIVES & FORKS CLEANING

PANTRY

MEAT LARDER

GAME LARDER

SERVANTS HALL

LAUNDRY

BREWHOUSE

WC

WC

HOT DRYING

WOOD

ASHES

COALS

120 Stoke Rochford hall, plans of the principal floor and the basement (Redrawn from plans in RIBA Drawings J12 (1 and 2) British Architectural Library, Drawings Collection)

121 The kitchen at Minley Manor, Hampshire, part of the additions of 1885 and later by George Devey to a house of 1858–62 by Henry Clutton (National Monument Record. A Bedford Lemere photograph)

122 *above left* A Victorian fernery: one kind of
specimen garden (Alfred Smee, *My Garden, its Plan
and Culture*, 1872, pl. 10)

123 *above right* Architectural gardening by Sir
Charles Barry at Shrubland Park, Suffolk, 1848 (Alfred
Barry, *The Life and Works of Sir Charles Barry*, 1867,
pl. 17)

124 *opposite above* Parterres in Trentham Park laid
out by W. A. Nesfield in the 1830s and 1840s,
photographed at the end of the century (*Country Life*,
1889, III, 273)

125 *opposite below* Tortworth Court. The park was
landscaped in the eighteenth century, though the
conifers and specimen trees are younger. The formal
terraces lie between the house and the park (*Country
Life*, 1899, V, 592)

126 *above* East Lockinge, Oxfordshire. This view shows the main street after it had been re-aligned by Lord Wantage in 1860 to remove it from the view of Lockinge House. The model cottages with their mixture of traditional Berkshire and Victorian Gothic styles were designed by Lord Wantage himself (Museum of English Rural Life)

127a, **b** and **c**   *below and opposite* Somerleyton, Suffolk. Built for Sir Morton Peto, a successful building contractor and Liberal MP for Norwich, about 1850, Somerleyton contains 28 cottages and a school built round a large green. It is perhaps the best surviving example of a 'picturesque' model village, still remote and rural

128 *left* Scene at the homecoming of Lord and Lady Heneage of Hainton, July 1896. The venerable figure standing close to the carriage is Mr Harrison, the oldest tenant on the estate (Hall Collection)

129 *below* An estate banquet for tenants held in the forecourt of Coleorton Hall, 1849 (Leicestershire Museums, Art Galleries and Records Services)

130 *above left* Drinking a stirrup-cup at a meet at Culverthorpe, near Sleaford in Lincolnshire (Hallgarth Collection)

131 *below left* The eighth Earl of Harrington with his hounds. The Earl brought hounds from Nottinghamshire to hunt part of the Quorn territory in Leicestershire (Leicestershire Museums, Art Galleries and Records Services)

132 *above right* Two gentlemen pose with their bag, at Hainton, a village on the Lincolnshire wolds south-east of Market Rasen (Hallgarth Collection)

133 *below right* A shooting party pose at Holton le Moor, Lincolnshire (Hallgarth Collection)

134 The squire and friends wreak havoc among the partridges. This scene of 1895 shows a breech-loading shotgun in use (*Illustrated London News*)

styles for his estate employees. The cottages are mostly detached and are well-built of local stone, but their styles range from mock-Tudor, castellated Gothic and Italianate renaissance to sturdy Swiss 'chalets', with a weird variety of intermediate decoration attached. In some ways it is the ultimate in model village architecture.[17] Although the picturesque and the eclectic were perhaps the most characteristic architectural manifestations of model villages, they did have some more sober rivals. An unadorned utilitarianism inspired Henry Roberts's cottage designs for the Society for Improving the Condition of the Labouring Classes, and it had a widespread influence, notably in villages on the Duke of Bedford's estate, and also those of the Duke of Grafton, like Potterspury in Northamptonshire.[18] The revived classic and Gothic styles had only limited influence, being too imposing for cottages; though elements of the former may be seen at Saltaire, and of the latter at Akroyden, near Halifax. These styles were not only too imposing but also too expensive.[19]

A more sensible response to the question of style was employed by those architects who sought to conform to the local vernacular style prevailing in the district while adding any minor improvements which may have seemed necessary. Thus at Penshurst in Kent the nineteenth-century additions conform more or less to the prevailing timber-framed Tudor style; and this approach was also adopted by Lord Wantage at East Lockinge, although admittedly some picturesque additions (particularly in the strange shape of dormer windows) were allowed to creep in.[20] This modified vernacular approach was fairly widespread. At Baldersby St James in Yorkshire William Butterfield adapted a local vernacular style in brick which was neo-Georgian except for its steeply pitched roofs. An even more modern type of vernacular was used by Raymond Unwin and Barry Parker at New Earswick, built for the Rowntree chocolate workers outside York, *c.* 1901–10. Here steeply pitched tiled roofs were combined with simple, often whitewashed, exteriors and fairly large windows, which were characteristic of what was then regarded as 'modern' architecture. As a garden suburb New Earswick, of course, occupies an intermediate position between village and town. Its ambience and feel are rural, but it is in fact part of the urban area of the city of York.[21]

Standards of housing varied very much from village to village, but with a tendency towards improvement as the nineteenth century progressed. The earliest picturesque villages, like Blaise Hamlet, provided only rather limited, dark and poky living space, but after the middle of the century most cottages offered a living room and kitchen downstairs, and three bedrooms above. The moral aspects of overcrowding particularly alarmed the Victorians, and it became increasingly seen as important that children should not share their parents' bedroom and that separate bedrooms should be provided for boys and girls. As families tended to be large this could still mean that three or four boys or girls might share a bedroom, but it was a great advance on the conditions which had often existed in the early part of the century.

An example of earlier conditions is provided by Ardington and Lockinge in 1860, before Lady Wantage and her husband started their work of amelioration. In later life (1907) she pungently described the old-world cottages as 'fast-decaying hovels through whose wattle and dab walls a walking stick could easily be thrust'.[22] When it was decided to remove part of the village which was too close to the Wantage residence to a more congenial site, Lady Wantage described the part to be destroyed as 'farm sheds, muck yards and hovels'.[23] The Wantages set about building the new model cottages with enthusiasm; and it may not be a coincidence that Lord Wantage had previously served as an equerry to the Prince of Wales, a position for which he had been selected by Prince Albert, some of whose enthusiasm for model cottages may have rubbed off on the young equerry. Lady Wantage stated:

> An architect was rarely employed; plans of buildings have always been made and executed under Lord and Lady Wantage's own superintendence. The picturesque character of the old style of cottage building, with its 'wattle and dab' walls, rough timber beams and thatched roofs, has been as far as possible retained, with the view of preserving the irregular character and charm of the old Berkshire villages.[24]

By the standards of the time these were sturdy and roomy cottages. Downstairs they had a living room 15 feet square and 8 feet 6 inches high, a small kitchen and out-houses containing a coal-stove, a built-in copper with fireplace beneath for boiling water for washing, and an earth-closet. Upstairs they had three bedrooms, one measuring 15 feet by 12 feet, and the other two 12 feet by 8 feet.[25] However there was one aspect of residence which never occurred to the Wantages: present-day residents find great difficulty in getting any furniture into the upstairs rooms because of the steep roof gables and narrow twisting stairs.

Modern sanitation was inevitably a late development since very few villages had piped water supplies, but it is interesting to note that Henry Roberts's 1848 design for model cottages contained water-closets if only with outside access, whereas when Prince Albert and Roberts designed a pair of model cottages for the 1851 Exhibition water-closets were provided with internal access, not only on the ground floor, but upstairs as well. These cottages were reconstructed at Kennington in south London after the Exhibition, where they still stand.[26]

However it is unlikely that many villages had piped water before the twentieth century, and it was in the industrial villages close to towns that progress was most rapid. In 1859 Akroyden was supplied with water and gas, and drainage was by 'sanitary tubes'. Bathrooms were still unknown, but an interesting variation on the usual tin tub before the fire was provided at Bourneville (*c.* 1895) where a sunken bath was built in the kitchen floor in front of the range. When required its cover was removed and it could be filled from large kettles warmed on the range.[27]

Generally speaking, model villages almost certainly provided above-average accommodation by the standards of the time, and usually supplied it at an artificially low rent as well. If the quality of the housing seems inadequate today that is merely a reflection of how much the general standard of living (and its associated expectations) have risen since Victoria's time.

III

The greater wealth (and often the greater needs) of industrialists enabled them to pioneer some of the improvements in housing standards and introduce them before they became practical in agricultural villages; but conversely it may have been the latter which inspired some industrialists to provide housing for their workers in the context of a village or garden suburb rather than in the densely packed urban tradition.

An interesting example of the industrial village approach is provided by Street in Somerset, now a small town virtually attached to Glastonbury, but for many years a model industrial village. Street is the home of the shoe-making firm of C. & J. Clark Ltd, one of the largest shoe manufacturers in Britain. This is very much a family firm, founded by Quaker farmers in 1825 when Street had a population of around 800 people. Shoe-making was at that time a cottage industry which provided employment for people living in Street and a number of surrounding villages. Clarks, however, were so successful with their shoes that it became necessary to bring in machinery to meet the expanding demand of the 1850s, and by 1861 the firm was producing 208,000 pairs of shoes a year. The population of Street was then 1,900, of whom practically all worked for Clarks. By 1901 the population had reached 4,000 (and shoe production 800,000 pairs), but Street still retained its village character.[28]

The Clarks had built their factory in 1857 right next to their own house in the main street, and there it still stands, though considerably enlarged. From the beginning they decided to provide housing for their workpeople, and the roads and houses were carefully planned and laid out to ensure that ample gardens and recreation space were left. The local lias stone (called blue, but actually a light grey) provided an excellent building material, and the company houses were built in a modified vernacular similar to that which is so attractively displayed in nearby towns and villages like Somerton and Compton Dundon.[29]

Although now too big to be regarded any longer as a village, Street yet retains the physical limits and the small community atmosphere which the more widely celebrated industrial garden suburbs, like Bourneville, Port Sunlight and New Earswick, have to some extent lost because of their proximity to large cities. The outward sprawl of Birmingham, Birkenhead and York has threatened them with encirclement and absorption, and although they have managed to retain a semi-rural atmosphere the village community aspect has inevitably tended to wither. However, all these industrial communities (Street included) share with traditional model villages the overriding influence (though not always the dominance) of one employer family. Lord Leverhulme at Port Sunlight clearly revelled in his paternalistic role, though the other three, the Cadburys at Bourneville, the Rowntrees at New Earswick and the Clarks at Street (all Quakers), were more concerned to try to reduce this aspect of their role so as not to induce hostile reactions amongst their employees. For the feeling of resentment at obligation, which can arise even towards the most beneficent of patrons, has always been the

421

most troublesome fly in the ointment of the model village. With this aspect of the subject we may conclude this chapter.

IV

In a situation where a landlord was providing the housing and, as frequently happened in model villages, other amenities as well, such as allotments, sports grounds, clubhouses ('reading rooms' as they were often called) and generally a well-organized and pleasant environment, he would inevitably expect to receive the gratitude, respect and obedience of his tenants. Equally inevitably they were inclined to feel a sense of being manipulated and a loss of self-respect. This feeling was no doubt accentuated in cases where the landlord disapproved of public houses (as many did), or expected regular attendance at church (as Lady Wantage did). At Selworthy in west Somerset Lady Acland provided red cloaks for the old-age pensioners to wear. This may have made the rural scene more charming, but must also have added to the feeling of diminished independence.[30]

All these issues were ventilated in a pointed way in relation to the Lockinge estate in an article which appeared in the Liberal *Daily News* of 25 September 1891. It was written by a 'special commissioner' who paid a visit to the estate, and appeared under the title 'Arcadia Realised', together with Lord Wantage's reply. The main points are given in the following quotations.

> One of the most interesting and instructive scenes of rural life in England may be found in the villages of Lockinge and Ardington. . . . I went over yesterday because two or three years back I understood that the owner of this vast estate was going to crown and complete the remarkable little social system he has created here, by admitting his people to a share in the profits of his farming, and I wished to learn a little about the result of it. . . .
>
> 'These villages of Ardington and Lockinge' the special commissioner went on,
>
> are well worthy of a visit. Seen in the early summer especially, as I saw them on a former occasion, they strike one as quite a little rural paradise. The estate is beautifully timbered; the cottages with their ornamental eaves and pointed gables, their fanciful chimney-stacks and pretty porches overgrown with ivy and roses, their grassy slopes and lawns and shrubs and flower-beds, all present innumerable points of view with which the artist would be enraptured. Every villager has, or may have, his allotment. There is an admirable reading room and a public house in charge of a salaried manager who has no interest whatever in pushing the sale of drink, but who is especially required to provide soup in winter, and tea and coffee and other non-toxicants at all times. There is a first-rate co-operative store, with commodious

premises, at which the people can get all the necessaries of life, clothes, grocery, bread, meat, and provisions, on profit-sharing terms. The bakery is a beautiful little place, with patent ovens and the newest machinery. In addition to all this, over a hundred villagers are employed in municipal workshops, so to speak—shops fitted with all kinds of the latest machinery and the best appliances—saw-mills, carpenters' shops, blacksmiths' shops, painters' shops, wheelwrights' shops—all for the building and repairing and general maintenance of the property on the estate. There are two churches and an excellent school. In short, it is a little self-contained world in which nobody is idle, nobody is in absolute want, in which there is no squalor or hunger, while in the midst of it all is the great house of Lockinge the beautiful home of Lord and Lady Wantage, always ready to play the part of benevolent friends to all who need their help, and who indeed, by all accounts, seem sincerely desirous of promoting the happiness and well-being of their people. The regular pay of the labourers on the estate is not higher than elsewhere. I understand that it was a shilling or so higher at one time, and that in consequence Lord Wantage has the very cream of the labourers in that part of the world, but that it was reduced to ten-shillings a week when the profit-sharing scheme was promulgated the expectation being that this reduction would be more than counterbalanced by the dividend that would be distributed when the farm accounts were made up.

Having found so much to praise at Ardington and Lockinge the special commissioner turned to what he thought 'radically rotten and bad':

The whole system of things here is another illustration of that 'model' village life which is merely another name for social and political death. Lord Wantage is not to be attacked. He stands high in the esteem of all his neighbours and friends—unless maybe some of the tradesmen in the little town of Wantage, who are naturally angry with co-operative supply stores—and he has most laudably and consistently carried his Conservative principles into action. Materially, the result on the face of it is delightful and as a means of keeping the control and management of the people by the aristocracy nothing could possibly be better. But for all the purposes of political life and social progress and human development it is utterly bad. Lord Wantage has done for the people, in the true spirit of benevolent Toryism, what the people ought to be able to do for themselves—not individually, of course, but collectively and unitedly, and by their own sturdy independent and manly effort. I don't know what Lord Wantage's personal wish may be with regard to the voting power of his own people but I am sure that those people themselves have no idea whatever that they are free electors. 'Any

423

politicians here?' I asked an old man as I walked up the road with him through Lockinge. 'What's them?' said the man with a puzzled air. 'Politicians,' I bawled, thinking the old man was a little deaf or very stupid—'Politicians—you know what politicians are'. 'Be-em animals they goes out to shoot?' said the old fellow. Then I saw the waggish twinkle of his eyes that told me plainly enough he was only making a fool of me. He knew very well what politicians were, but he wasn't going to talk about such matters at Lockinge, and I couldn't induce him to. All around I heard Ardington and this village spoken of as a political dead sea, in which no public opinion ever was known to manifest itself. Nobody would say that Lord Wantage was a man to exercise any improper influence on his people; but he is a strong Tory, has been a member of the Tory government, his agents are Tories, and he owns all the land and houses, and can give or take away employment. I could not find anybody who knew of a political meeting having been held in these places. I heard it rumoured that there was one man who dared avow himself a Liberal, but I couldn' find him. 'O yes, Sir', said a woman in the place, 'they all votes Lord Wantage's way, of course. It wouldn't do for em to go again 'im.'

And according to the *Daily News* reporter, many of the amenities of Lord Wantage's villages were accompanied by irritating restrictions on individual freedom:

> I am assured that the admirable little public house in Ardington is to a great extent a failure, because the men find that they are not free to talk there, and that whatever they say is liable to be carried by the birds to the agent's or bailiff's ears. The people are managed and governed and controlled without the least voice in their public and collective affairs, and, though they undoubtedly have strong opinions on certain matters, they dare not give expression to them. For instance, the people have allotments for growing their own vegetables, but they must not keep a pig. They have flower gardens in front of their cottages; if they don't keep them in order the bailiff will be down upon them. A labourer doesn't quite like his cottage; there is no possibility of shifting without the bailiff's consent and arrangement. 'They daren't blow their noses over at Ardington without the bailiff's leave,' said a labourer in the neighbourhood. The people control nothing, have no part whatever in anything like public life, nor any voice in matters directly affecting their own welfare. . . .

For their village stores the men ought to subscribe their own capital, pay interest, if at all, into their own coffers, and pocket the profit of the whole business. The management would, of course, be in the hands of the people themselves, who would elect their own officers and control their own affairs. Whatever advantage there might be would be public advantage, and it would all be consistent with everybody's perfect freedom and independence. There need be no fear of anybody, no cringing to agents, no concealment of opinions—absolutely nothing inconsistent with free, individual, manly life and sturdy citizenship. . . .

To the Editor of the '*Daily News*'

Sir, . . . It is not my desire or intention to enter into any controversy; but I feel it would be unfortunate if some of the systems in operation on my estates, which your commissioner describes, were to be discredited by erroneous statements which would have the effect of discouraging their adoption elsewhere.

A correspondent of yours who signs himself 'Lockinge' makes many and varied complaints on behalf of the labourers of this district. Among these the allegation that the 'bonus' system has caused universal dissatisfaction among the labourers on this estate can only have a misleading and mischievous effect. In spite of what this correspondent says, I strongly (after experience of some years) recommend the system as an incentive to industry, and as conducive to a widening of interest on the part of the labourers in the prosperity of the farm on which they work. The bonus is, as your commissioner points out, given over and above the regular wages paid to farm labourers on this estate, which are in no way affected by it, and which rise and fall according to the fluctuation of supply and demand. It is not intended that the bonus system should be worked on strictly profit-sharing principles, which at present involves considerable practical working difficulties, but which further experience may possibly overcome. But the amount of bonus given is dependent on the profit realised. Certain farms of mine, which till recently made no profits, and consequently gave no bonus, have since last year paid their way, and have yielded a bonus, which I hope may be gradually increased in amount as the farm profits improve. The enforcement of sanitary regulations naturally falls upon the landlord, whether he happens to hold town or country property, and the insurance of healthy conditions by means of estate rules must in some cases override other considerations. The convenience of a pig-sty close to the cottage backdoor is more than counter-balanced by the contamination of the neighbouring well. But it by no means follows that, because a pig-sty is not allowed close to a cottage, the cottager is forbidden to have one elsewhere. The allotment is the most suitable place for a pig-sty, and on this estate every man, can, if he wishes, have one put up at cost price, and removed at his convenience. Allotments should, where possible, be in near proximity to the village. Such is the case on this estate, and the proof that they are not 'failures' is that the demand for them is such that none are ever vacant. The management of the public house is so well described by your commissioner that I need say no more about it, except to observe that the sole restrictions enforced are such as the law of the land imposes, namely, those restricting the supply of liquor when men are in a state of drunkenness. The co-operative stores established in these villages distribute the whole of the profits among their customers, being worked on what is known as the Rochdale co-operative system. This mode of distribution was adopted, after full consideration, in preference to another plan, also on the Rochdale principle, which disposes of the profit in the shape of dividends, among the shareholders. But when there are shareholders who take these dividends, the money returned to the customers on their purchases is to that extent diminished, and this consideration has guided the managers of these stores in their adoption of a system which is working very satisfactorily.

It has been said in your columns that it is easy to draw pleasant pictures of the condition of the agricultural worker under the care of a beneficent landlord. But why assume that such a condition can only be purchased at the expense of freedom to think and act for himself? The fact that we live in democratic days is no reason for disparaging and discouraging the legitimate influence landlords may exercise over their neighbours and tenants by helpful supervision and by friendly interest in their affairs which ought not, and which do not, interfere with the freedom of speech and liberty of action which are the right of all alike, of labourers as well as landlords.

I am, Sir, your obedient servant,
Wantage
Lockinge House, Wantage, Berks, October 3 [1891].[31]

These two quotations provide such an excellent summary of the conflicting contemporary views of model villages that further comment is hardly necessary; except to point out that the economic advantages of residing in one could be very real. Those who wished to maintain a more independent and self-reliant way of life had a high price to pay.

In conclusion it should be noted that model villages (both rural and industrial) had a far wider influence than their limited numbers would imply: for if a few landlords could aspire to remodelling a whole village, there must have been hundreds who were inspired by the example to tackle the housing problem on a smaller scale. New cottages were built to ampler and more convenient standards, and older cottages, which might otherwise have been neglected, were refurbished or extended. Thus was the influence of the model villages filtered through the whole of the Victorian countryside.

Notes

1   See Havinden, 1966, for a general history of Lockinge and the Wantage estate.
2   See Darley, 1975, for an excellent and wide-ranging discussion of the many types of model village.
3   See F. M. L. Thompson, 1963, *passim.*
4   Cited by Darley, 1975, 8.
5   Cited by Cooper, 1967a, 1454.
6   Pevsner, 1958, 468–9.
7   Darley, 1975, 45–7.
8   *Country Life*, 10 December 1904, 881–2.
9   Holderness, 1972b, *passim.*
10 Allen, 1846, *passim.*
11 Alice M. Hadfield, 1970, *passim.*
12 Boyson, 1970, 115–40.
13 Holroyd, 1871, *passim.*
14 Wilson, 1954, I, 142–58.
15 Darley, 1975, 30.
16 Cooper, 1967a, 1456.
17 Pevsner, 1953, 129–31.
18 Cooper, 1967a, 1456.
19 Darley, 1975, 67.
20 Havinden, 1966, 105–11.
21 Darley, 1975, 92–4.
22 Havinden, 1966, 54.
23 *Ibid.*, 68.
24 *Ibid.*, 69.
25 *Ibid.*, 95–6.
26 Darley, 1975, 45–6.
27 *Ibid.*, 67, 70.
28 Clark, 1975, *passim.*
29 Little, 1974, 129–34.
30 Acland, 1976, 9.
31 Havinden, 1966, 113–18.

31   Landlords and Tenants

T. W. Beastall

I

The landlord–tenant system depended upon the great wealth of landowners and the security, coupled with a freedom to make the best of their farms, that this gave to tenant-farmers. Landlords were expected to put their capital into their estates, to protect their tenants in bad times, to stand for fair or sympathetic conduct towards farmers and to eschew all appearances of rapacity or ruthlessness. Not all landlords were wealthy but their conduct had to suggest that they were, and their standards in estate management were set by those who from agricultural rents, woodlands, mines, railways, docks and urban building, were possessed of great incomes and vast assets.

Many landlords had gradually developed a relationship with their tenants which was relaxed, interested and encouraging. Showing concern for the condition of one's tenants was as essential a part of rural life as participating in the many sporting activities that went with the ownership of a great, or indeed a small estate. The landlord owned the soil, and through his agent made sure that it was kept in good heart by holding his tenants to certain conditions of practice. It had to be as well-drained as possible, enclosed, served by convenient roads or lanes, protected from the ravages of rabbits, and its function as a crop- and livestock-raising asset reconciled with the claims of hunting, shooting and fishing. The farmhouse and buildings, with walls and some hedges, were usually the landlord's responsibility. Perhaps his chief contribution for being spared the direct risks of farming was that in capitalizing the holding he was enabling the farmer to use all his resources for implements, seeds,

428

fertilizers, the purchase or hire of better livestock, the use of more horse power, and the employment of good shepherds, wagoners and labourers. This made possible the traditional aim of tenant-farmers, the one held in the 1840s by occupiers on the north Lincolnshire uplands, who tried to make in a year at least three times the amount they had to find for rent and tithes. If rent and tithes stood at £1,000 a year, then that sum could be spent on labour, fertilizer and family living costs, and £1,000 would be looked for in addition as profit.[1]

Cottages for the farm's labourers were often built and maintained by the landlord. Sometimes he would keep them in his own hands and let them to farm workers himself. On other estates cottages were let with the farm and the tenant had control of their occupation. For tenant-farmers there were advantages in not owning the land they farmed. It was easier to raise the capital to rent a farm than it was to buy one, and cheaper to set up one's sons as tenants than it was to buy holdings for them. Mobility in bad times was easier for tenants than for owner-occupiers, and yet ownership of land could be combined with tenancies. When prices fell during a run of bad seasons the landlord acted as a 'buffer between the tenant and the adverse conditions of the time. Rent reductions or returns eased matters until the crisis passed.

Residence was another feature of the landlord-tenant system that gave to English farming an enviable degree of stability and commitment by both farmers and owners. Tenants were expected to live in the main residence of a holding or to install there a responsible member of their families. Landlords, whose seasonal migrations took them to London and elsewhere, were expected, nevertheless, to spend part of the year on their estates. The Dukes of Devonshire had to know about their tenants in Ireland and in eight English counties. The better communications of Victorian England enabled landowners to keep in close touch with the affairs of their estates, and to have early reports on the meetings between their agents and the tenants at events like the biannual rent or audit dinners. Many landlords maintained a home farm, from which to feed their households at cost price and to practise farming themselves with the aid of farm managers or bailiffs. This tradition brought them into contact with their tenants, but movement about their estates in the course of hunting and shooting probably did as much or more to familiarize them with the farmers' mood and the condition of their farms. Landlords had to make some effort to provide balanced holdings. They had to break up inconveniently situated farms, and attempt some redistribution of difficult land so that those with capital and skill could tackle it successfully. The purchasing policy of many estates was to buy up the land of interlopers and round off the property in a ring-fence layout. A resident landowner was of value to a tenant, too, in dealing with difficult neighbours.

Through his landlord a tenant enjoyed access to political affairs and business knowledge. For example, landlords appreciated that Repeal of the Corn Laws would affect their estates, and some provided leadership for their tenants in preparing for it. Under the Land Improvements Acts landlords negotiated loans for draining and building. New ideas were introduced through agricultural shows and ploughing competitions. Aristocratic owners recommended practices found in distant counties, and urged upon their agents comparisons which otherwise would not have been readily available to the local tenantry. The earls of Scarbrough, for instance, made comparisons between their tenants in Lincolnshire, Yorkshire and Durham. Lord Willoughby d'Eresby would call for the use of hedge bills on his Lincolnshire estate such as he saw in Scotland, and he could show his staff on the Grimsthorpe estate the 'Scotch method of sowing turnips upon ridges'.[2] Size and diversity gave to large owners and their agents a breadth of knowledge which must have benefited their management. The advice of a landlord was useful, too, when railway promoters were seeking support for their schemes. He usually had knowledge of alternative proposals and his response to overtures was likely to be more discriminating than that of an owner-occupier who lacked his contacts and his political influence. The tenth Earl of Scarbrough wrote to his Yorkshire tenants in 1900 telling them to be on their guard when railway promoters approached them. The demands of the coal interest were strong in the county at that time, and it was important for agriculture to speak with a single and influential voice.[3]

The landlord–tenant system as represented by the great estates of the aristocracy was not spread evenly over the country, but since it was to be found in all geographical and farming regions its example and influence were strong. In Victorian England most counties had from one fifth to a half of their total acreage farmed under the system. While there were counties like Kent, Surrey, Essex and Middlesex where London's purchasing power had prevented the creation of really great estates, there were others like Lincolnshire where formerly poor land had been bought cheaply, welded into estates, and improved. The north and the west of England were more influenced by the landlord–tenant system than the south and the east, but the style and the assumptions of the system were widely known and served as standards of comparison, if not always of imitation, in areas where great aristocratic estates were few.[4]

II

That on the whole good landlord–tenant relationships were the norm is confirmed by the substitution in the second quarter of the nineteenth century of tenancies-at-will or annual tenancies for leases of three, five, seven or twenty-one years. Farmers were willing to risk their capital at a time of uncertain farming prospects on the strength, sometimes, of nothing more than a verbal agreement with the landowner. Of course, there were strong economic forces supporting this informal arrangement. Tenants with capital and skill were hard to find, and they knew that an annual agreement left them free to move if they were not making a profit, and moreover the landlord was unlikely to hazard having to take his farm in hand by evicting his tenant. Leases had been useful to both tenants and landlords when waste land was being broken into tillage, but after the Napoleonic wars farmers had to watch profit margins carefully as cereal prices levelled out well below the inflated peaks of wartime. They did not want to be tied to the terms of a lease, and the freedom to assess their position each year at Candlemas or Michaelmas appealed to them. Not only were landlords denied access to their farms by a lease, but when prices fell tenants would throw up the lease unilaterally. This left the owner with either the unwelcome prospect of accepting the situation or exacting some form of penalty; a time-consuming and unpopular activity. For him, too, the annual agreement was therefore more acceptable. It was for these considerations, which made good sense in the early Victorian farming context, that leases fell into disfavour, and it was not a crude attempt to wield political power over a proportion of the electorate enfranchised by the Chandos amendment in the 1832 Reform Act. The new importance of the tenant with the ability and capital to tackle large farms now that price levels were lower and the protection of the Corn Laws might be removed was in itself a good reason for enfranchising a vital interest in rural society.

Tenancy arrangements varied within farming regions and even within individual estates, but while encouraging the tenant to invest in his holding most agreements were designed to preserve ancient or valuable pasture, keep the arable in good heart, and ensure that when vacated the farm was fit to hand over to a newcomer. A smooth take-over, an absence of disputes, and a short period of dual occupation of either farm buildings or the land, were also important in any agreement. On the Durham, Lincolnshire and Yorkshire estates of the Lumley family new annual agreements were drawn up in 1864. Six months' notice on either side was to be given, and mineral, timber and game rights were reserved by the landlord. In Yorkshire land was let on 2 February and farm buildings from 1 May. Written consent was needed before pasture could be ploughed: a fine of £10 an acre could be imposed on a tenant ignoring this clause. Rents were to be paid biannually, and the occupier had to meet all other outgoings, except the landlord's property tax. Tenants were also to keep a foxhound free of charge. The land was to be farmed according to the best methods of the district, and no straw, chaff, hay, fodder or turnips sold off without permission. A four-course rotation was to be followed, and no two white crops sown in succession. On leaving, the tenant was to be compensated for his improvements under the terms of the local custom. In 1897 an amended form of the agreement required the tenant to insure his stock and produce, to live in the farmhouse or to place a member of his family there, to paint the buildings every fourth year, trim hedges and clear ditches every year, and, for the convenience of hunters, remove all barbed wire between 1 November and 1 April.

The first twenty-five years of Queen Victoria's reign saw much investment by tenant farmers in bones, guano, marl and lime. Many developed mixed enterprises, balancing their resources between stock-rearing and cereal-growing, and by keeping their sheep in the fields to eat clover or turnips they consolidated the soil, manured it and raised its fertility. Cattle were fed artificial 'cake', the manure from which, when collected in the fold or crew-yard of a farm, became a valuable commodity. Farmers were willing to put their capital into horse power, labour and farm carts to transport the manure to their hungry croplands, and in some of the upland regions of Yorkshire

431

and Lincolnshire even to help their landlords build new barns and crew-yards out in the fields so that mixed farming could advance. But some farmers grew difficult as their leases ran out. William Dawson was the tenant of the 2,300 acres of Withcall farm, near Louth on the Lincolnshire wolds, under Lord Willoughby d'Eresby. In 1842, with six years to run, he became anxious to buy his farm, which stood detached from the other estates of his landlord. He threatened to spend no more on bones, linseed cake, artificial manure, draining, building or fencing, and threatened, too, to sow the whole acreage with wheat. Leases, in fact, might encourage an occupier to think that he had a right to be given a first refusal to purchase his holding at a low price; or that as he had enjoyed a long lease the landlord was bound to refuse him a renewal and offer it to a newcomer for a higher rent. Tenancies-at-will, on the other hand, could continue indefinitely in a flexible arrangement undisturbed by the crisis which inevitably came when a lease was due for renewal. The Earl of Yarborough boasted that he did not *get* tenants in Lincolnshire, he *bred* them! Many of the families listed late in the nineteenth century as walking puppies for the Brocklesby hunt were already there in 1754. This continuity of association with the estate, if not occupation of the same holding, was achieved by a system of mutual respect, relatively low rents and tenancies-at-will. In Nottinghamshire, too, by the 1840s leases were neither wanted nor expected as sons succeeded fathers on farms in many cases.[5]

Farmers were willing to exchange leases for annual tenancies because county customs for tenants' compensation ensured that investment in their holdings would be safeguarded. Compensation varied within counties and even within farming regions, however. In parts of the West Riding tenants were paid for what they had put into the land by way of seed and fertilizers in their last year of occupation, and for half their costs in the penultimate year. This strong custom meant, it was believed in farming circles, that a tenant could fail in Yorkshire, set up again in Nottinghamshire with his tenant-right award, fail again and set up once more in Lincolnshire. Heavy tenant-right payments discouraged younger applicants for farms who had skill but little capital. On the other hand, the custom encouraged tenants' investment, gave security to the tenant-at-will, and helped the landlord in that fewer farms were run down. Landlords could buy up the tenant-right of an outgoer and offer the farm to a newcomer without a demand upon his capital. The tenant-right would then be paid off over a period of years as part of the rent. It also saved landlords the unpopularity of taking action against a man who left owing large arrears of rent. Although landlords were possessed of considerable powers in law to seize the goods of defaulting tenants, they were reluctant to exercise them, and the spectacle of a tenant committed to prison was not one that many landlords would contemplate. By deducting some or all of the arrears of rent from the sum to be paid the outgoer by the new occupier, the landlord could recover his rent without attracting adverse publicity in the press.

In the Lincolnshire uplands farmers were prepared to take large farms without even a compensation clause in their annual agreements. Their security, they said, rested in the high repute of valuers, the strength of local custom and goodwill. William Loft of Trusthorpe, who farmed 500 acres of wold and 500 more of marsh, converted his fourteen-year lease into an annual tenancy in 1847.[6] On the Leveson-Gower estates in Shropshire and Staffordshire farmers were not interested in leases in the years after the Napoleonic wars. James Loch, the agent, believed

> The attention and capital of the landlord should be bestowed upon the permanent improvements which, in their execution, would withdraw too large a portion of a tenant's capital from the cultivation of the land . . . this is the landlord's proper line of duty, and well suited to his station and position in society.

The landlord having helped the tenants to weather the difficult years for farming in the 1820s, the Lilleshall and Trentham estates were praised by James Caird when he saw them in 1850. Loch was delighted by his verdict. By then his work of over forty years was having its effect. Lilleshall was thought to be the lowest-rented estate in England and arrears were few. During the 1840s the agent had thought the farms were under-rented, but because of uncertainty about the future of the Corn Laws the landlord was prepared to bear some of the cost of Repeal by forgoing the rent increases. He pointed out to another landlord that the Leveson-Gower rents had been reduced by about 26 per cent in the late 1830s: 'no wonder your tenants bellow and scream'.[7]

Landlords were reluctant to raise rents until tenants had reaped the reward of their improvements. So in districts where tenants had helped bring marginal land into cultivation rents were allowed to remain low. In addition, though between 1815 and 1840 rents went up by only small amounts or not at all, prices fell, and therefore in real terms landlords were not losing and were willing to postpone rent increases. On the Brocklesby estate of the Earl of Yarborough wold land was let at 10s. to 12s. an acre in 1833 when on a valuation it was deemed to be worth from 20s. to 27s. Yet within roughly the previous forty years the gross income of the estate had increased three-fold, an increase which in real terms was even higher. Nevertheless, rent took only about a third of the returns accruing to the tenant-farmer. James Caird thought in 1850 that rents were a function of landlords' attitudes and of those of their agents, rather than of the land's intrinsic value or the ruling level of prices for agricultural produce. On the larger estates rents tended to be low: the owners had other sources of income. Where a few large estates dominated a district then the 'custom of the neighbourhood' was to offer and ask for low rents. In Lindsey the 40,000 acres of wolds land owned by Lord Yarborough influenced rents in the whole region. Although land was generally low-rented, the agent said of one tenant on land worth 34s. or 35s., 'I cannot think how Atkinson can have the conscience to accept it at 25s an acre which is what he pays.'[8]

In the 1850s, when the shock of Repeal had receded and some of the benefits of improvement showed returns, rents were raised on many estates. In 1850 an applicant for a farm on the Cowdray estate in west Sussex was refused a low rent on the ground that other tenants would be encouraged to ask for the same. When rent abatements were discontinued or rents were raised agents tended to record their relief in letters to their employers. In September 1854 there were fifty-six tenants at the Cowdray estate audit dinner and thanks were conveyed to Lord Egmont for the previous rent abatement 'and not one remark on its discontinuance'.[9] In July of the same year, after attending a dinner at the White Hart in Lincoln, Weston Cracroft Amcotts noted: 'Cordial reception from my father's Hackthorne tenants at their rent dinner . . . —not a murmur at having their rents raised.'[10] At Cowdray on 13 September 1853 Lord Egmont was told by his agent of a good rent audit. There were few arrears, and at the Angel, Midhurst, there was 'quite a roomful, and all were gratified with the treat your lordship gave them, the buck was a very fine one, and the grouse in fine perfection'. The workpeople on the estate had a dinner of beef in October, 'and all were highly gratified and very thankful, the high prices will make the coming winter a severe one for the working people'. This was a time of agricultural prosperity, however, when rents climbed back to the levels of 1815, arrears were few, and the high noon of Victorian farming was enjoyed by both landlords and tenants.[11]

III

The golden years of high farming ended with a succession of bad seasons in the late 1870s. Heavy imports of cheap grain shook the confidence of farmers, and landlords were again obliged to help. Rent returns and reductions, with drainage schemes and measures to convert arable land to pasture, were employed to ward off the nightmare of landlords—the taking in hand of untenanted farms impossible to let without massive capital expenditure. In Essex extra out-buildings for milking parlours were built as dairy farming was introduced to traditionally arable districts.[12] On the Bedford estates the nature of the land precluded a swing to pastoral or mixed farming, and on others the management's assessment of how best to help the tenants reinforced the traditional style of farming. Estates in livestock-raising counties fared better. Landlords avoided having to make large reductions in rent, and by keeping up expenditure on buildings, drainage and other land improvements, they obviated a steep fall in net incomes. This was true, for example, of a property in Northumberland, the Earl of Harewood's estate near Leeds, and Lord Fitzhardinge's estate in Gloucestershire.

On the Duke of Bedford's estate near Woburn the cost of farms in hand between 1879 and 1896 worked out at £1,284 a year. But on the Duke of Sutherland's estates in Staffordshire and Shropshire, where a change away from cereals to mixed farming was actively encouraged, the burden of farms in hand from 1880 to 1899 was only £220 per annum. Dutch barns for the storage of winter fodder were provided. These, with their galvanized iron roofs on iron pillars, were cheap to erect and maintain, and saved the farmer the cost of thatching his hay ricks. Covered fold-yards were built to help the winter fattening of cattle, and, where possible, heavy land was drained and put down to permanent pasture at a cost of £10 to £15 an acre. This was preferable to allowing tenants to let uneconomic arable tumble down to poor grassland.

On the whole, landlords had been quick to make use of public funds to help drain the heavy clays which were so expensive to farm. The Duke of Cleveland spent great sums on draining his Northamptonshire estate on boulder and Oxford clays. In Northumberland, on the estate of Earl Grey, much had been done in the 1850s and 1860s to drain the heavy land, while near Alnwick on the Duke of Northumberland's farms draining had been carried out without a change to permanent pasture. In Devon tenants on the Duke of Bedford's estate were enabled to grow better turnips, and others, also thanks to better draining, could turn to a wider variety of green crops. Landlords helped tenants to meet the difficulties of the period 1873–96 by creating confidence where possible, dealing promptly with complaints, and encouraging the enterprising. Even so, landlord–tenant relationships were put under considerable strain. Edward Heneage said in 1886 of his tenants on the central wolds of Lincolnshire: 'I am afraid I shall lose some tenants of the larger farms even at reduced rents.' Of his neighbours he observed: 'Landlords are in such a panic that they are letting at any price and giving thirty and forty per cent reductions . . . farmers will not be practicable and reduce their own expenditure.' By 1881 his own rents had to follow the levels of 1847 despite the £100,000 spent since then on improvements.[13]

On the estate of the Foljambe family in north Nottinghamshire the larger tenants suffered most and their farms were the hardest to let. Those with farms of under 150 acres who relied on family labour and combined dairying with cereal production needed less assistance from their landlords. While one good tenant on the Scarbrough estates in 1885–6 was given a rent reduction and an installation of water power for chopping and grinding, with no interest charged, a neighbour was refused a rent abatement: his land was 'full of twitch and altogether unfit to grow anything. The fences are neglected and full of gaps', the agent observed. In November 1886 some Yorkshire farmers meeting near Doncaster passed a resolution claiming:

> The present low prices of corn and stock and the prospect of agriculture in general warrants a substantial return on the rent and they trust that landlords will make their tenants large returns . . . the whole half year's rent will not compensate for the loss sustained through the depression in value of farm produce.

By the 1890s, however, tenants were coming to see that rent reductions alone would not solve their problems. Lord Scarbrough's agent told him in 1892: 'All paid up and there was no feeling expressed asking for a reduction of rent—the general impression was that your lordship had met them fair as to rent and they must look to some other source to improve matters.'[14] Although numerous tenancy changes were not averted, the estate's management did give confidence to the more resilient of the tenants, and those who held on until the 1890s survived to enjoy a limited prosperity in the new century.

IV

Though disputes about annual tenancies, rent, leases and compensation for improvements strained landlord–tenant relationships, they were internal stresses within a paternalistic society. To its critics from the industrial and urban classes, rural England presented a united front. Loyalty, custom and a genuine wish for guidance at election times caused tenants to welcome advice on how to vote. Many had little time for, or interest in, politics, yet in the days before universal suffrage to cast a vote was a privilege not to be forgone. Traditions of voting for the landlord's candidate went with the handing down of farms from father to son as a natural expression of a mutual interest. Only when a landowner switched from one party to another had he to be explicit about his expectations at the polls. And when parties divided, as did the Liberals over Irish Home Rule or the Conservatives over Imperial preference, landlords made their wishes plain, as some of them were to do again in 1931 when their tenants faced the prospect of a national government.

Guidance was expected, too, on ceremonial occasions. In 1894 the agent at Cowdray wrote to the tenants telling them when they were to present plate and addresses to Lord Egmont on the occasion of his silver wedding, and when the gifts would be on view. In September 1897 they received instructions about attendance at the earl's funeral.[15] National and family occasions were marked by well-ordered ceremonies. Seating plans were drawn up in estate offices and the steward would be their unobtrusive stage manager. These gatherings always helped to bring an estate together, but the activity that above all others emphasized the leadership of the aristocracy was fox-hunting. Tenants were expected to help protect foxes, and to shoot one was an outrage in most English counties. Tenants were invited to subscribe to hunts, and the sixty or seventy well-mounted farmers in scarlet who followed the Brocklesby were living proof of the success of improvement on the north wolds of Lincolnshire. Yet in the last quarter of the century there were complaints about the cost and the risk of keeping a foxhound puppy. A tenant in Yorkshire, who had lost 'into teens' of lambs and two ewes, refused to repair a bridge on his farm 'owing to the foregoing losses, high rent, bad seasons, bridge more convenience to hunters than self ... I absolutely refuse to do more because I cannot afford to or I should not stick at such a trifle'. His confidence that his complaint would meet with a sympathetic response was justified.[16]

Shooting was wholly reserved for the landlord and his friends, but occasionally leading tenant farmers would be invited for a day with the guns. Although a radical observer of the rural scene emphasized the damage done by corn-eating pheasants, tenants objected more to the losses inflicted by rabbits and hares. The last, with a taste for the crops of improved husbandry like turnips and carrots, were the subject of

436

bitter complaints, especially in times of low prices. The Ground Game Act of 1881 allowed tenants to destroy rabbits and hares without their landlord's permission, but traditions of deference made many occupiers rely upon a drive against rabbits by their landowners' keepers or compensation in the shape of lower rents. The custom of giving game each year to tenant-farmers and parsons as a seasonal present was well-established by Queen Victoria's reign, and the worst features of game preservation, savage sentences on poachers and the use of spring guns, became things of the past. On many estates tenants were allowed to shoot freely once the flying game season was over, but landlords were suspicious of farmers whose sporting interests might conflict with theirs; and a strong reason for rounding off estates by the purchase of inlying fields was to exclude the guns of owner-occupiers or urban speculators. A 'quiet' applicant from Pulborough for a farm on the Petworth estate in 1850 was eligible in every way except that he wanted to keep two greyhounds for coursing on the farm and the common. In October 1850 at Rufford Abbey in Nottinghamshire a great £100-a-side, two-day shooting match between a team from Melton Mowbray and another from Market Harborough saw the shooting of 172 brace of partridges by one side and 132 brace by the other. Squires led the teams and the Earl of Scarbrough provided 'sumptuous entertainment', though he did not take part in the competition. Steeplechasing, considered a plebeian diversion, might be patronized by land agents and stewards but was not thought suitable for their employers. Landlords would play cricket with their tenants, gamekeepers and local clergy, but hare-coursing, appropriate enough for estate servants, was not indulged in by landowners and leading tenant-farmers.

Deference to the landlord's wishes in sport and personal conduct could be irksome, but in return the tenant could expect an active interest in his welfare. The reports of nineteenth-century land agents included many personal details about tenants and their families, and for those who were content to live and work within the social assumptions of the Victorian estate there was a degree of security that counted for something in an age of accelerating change. When, at the turn of the century, a duchess addressed a gathering of tenants' children on an estate in Yorkshire, she said that it was nice to cross the county border to see 'other people's people'. Though later generations might think it a patronizing observation, they could not, with justice, see in it indifference or lofty disregard.[17] Landlords and tenants worked within an informal partnership which took account of both social deference and economic reality. There were limitations as in all partnerships, but it produced social stability in the English countryside and improved standards of farming—advantages which drew favourable comment from observers of the agricultural scene, both in bad times and good.

Notes

1   Perkins, 1976, 130–1.
2   Lincs. RO: 3 Anc. 7, 23/33/44, 34/55.
3   Lumley MSS, Letter Book 1900, 761.
4   F. M. L. Thompson, 1963, 27–44.
5   Lincs. RO: 3 Anc. 7/23/7/18; 23/43/16; Collins, n.d., 17; BPP 1848 VII 409.
6   BPP 1848 VII 7160–2, 7163–4, 7698.
7   Richards, 1974c, 11, 105, 116.
8   Lincs. RO: Yar. 5, 25 September 1841; Perkins, 1976.
9   Dibben, 1960, No. 1907, 4, 22.
10 *Lincolnshire Life*, September 1974, 48.
11 Dibben, 1960, No. 1906, 14, 15, 20, 22, 28, 41.
12 Gavin, 1967, 86; BPP 1896 XVI R.C. 1894–7, 4; Perren, 1970.
13 Lincs. RO: 2 Hen. 5/14/39, 42, 44, 96; 2 Hen. 5/8/63.
14 Beastall, 1975, 163–9.
15 Dibben, 1960, No. 1899.
16 Beastall, 1954, 137.
17 Author's conversation with member of a Yorkshire farming family.

32   The Land Agent

Eric Richards

I

The foundations of country house life in Victorian Britain and its splendid façade of conspicuous consumption and social ritual rested upon an elaborate structure of rural management, with, on a large property, a bureaucracy of bailiffs, stewards, ground officers, clerks, mineral managers and sub-agents of all sorts. At their head stood the land agent, sometimes referred to more grandly as 'commissioner' or, in Scotland, as 'factor'. Land agents were the men who administered rural Britain in the age of the great estates and their managerial responsibilities were heavy by any standards: the great landed estate was one of the largest business enterprises of the Victorian economy. Between 1816 and 1895, for instance, the agents of the dukes of Bedford presided over the expenditure of £4¼ million on the equipment of the Bedford estates.[1] By the middle of the century turnover of rental income on several large estates exceeded £200,000 per year. And in many respects the management of an estate was more complex and subtle than that of a factory or railway company or house of commerce.

Many proprietors handed over to their agents almost all responsibility for running their properties, to the point where the agent became the *alter ego* of the landlord. 'Sometimes, when that owner is an absentee, almost the whole power and control conferred by the possession of such a territory is vested in the landlord's representative.'[2] He could influence the direction and volume of agricultural investment, modify the entire social climate of an estate, manipulate electoral behaviour and greatly affect the level of efficiency and welfare in the landed community. Some agents behaved with as much patrician style as their masters; others were of a rougher breed, technicians with plans to pursue, men who enjoyed the daily exercise of authority. A few agents managed to tyrannize entire rural populations, creating riot and an undying legacy of hatred. But most were honourable, serious and trustworthy men, key managers in the growth of the Victorian economy, and they were not easily found or trained. In an age when many estates diversified their enterprise into industry, mining, transport and urban development, the versatile skills of the agents were visibly stretched. Yet they were also a vital link which sustained the traditional framework of rural Britain, that element which David Spring called 'the coherence of landed society'.[3] Their conviction in this system was sometimes even greater than that of their masters, and their identification with the old agrarian order made them its stoutest defenders. At the end of the Victorian age they mounted a noisy corporate resistance to the impending break-up of the great estates.

A good agent was a man who improved the agricultural practice and value of an estate, who was self-effacing enough to channel all public credit to his employer, and who cultivated the expected reciprocation of respect between the landlord and the community. His work was most easily performed in modern farming areas in prosperous years; it was most difficult among the congested, poor and mutinous populations on the peasant fringe of the Victorian economy. In England the land agent was often regarded as the respected, knowledgeable and even impartial conductor of the rural scene. In Ireland he was as likely to be the hated symbol of landlord neglect and exploitation. Captain Boycott was the best-known agent of the century, mainly because his name has passed into the language. Most agents lived less dramatically and with less controversy. It is a testament to their ability to organize paper that much of the history of modern agriculture is derived from land agency records.

The public reputation of the land agent was extraordinarily mixed. Professionalism and a high moral responsibility, together with expertise in man-management and technical mastery, were the virtues to which the leaders aspired. But the business was too varied to allow a stringent and uniform code of conduct, and land agents at all times had the greatest difficulty in creating a collective professional identity. They were, inevitably, the instruments of unpopular agricultural change, and it was an acknowledged part of their function to absorb as much of the obloquy as they could manage. It was expressed in an Irish opinion that 'the landlords were sometimes decent men, they will tell you, but the agents were devils one and all'.[4] It was a profession which probably attracted more than its share of unsavoury characters. In part this was a consequence of the open nature of recruitment to its ranks: virtually anyone could set up as an agent. In part also it reflected the lack of systematic training in the business of land agency. The problem was compounded by the rapid increase in the demand of the Victorian economy for the skills of managers. The scale of management, in terms of turnover and investment, continued to grow at a time not only of rapidly changing technology but also of shifting assumptions about social, political and economic roles on the land. For instance, many agents in the middle of the century found themselves saddled with the task of managing political influence, while their masters equivocated about the morality of the exercise. Moreover, the organization of farming created problems no less than those of industry and, after Repeal, agriculture was more vulnerable to seasonal and external instability than any other part of the economy. Able and trustworthy agents were always scarce. When the superintendent of the Bridgewater Trust was asked if he could recommend a man for a position on another estate, he replied of agents in general:

> If he is clever and has learned his business, he is tempted away by high wages . . . and if induced to stay he immediately supposes we cannot do without him and becomes an idle, impudent Rogue—*au contraire*, if he turns stupid and incompetent for any situation, he is sure to remain on our hands, and I can readily send you half a dozen of this sort.[5]

It was a scarcity reflected also in the very substantial salaries commanded by the elite of the profession. As early as 1811 Earl Fitzwilliam's agent was paid as much as £1,200 per annum, while in the middle of the century Christopher Haedy, chief agent to the Duke of Bedford, received £1,800, salaries comparable with the top railway managers of their day, and which understate the value of a position which was normally associated with lucrative perquisites.[6]

II

Regular methods of land management had emerged by the end of the eighteenth century and the land steward was one of the main instruments in the rationalization of technology and tenure. While there remained a great deal of overlap between the trades of agent, surveyor and lawyer, on the larger estates management became more systematic, even scientific. Smaller estates tended to be administered either by the owner himself, or by a local farmer, an attorney or a clergyman, usually on a part-time commission basis. In the Victorian age there were endless efforts to gain professional recognition for land agents, and a dissociation from the previous low opinion of lawyers and attorneys—partly incurred by well-known cases where local land markets had been manipulated for the personal gain of the landlord's representative, or where bribes had been taken from tenants in return for special favours. Large estates required residential agents who gained in both income and prestige since they deputized for the landed aristocracy: men 'for social and political reasons who could be continuously on the spot to demonstrate the owner's authority'.[7] The employment opportunities for land agents, and consequently for their professional status, were much advanced by the tasks generated by the great body of legislation associated with parliamentary enclosures and tithe commutation, measures which drew upon the accumulating expertise of land agents. In the late nineteenth century the spate of land legislation and regulation persuaded more landlords to reform the administration of their estates and this had a favourable effect on the public esteem of land agents.

Adam Smith had warned landlords against over-enthusiastic agents who took over too much of the initiative and enterprise in agriculture. The danger, he wrote, was that eventually

> the country (instead of sober and industrious tenants, who are bound by their own interest to cultivate as well as their capital and skill will allow them) would be filled with idle and profligate bailiffs, whose abusive management would soon degrade the cultivation.[8]

J. R. McCulloch, by contrast, thought that landed estates (and indeed the nation) were generally better placed when the landlord was an absentee and the management left in the hands of intelligent agents with whom the tenantry preferred to deal.[9] In reality land agents provided much of the driving force behind the remarkable improvements in agricultural productivity, partly as managers, but also as technicians and propagandists for the ways of improvement. The duties of agents were never-ending: letting farms, keeping accounts, drawing up leases and tenancy agreements, checking farming practice among the tenantry, evicting the recalcitrant and the bankrupt, presiding over institutions of local government, encouraging improvements, supervising plantations, keeping the peace between tenants, labourers and cottagers. These were likely to include also the supervision of domestic arrangements of the landed proprietor and the complex delegation of authority for the exploitation of urban, industrial and transport resources of the estate. It was hard work and it broke the health of many good men. They took few holidays, often worked on Christmas Day, and normally spent a large part of their life on horseback dealing with every mundane detail. Sometimes their employers sensed the strain and packed them off, perhaps to Harrogate, to renew their energies. The very large agencies often managed, in a general supervisory fashion, many different estates. Thus Messrs Rawlence & Squarey in the 1890s supervised about a quarter of a million acres in twenty-four counties.[10] On the great estates there was usually a complicated hierarchy of offices, with a central office in London which co-ordinated the diverse estates. Some properties, such as those of the dukes of Bedford and Sutherland, would daily generate small mountains of correspondence. At the local level there were two functions of surpassing importance. One was rent collection, which required the efforts of sub-agents, auditors and bailiffs, helped along by a modest degree of hospitality to ease the money from producer to rentier. Here it was important to judge the degree of rigour appropriate when dealing with tenants in arrears. The second vital task was the selection of tenants: the highest bidder was not necessarily the best, for an estate would need men of capital, technical ability and general reliability rather than mere speculators. An informal network between the large estates helped in the vetting of tenants.

Most land agents were drawn from the middling ranks of society, younger sons of country gentlemen, or farmers, lawyers or clergy. Many agents had no formal training at all, and some of those who specialized in the management of mining property in the early Victorian period were barely literate. But informal solutions emerged, particularly in the form of unofficial 'schools' of agents. The best training was an apprenticeship in the offices of one of the top managers of the day, with Clutton or Sturge or Squarey or Woolley or Thomas Smith or the Lochs—all of whom raised a stream of articled pupils who were able to move into senior positions on other estates.[11] There were internal controversies about the relative importance of theoretical knowledge and practical experience; there was unanimity that the profession was continuously undermined by the easy entry of amateurs and incompetents. In the early nineteenth century Scottish agents enjoyed an unusual prestige which was partly based on the fame of Lothian farming, but they never came to dominate the profession. The most important source of talent was hereditary: there was an extraordinary number of sons and nephews of agents. As Edward Hughes put it, 'Like the civil servants they not infrequently died in harness, and in the hope that the mantle would eventually fall on their sons or relatives.'[12] There were many instances of dynasties of land agents whose hereditary claims on the position were almost a parallel to those of their patrons.

Aspiring to a status comparable with the medical and legal professions, the leading land agents were endlessly indignant at the dilution of their reputation by untrained interlopers. C. G. Grey of Dilston fulminated at the regiments of retired soldiers, sailors, butlers and house stewards who inhabited the profession, the failed farmers, pernickety lawyers, and former head clerks. Worst of all were the relatives of the landowner: 'Poor relations, for whom some provision is desirable, would generally cost an owner less if he were to make them an allowance to live at Bath or Cheltenham.'[13] James Caird, perhaps the most penetrating observer of land management at the middle of the century, castigated some of the weaker arrangements of the day. In Oxfordshire, for instance, he blamed landlords for their ignorance of agriculture: 'And what is equally unfortunate . . . they have not yet seen the necessity of making amends for their own defective knowledge by the appointment of agents better qualified.' In Northamptonshire some landlords were merely interested in rent returns and employed maximizing agents who had no expertise and felt no responsibility for the care of the soil: 'Some employ men of low standing with a small salary, and in a dependent position, butlers, gardeners, and sometimes gamekeepers, performing the function of land agent. Lawyers are employed by some, but merely receive the rents.'[14]

Incompetent agents, wrote Caird, were a menace to the agricultural community. The weakly old gentlemen and the retired officers in charge of valuable property could easily let slip the reins of improvement and eventually rents would decline. A good agent would provide the foundation for a general improvement of productivity and rising rents from 'an active and intelligent tenantry'. Some agents were paragons: Bright, Lord Hatherton's man, not only managed to double the stock and the output of the home farm in Staffordshire, but invented a revolving harrow and a furrow press which sowed and rolled seeds in one operation. Caird warned landlords against expecting such services too cheaply. Even the most bigoted landlord, he said, knew that rents could only be maintained if the tenantry were given the facilities and professional advice that were required. 'An experienced sensible agent, with the aid of a willing tenantry, will effect as much with £100 as an inexperienced or incompetent man can with £200.' G. C. Brodrick[15] calculated the costs of management in the 1880s and found them extremely variable. On large, well-managed properties in the Midlands costs could be as little as 4 per cent of the rental, compared with more than 20 per cent in other places.[16]

John Lockhard Morton also railed against the type of ignorant agent who had no science, no knowledge of the land, and whose one idea was 'that the exaction of exorbitant rents from the tenantry is his chief business'. Morton would not absolve a landlord from the responsibility of management for otherwise he would be at the mercy of his agent:

> Then, in such a case the landlord is separated from his tenants by an
> impossible barrier, and, in most cases, can only reach them at second hand.
> He wants that knowledge of the farmer's life, habits, modes of thinking, and
> general hopes, which are necessary to create a sympathy between him and
> them.[17]

In rare cases, such as that of R. H. Bradshaw of the Bridgewater Trust, an agent could manipulate his masters and tie them in such legal knots that quite extraordinary stratagems and inducements were required to dislodge him.[18] In the 1860s most landed property in England remained in the hands of solicitors 'who are usually little more than receivers without much knowledge of the details of management',[19] and there were frequent public criticisms of bad agents who 'would wish to act a despotic part towards tenant farmers'.[20] Even at the end of the century the profession had made little progress in its efforts to control entry. Henry Herbert Smith observed that agencies were overstocked with 'a large body of persons who have failed in every other walk of life, or have been obliged . . . to retire from other professions . . . the waifs and strays of the professional world'. Anyone could walk into the agency trade without qualification or restriction: 'The most incompetent tiro can advertise himself as a learned specialist', he wrote, and the worst sort were attracted by visions of an agent's life full of hunting and shooting. Worse still were the retired military men whose background disqualified them 'because they are accustomed to handle men like machines'.[21] Ireland appears to have suffered more than its share of this sort of recruit.[22]

There was no separate Land Agents' Society until 1902, although the elite of the profession had gained entry to the exclusive Surveyors' Club formed in 1834. In 1886 it was claimed that the great majority of the leading agents of the day were members of the Surveyors' Institution.[23] There was no separate category of agents in the Census, but there were informed guesses that in 1877 about sixty agents controlled approximately two-thirds of England,[24] and though this may have been an exaggeration it pointed clearly enough to the concentration of ownership and the extent of the authority wielded by agents. By the end of the century the levels of education had probably improved; in 1882 the Royal Agricultural College at Cirencester reported that most of its students became land agents.[25] There was also an evident decline in the importance of solicitors doubling as agents; by the 1890s, it was said, the 'times have beaten that class of men', and 'their places are taken by practical men who are able to farm the land for the landlord when he gets it in hand'.[26]

A recurrent theme in the credos of the most influential agents was that they should strive to transcend the raw fact that they were the creatures of the landlords and that they should administer the rural community with Olympian impartiality. It was an ideal of moral responsibility emphasized by Thomas Smith Woolley in 1871. Estate agents, he thought, should not regard themselves merely as 'machines for carrying out their own wishes and decisions of landlords'; they should indeed have equal regard for 'the rights or claims of their tenants or dependants'. Thus, as he phrased it,

> he should regard all questions between them with judicial impartiality, being neither led by amicable weakness, or a desire for popularity, into trifling away his employer's rights, nor by even less worthy motives, into an unjust or arbitrary dealing with his neighbours.

Land agents very rarely questioned their belief that, of all forms of rural property, the estates of the landed aristocracy were the best managed. Nor did they doubt that this happy circumstance rested ultimately upon a natural sympathy and understanding between the strata of rural society. It was striking that, after a century of agrarian rationalization, land agents were advised against too rigid an application of the rules of political economy, and against that polarization of rural society which was associated with 'the further development of the terrible tendency of modern society to crystallize as it were into a few strata, more or less bitterly antagonistic to each other'.[27]

III

Land agents managed all aspects of estate business including the mobilization of electoral support and political information. After 1832 the exercise of political influence became less obvious and, indeed, more ambiguous. Symptoms of independence among the tenantry raised the blood pressure of many estate agents, but most landlords by the middle of the century appear to have relied upon a continuing tradition of deference in rural society: 'the tenant voted with his landlord not out of fear, but because he accepted the traditional nature of authority, unquestioningly'.[28] It was a tradition, however, reinforced by the informal powers of influence exercised in practice by the agents. In the parliamentary inquiry into electoral proceedings in 1868 there was investigation of a case which involved the mass switching of votes to a landlord in Cheshire. Asked if direct pressure had been applied by the landlord, the local magistrate replied to the contrary, but explained, however, that

> he allows his agent to go to the tenant, and he allows him to say how much it would please the landlord, if the tenant voted in a certain way, and gives hints that if the tenant does not vote as his landlord wishes, all sorts of petty indulgences, in the shape of small repairs, additional gates, and perhaps a little time to pay his rent, will be withdrawn, and the landlord, except in very few cases, has not the straight forwardness to say 'You may vote as you please'. He stands by and lets the agent hint all these things.[29]

In 1859 it was reported of a Buckinghamshire election that

> Mr. H. Bull was a land agent, and had considerable influence at Aylesbury. He had an opportunity of being of service to small farmers in many ways in regard to loans, mortgages etc., and by merely lifting his finger and saying for whom he could vote, he would probably carry between thirty and forty voters with him.[30]

There was similar evidence for Wales in the 1890s. One witness before a parliamentary committee remarked that he had 'known agents going around to the tenants to tell them how and for whom to vote. I have also known them to meet tenants and walk them in a body to the polling booth.'[31] In Ireland the exercise of political manipulation was less veiled and the role of the agent more muscular. The landlord was less able to draw upon the assumption of deference, and there was more blatant resort to the threat of eviction at times of electoral conflict. When Lord Hertford came to recognize the practical independence of his tenants he took the logical step of raising his rents to the full value of the land. The land agent in Ireland was thus the 'physical reminder of proprietorial power . . . . As members of a notably beleaguered profession, they stood at the intersection between landlord and tenant, a location at once exposed and dangerous.'[32]

There was always a social distance between land agent and master; even the brilliantly successful agents like James Loch and Rowland Prothero, men who became lesser gentry in their own right, maintained a dutiful deference that seems mildly incongruous in retrospect. Very often such men dealt with employers who were wilful, prodigal and unintelligent, who had to be mollified and coaxed into commonsensical ways. Agents like Loch and Haedy perceived their function as, in part, to preserve the aristocratic empires over which they ruled, rather like ducal prime ministers, despite the recurrent waywardness of some of their patrons. Some agents acted as highly respected consultants to other estates, called in for overhauls of administrative structures and for major policy changes. The country house network facilitated this important interchange of expertise. Sometimes an agent would plead for retrenchment with superhuman stoicism. The Duke of Bedford observed the extraordinary efforts of his family auditors, the Adams, who 'continued for more than thirty years to remonstrate with his father (and in pretty strong terms too) at his annual excess of expenditure over income and his consequent increasing debt. It is very creditable to them.'[33] At the other end of the scale from the great ducal commissioners were the unglamorous agents of the very small landlords, one of whom was pictured at breakfast with his employer by Richard Jefferies:

> The steward was usually in attendance. He was a commonplace man, but little above the description of a labourer. He received wages not much superior to those a labourer takes in summer time, but as he lives at the Home Farm (which was in hand) there were of course some perquisites. A slow quiet man, of little or no education, he pottered about and looked after things in general.[34]

The devotion of many land agents to efficiency, good relations and profit made possible the pursuit of pleasure and extraordinary feats of consumption by their masters. There is little evidence of the attitude of agents to this curious arrangement though many of them seem to have regarded it as the natural ordering of society.

IV

Individual land agents of the Victorian age are remembered because they were successful, notorious or simply well recorded. Francis Blaikie, steward at Holkham, represents the early nineteenth-century model. Previously agent to Lord Chesterfield, he entered Coke's service in 1816 and set about the regularization of some of the famous Holkham innovations. Within a few years he was receiving a salary of £650, and in charge of a substantial bureaucracy of sub-agents. He was a proselytizer of improvement, a writer of treatises, a Scot who considered it 'a duty incumbent upon man to diffuse to his fellowmen the fruits of his experience in this life. All men have not the same advantages in acquiring information. Those advantages are bestowed upon us by the providence of God.' Blaikie was exceedingly expert in the details of agricultural method, a penetrating critic of bad practice, a somewhat solemn figure of efficiency and rectitude, and inexhaustibly devoted to his employer. His was a total identification with the interests of the Coke family and he saw his role as that of saving his masters from their best instincts. During one financial crisis Blaikie remarked with some feeling that 'Mr. Coke's benevolent mind outstrips his resources.—It is a virtue in him carried to excess, and for which I see no remedy in this world', and he felt intensely frustrated that Coke could not see the matter in the same serious light.[35]

The Oxley Parker agency, a dynasty which spanned most of the nineteenth century, was developed by Christopher Comyns Parker, a member of the select Surveyors' Club, and second son of a Chelmsford attorney. The Oxley Parkers became substantial country gentlemen in Essex society, men with a superb grasp of the details of how the country worked and of the vagaries of agriculture. They managed many estates and trained themselves to the task. Their business was greatly enhanced by work associated with tithe commutation and their success depended on accumulated trust and reputation with landowners. They took virtually no holidays and frequently worked more than twelve hours in a day, much of it in the saddle. John Oxley Parker, the son of the founder of the land agency business, began his day early, and a visitor wrote: 'Being aware of your early rising habits will plead an excuse for my making an appointment with you at your House at 5 o'clock tomorrow morning.' His biographer described his work in this way:

> He served landlords who often expected to reap where they they had not sown, parsons who depended on his services for their livelihood, parishioners and tenants who relied on him somehow to save them from ruin in evil days, companies established to make new railways, and landowners who wanted to make a profit out of them, and all the time he had to hold in his mind one prime consideration—not just what was expedient, but what was right.

When the Oxley Parkers selected a tenant, possibly the most important task, they looked for sobriety, a good churchman and communicant, preferably married and of a good family, Conservative in politics—'A fast young man would terrify us quiet people' was a typical comment. The Oxley Parkers made considerable money both as farmers and as land valuers. Conservative though they were, they felt it necessary to remind their patrons repeatedly of their social obligations and their identity of interest with the welfare of all classes on the land. No agents were more conscious of the fragile basis of trust upon which all relations in agriculture rested.[36]

Some land agents became national figures in the Victorian countryside. John Grey of Dilston (1785–1868) took charge in 1833 of the Greenwich Hospital estates in Northumberland, over which he presided for thirty years. In this case the agent possessed considerable effective autonomy: 'He was as free in action as if he had been an independent Landlord . . . it was for the interest of the Hospital as well as for the tenantry under his control that he was left thus unfettered.' A dynamo for improvement, Grey developed the estates with enough success to increase the rental by £20,000, and its food output by half, while simultaneously enchancing the condition of its people. He reduced the number of sub-agents from twelve to three, and it was widely claimed of him that he was 'guide, philosopher and friend to all the tenantry'. 'He constantly bore in mind the real and fundamental identity between classes which becomes more marked in an advanced and complicated social system, where everything is mutual and reciprocal.' He established agricultural societies, farmers' clubs and libraries; he often spent between five and eight hours a day on horseback. His great reputation as an agent reflected upon his own trainees, whose services were solicited by proprietors across Britain as well as by the Emperor of Austria and the manager of Public Works in Sardinia. 'He sent many a stalwart

Northumbrian in this way to disseminate his advanced notions in different parts of the world, or to carry out the plans of enlightened noblemen on their parks.' And in 1858 the French government asked him to estimate the effects that free trade in corn had wrought on England. He was described on his death as 'a leading name in English agriculture, a leading exemplar of the duties of landowning, a leading teacher by example and precept, of good farming in every department of it'. He had the unusual habit of making extremely frank public statements which were critical, for example, of absenteeism and the poor provision for cottagers on many estates. In 1840 he expressed displeasure at the 'grandees who lavish expense upon their castles and deer-parks but disregard the dwellings of the cultivators of the land'. In 1846, at a meeting of the Royal Agricultural Society in Newcastle, he told the Duke of Cleveland that he was wrong to think that there was a limit to improvement—such a limit could never be reached while unimproved properties and annual tenancies persisted, and he went on to remind landlords of their palpably unfulfilled obligations to the working classes, notably in the provision of education and accommodation.[37]

One of the best-known agricultural writers and ideologues of the old rural order was Rowland Prothero (created Lord Ernle in 1919) who became agent-in-chief to the Duke of Bedford in 1898. This was after a diverse career in law, academia and literature. He had been editor of the *Quarterly Review* from 1893 to 1899, but he had a passion for agriculture which the Bedford appointment brought to a focus. He recalled the suggestion that his new employment would entail a loss of social status, that he would indeed 'be lucky to get a glass of sherry in the dining room'. This fear was outweighed by his sense of the challenge of the huge Bedford estates. The terms of his appointment also helped. In addition to his salary Prothero was given a rent- and rate-free country house in Bedfordshire, a staff of three indoor servants, seven gardeners and three keepers. Heating and lighting were also free; moreover

> Cream, milk and butter were supplied every day from the dairy at Woburn. Game and the produce of the fine garden were at my disposal. Port, whisky and mineral water were all allowance, and I was given the run of a cellar of Vintage Hocks.

The hunting was excellent, too, and Prothero had the use of two tennis courts and a squash court. Much of this comfort was duplicated at the second country house he was given in Cambridgeshire. Prothero administered a structure which delegated much authority to local agents, 'men at the top of the tree in their profession', and he exercised control 'mainly through the financial checks on independent action'. His most important function was probably that of defending the system of vast aristocratic estates, especially their role, as he saw it, of nursing agriculture through the many years of adversity, and in which the Duke of Bedford had been 'typical of the standard of social and moral obligation towards the tenants and workers'. He particularly sought to improve the comfort and security of cottagers, and attempted to act as a benevolent buffer between workers and farmers. He was a great believer in the powers of cricket as a social solvent, for 'no better opportunity exists for making real friends with rural workers than that afforded by a village club for which you play regularly'. He thought that the old integrity of English village life had shrivelled into a mockery of its former self. 'Sober and industrious, the . . . villagers lived narrow, self-centred lives, knowing no interests outside themselves. They seemed to be passing through life without really living. They were my neighbours. Could I do anything to vary and widen their experience?' One of his answers was to offer village talks on historical figures such as Bunyan, Wesley, Wyclif and Savonarola. Prothero subsequently entered politics at the request of the duke. In his first campaign his opponent described him as 'the pampered pet of a Noble Duke'. In fact Prothero's agency spanned the period of the dissolution of half of the Bedford estates, and he found increasing opportunity to develop his public career. In the First World War he became president of the Board of Agriculture and was charged with the responsibility of organizing the food supplies of the nation. He is now best remembered for his classic and controversial history, *English Farming, Past and Present*, which accurately reflected his own conservatism and nostalgia for a bygone harmony in the countryside.[38]

V

In Wales land agents seem to have come into their own during the time of the enclosures, and there was a current of nationalist feeling against those brought in from England and Scotland to administer the large estates. They had 'a passion for raising rents, shortening leases, consolidating farms, and enclosing land hitherto little used'.[39] In general the Welsh estate agent was more unpopular than his English equivalent: it has been said that

> As representatives of a largely anglicized and Anglican landowning class, some of whom were absent from their estates for a greater or lesser part of the year, the agents were frequently the recipients of abuse and vilification, both from radical writers and from the chapel pulpit.[40]

One English agent, Thomas Cooke, remarked bleakly in 1842:

> My English ways do not suit Welsh customs, and my opinion of the Welsh farmers generally is that they know less than their horses. They are too ignorant to be taught. They are a hundred years behind the worst English districts.[41]

The tradition of anti-agent criticism found voice in the Welsh Land Commission of 1893–5. It was said that the influence and social status of the agent in Wales were greater than in England because the gulf between the landowning and tenant classes was greater. Daniel Jones remarked in evidence: 'We are of opinion that the management of estates is too often entrusted to men of other nationality than our own, inasmuch as difference of language between agents is a source of great inconvenience.' One agent was remembered as the great tyrant and depopulator of the Mostyn estate, another as 'the curse of the country', while another was reported to have vowed an intention 'to exterminate Nonconformity in Cardiganshire and starve the damn preachers'. The report of the commission noted such allegations and remarked:

> There is an impression in Wales, as elsewhere, that owners sometimes employ as agents men of a hard and grasping temperament, strict in their view of the duties of others with the intention that they should act in a way more rigid and exacting than they as owners should venture to act without incurring censure or resentment—men willing for the gain of office and its individual profits to run the risk of any amount of unpopularity and to take upon their own shoulders the social obloquy that rightly should fall upon their employers.

Although Welsh agents were generally absolved of charges of merciless rapacity, the commission did not scotch all the adverse criticism of ignorant, corrupt and truculent agents in the country, and it expressed the view that the level of competence of agents was generally inadequate.[42]

Some agents in Victorian Britain behaved like colonial administrators or missionaries, as though they were carrying the benefits of civilization to retarded outliers of the world. This was especially irksome when the agent was a stranger, vested with powers to bring about radical changes, and yet worse if he could not speak the language of the people involved. Agents from the Scottish Lowlands often possessed such a reputation. James Loch (1780–1855) was probably the most influential estate administrator of his day. The son of a bankrupted proprietor in Kinross, Loch was given a legal education during Edinburgh University's golden age. In 1812, instead of entering politics, he took over the supervision of the vast Sutherland estates, and remained at the helm until his death in 1855, when he was succeeded by his son, George. The Sutherland estates were among the greatest managerial challenges of the Victorian age. In Scotland were the million acres of unreformed Highlands, seething with poverty, corruption and discontent. Here Loch found a bickering and astonishingly prodigal body of factors mismanaging the colossal process of clearance and the associated regeneration of the coastal zones. In England were three substantial estates, full of coal and ironstone, potentially very productive and ripe for zealous improvement. There were four large family seats to maintain and a level of consumption to be made properly conspicuous. And as well there was the Bridgewater Canal, which gave the Sutherland family a vast income, in all more than £2 million net over a period of thirty years. It was an inherited asset, fraught with difficulty because Loch had no control in the management of the wonderfully lucrative canal. Moreover, he felt impelled to seek terms with the impending competitors—the Liverpool and Manchester Railway in the teeth of total opposition from the canal managers. Steeped in classical economics, liberal in politics, Loch was also for many years in Parliament and was widely consulted on political and legal matters throughout his career. Lord Wharncliffe was told that a few minutes of conversation with Loch 'would be worth guineas of manuscripts'.[43] He wrote books and pamphlets in defence of his Sutherland policies, and he faced the grilling of the House of Commons on the question of the Highland clearances. He acted in the management of five other large aristocratic estates, and spent much of the rest of his life in public service and antiquarianism, and in raising a large family, the sons of which became notable figures in late Victorian life.

Loch was totally dedicated to work; he stated many times that it was his function to shield his masters from any odium connected with the policies pursued by the family. All the estate administration was made systematic and centralized; the tenantry were required to communicate only through the agents and factors. Loch indeed had said that 'His Lordship's territories are a kingdom and ought to be considered in this light by those he employs', and he undoubtedly cast himself in the role of prime minister. His conviction never dimmed that aristocratic landed estates were the first instruments of progress, and he could not understand his own unpopularity, a matter which hurt him deeply. After the era of James and George Loch the Sutherland estates were administered by a succession of unhappy commissioners: Sir Archibald Kemball, a soldier-diplomat disappointed in his career, and then R. M. Brereton, a civil engineer and agent with experience in India, North America and Norfolk. Both found the crofter question almost impossible to cope with. Their resignations were mainly occasioned by interference from the Sutherland family, especially from the heir, Lord Stafford, who took over the administration in 1880 and tried to model it on the pattern of a railway company with regular board meetings. He lasted almost two years, his resolve defeated by bitter quarrels with his father. The turbulence of management in this period served to emphasize the previous achievements of the Lochs.[44]

James Loch had recruited many Lowland agents for both England and the Highlands. In the Highlands factors inevitably wielded great local authority and, in many instances, misused their powers. Sir John Sinclair in 1795 had warned that 'a Highland estate is populous and extensive, it ought never to be put under the management of one factor', and he believed that all factors ought to be held within a system of restraint.[45] Such men were charged with the responsibility of clearing large populations from extensive areas in the Highlands and many were hated figures; others agonized over the tasks they performed and wept for the people caught in their tragic economic dilemma.

As the crofting community developed means of political and physical expression in the last quarter of the century, the task of the factor became extremely difficult. One of the best-known, indeed notorious, factors was Evander MacIver of Scourie in Sutherland, a man of robust views and a sense of traditional order in the north. He refused to believe that the crofter system could be either profitable or prosperous, and he was angered and appalled by the rebellious attitudes of the people. A Lewisman, with a command of Gaelic, he reigned for half a century over a population which he regarded as far too large for its own comfort and too susceptible to infections of Irish land leaguism. He was highly critical of his superiors—men who, he believed, were too often ignorant and unfitted for their work, and a duke who thought more of his yacht than his estates.[46] In the evidence before the Napier Commission in 1883 a Free Church minister described the Sutherland family as benevolent, but 'the agents of his Grace are his hands, his eyes, his ears, and his feet, and in their dealings with the people they are constantly like a wall of ice between his Grace and his Grace's people'.[47] The factors came to feel much tension during the crofter agitation. One of them remarked in 1885 that 'every eye is upon the Factor, and his every action is liable to be construed as hostile to the Crofter Class'; it was a time when ground officers resigned for fear of their lives. 'To suit the present crisis', wrote another, 'a Highland factor would require to have a head of brass, and feet of iron.'[48]

Irish land agents enjoyed higher social status than others, mainly because they were more effectively substitutes for absentee landlords, and were the centre of the local community.[49] But they were also more exposed to abuse and actual danger than those elsewhere, and bore the main brunt of the controversy and disorder of the Irish countryside. In Ireland, it has been remarked,

> the post of the land agent itself conferred that kind of status i.e. of the gentry, and any Irish land agent moved virtually as a matter of course into the magistrate class: he lived, entertained, and hunted like a gentleman, and he took his part like a gentleman in displaying the authority of the established regime, and in maintaining order in a much troubled country. With this social and administrative position, Irish land agents were members of the upper class.

Their belief in the philosophy of the great estate was yet more total than that of their counterparts in the rest of Britain, and their fear of its break-up reached a proportionally higher pitch. Irish land legislation eventually left them redundant and without compensation.[50] Of W. Steuart Trench, land agent to several landowners in Ireland, and a man whose name is said to be abominated still in popular tradition, it was claimed: 'So evil was he that the rats invaded his grave and devoured his body.' His *Memoirs* were designed to place before England the serious problems of land management in mid-century Ireland. Nevertheless, he retained a note of optimism: Ireland, he considered, was not 'altogether incapable of management' because 'justice fully and firmly administered is always appreciated in the end'. His introduction to Ireland had been dramatic enough. He arrived at the Shirley estates in March 1843 to find the tenantry still exultant at the death of his predecessor, an agent named Mitchell. On the night of Mitchell's sudden death they had

> lighted fires on almost every hill on the estate; and over a district of upwards of 20,000 acres, there was scarcely a mile without a bonfire blazing in manifestation of joy at his decease. So remarkable an occurrence as this could not pass unobserved by one who was about to succeed him.

The tenantry then embarked on a campaign to demand rent reductions from the landlord, Shirley, by intimidating the new agent. Trench faced the people in tight-lipped, uncomprehending attitude. Kicked, beaten, punched, hat knocked off, threatened, prayed against, assaulted, his clothes stripped from his back, dragged across the main street of Carrickmacross, sticks whirling over his head—Trench (by his own account) came close to death in his resistance to the demands of the people. He eventually out-bluffed the amassed tenantry, following advice from other agents that any compromise on the question of rent would endanger every other proprietor and that the 'barony would be completely disorganised'. Trench stood firm and Shirley's rent roll, apparently, was preserved.[51]

For a later period in the century Samuel Hussey's *Reminiscences* serve to illustrate the extreme dangers facing many agents in Ireland. Hussey was described as 'the most abused man in Ireland', a man who survived attacks on his life including an elaborate dynamite attempt on his house in Kerry in 1884. A substantial owner in his own right, he was especially conscious of the elevated status of agents. His multiple agency was one of the largest in Ireland, and he appeared before no fewer than seven commissions. His *Reminiscences* thundered against what he termed the copious mendacity of the enemies of Anglo-Irish landlords, and he blamed Gladstone for creating most of the trouble in Ireland. The danger was so great that

> I never travelled without a revolver, and occasionally was accompanied by a Winchester rifle. I used to place my revolver as regularly beside my fork on the dinner table, either in my own or in anybody else's house, as I spread my napkin on my knees.[52]

The experiences of Trench, Hussey and Boycott were, no doubt, more memorable than most, but the life of an Irish land agent was not easily compared with that of his English counterpart.[53]

VI

It would be impossible to estimate with any degree of accuracy the independent contribution of land agents to the economic and social life of the Victorian countryside. There is no doubt that, in the highest ranks, the profession was peopled with men of considerable distinction and great ability. In terms of the organization of agriculture and the ownership and use of land, they were an extremely conservative force. The fact that they wielded such large measures of authority with, outside Ireland at least, relatively little social friction, was a tribute to their skills and to the resilience of agrarian traditions in Britain. Their extreme diligence, loyalty and identification with their masters certainly sustained the old aristocratic order and permitted many landowners to follow careers of extraordinary leisure or of political and social leadership. F. M.L. Thompson has argued, however, that the professionalism of land agents, and the diminished interest of the landed class in the actual work of the countryside, helped to hasten the eventual disintegration of rural society, that the 'roots of deference in a personally administered paternalism were being sapped'.[54] It is sometimes argued that land agents were powerful initiators of the rationalization of agriculture in the early nineteenth century, that they were a managerial elite who achieved rapid gains in food productivity. By the same token it is possible that their collective dedication to technical perfection *per se*, and to very high levels of investment, encouraged over-capitalization in agriculture in the last quarter of the century. Their acceptance of the assumption that the return on capital on the great landed estates should naturally be lower than elsewhere in the economy may have helped to undermine the competitive capacity of British agriculture. And, indeed, it is not self-evident that these attitudes were fully in conformity with the 'national interest'.

Notes

1   Bedford, 1897, 76.
2   Smith, 1898, 311; BPP 1896 XXXIV 249.
3   Spring, 1963, 53.
4   Quoted in Hughes, 1949, 186.
5   Quoted in Richards, 1974, 107.
6   F. M. L. Thompson, 1963, 161–2; Spring, 1963, 133.
7   F. M. L. Thompson, 1968a, 32.
8   Quoted in Hollander, 1973, 234.
9   Robinson, 1826, 58.
10   BPP 1894 XVI, Pt I, 451.
11   F. M. L. Thompson, 1963, 157.
12   Hughes, 1949, 198.
13   *Transactions of the Surveyors' Institution*, 1871–2, IV, 282–3.
14   Caird, 1852, 27, 417.
15   *Ibid.*, 493–5.
16   Brodrick, 1881, 422n.
17   Morton, 1858, 7–9, 23–9.
18   Richards, 1973, ch. X.
19   *Transactions of the Surveyors' Institution*, 1868–9, I, 60.
20   Morton, 1858, 29.
21   Smith, 1898, 295–9.
22   Donnelly, 1975, 183.
23   *Transactions of the Surveyors' Institution*, 1886–7, XIX, 3.
24   F. M. L. Thompson, 1968a, 32, 97.
25   BPP 1882 XIV 192.
26   BPP 1894 XVI pt II, 235; BPP 1894 XVI pt III, 265; BPP 1896 XVII, 141.
27   *Transactions of the Surveyors' Institution*, 1871–2, IV, 271–2.
28   Nossiter, 1975, 48–9.
29   BPP 1868–9 VIII 250.
30   Davis, 1972, 163–4.
31   BPP 1895 XL 2.

32 Hoppen, 1977, 90–1.
33 Spring, 1963, 34–5.
34 Jefferies, 1880, 182.
35 Parker, 1975, 189; Spring, 1963, 130–1; F. M. L. Thompson, 1963, 156.
36 Parker, 1964, *passim.*
37 Butler, 1869, *passim.*
38 Ernle, 1938, *passim.*
39 Jones, 1973, 7.
40 Colyer, 1977, 403.
41 *Ibid.,* 413.
42 BPP 1896 XXXIV 250–8.
43 Spring, 1963, 89.
44 Richards, 1973, *passim.*
45 Sinclair, 1795, 136.
46 MacIver, 1905, *passim.*
47 BPP 1884 XXXIII 2594.
48 Stafford R. O.: Sutherland Papers, D593/K/1/3/73, Purves to Kemball, 23 February 1885; Gunn to Kemball, 16 March 1885.
49 Donnelly, 1975, 187.
50 F. M. L. Thompson, 1968a, 259 ff.
51 Trench, 1868, VII, 64–78.
52 Hussey, 1904, 67, 235.
53 Maguire, 1972, ch. VI.
54 F. M. L. Thompson, 1963, 183.

33   Landowners and the Rural Community

F. M. L. Thompson

I

As the twentieth century knows very well, it is not too difficult for any tolerably well-organized and disciplined group in authority, adequately furnished with jackboots, machine guns, and bully boys, to hold the populace in thrall, extracting an outward show of respect and obedience from the inward experience of fear. One strand in the rural literature of the nineteenth century asserts, or implies, that rural communities were held in thrall to the superior and possessing classes through the exercise of analogous coercive power and the fear of the consequences of disobedience, even though these might be exercised in a more decentralized, more civilized, and less obtrusive fashion. It is a view which sees agricultural labourers and village folk harbouring a sullen resentment, dislike, and hatred of farmers, parsons, and squires, nurtured on poverty, oppression, and regimentation, which for most of the time slumbered and grumbled under the surface, and occasionally flashed out in explosions of violent words or deeds at moments of acute crisis.[1] The idea of the undeclared war of the countryside with scarcely veiled jackboot social relationships is vividly expressed in a well-known passage by Joseph Arch:

> We labourers had no lack of lords and masters. There were the parson and
> his wife at the rectory. There was the squire, with his hand of iron
> overshadowing us all. There was no velvet glove on that hard hand, as many
> a poor man found to his hurt. . . . At the sight of the squire the people

trembled. He lorded it right feudally over his tenants, the farmers; the farmers in their turn tyrannised over the labourers; the labourers were no better than toads under a harrow. Most of the farmers were oppressors of the poor; they put on the iron wage-screw, and screwed the labourers' wages down, down below living point; they stretched him on the rack of life-long abject poverty.[2]

A second view portrays the rural relationship not so much as one of conflict contained by coercion, as of potential disaffection or awkward independence massaged away by social leadership, social conditioning, and paternalism. In this version the underlying relationship is also one of conflict, but vigilance and calculated manipulation on the part of the gentry normally succeeded in mediating it into an outward social harmony resting on deference and obedience, although periodically the conflict broke surface in protests, riots, or strikes.[3] A third view, singing the praises of the happy harmony of village life, of simple thatched-cottage contentment nourished by landlord kindliness, is barely credible in the light of today's conviction that all societies function with tensions and frictions, but was nevertheless widely held by contemporary apologists for the existing social order.[4]

The attraction of all these views is that, in their different ways, they present the relationship between landowners and the rural community in a satisfactorily positive way, involve the attribution of clear-cut, strongly motivated, and purposive actions to the landowners and equally clear-cut and intelligible responses from the villagers, and lead on into exciting abstractions about social control or class collaboration. The difficulty with them is that they rest on assumptions about landowners' behaviour and attitudes, and precisely about the extent to which the effects of their actions were calculated and intended, and about the degree to which they felt any commitment or involvement—whether defensive or benevolent—with the rural community at large, that make the theories conveniently self-validating. There were certainly many individual landowners whose sense of the duties and responsibilities of their station led them to minister to the moral and material welfare of what they thought of as their people, in ways which they decided were most suitable and proper, discharging what was felt to be the pastoral care of their flock so as to condition, discipline, perhaps control, the recipients of attention and mould them into dutiful, God-fearing, obedient, industrious, useful, law-abiding, and quiescent people who knew their place, kept it, and did not question the social order which made it a humble one. There were also, no doubt, a few who did similar things more explicitly out of fear of social disorder and rural unrest, conceiving the effects of their actions on the minds and lives of the community as measures of moral police in support of formal civil authority. But many more, the silent majority as it were, were not sufficiently active, imaginative, responsible, or assertive to try to use their power and position to influence the rural community in any systematic way. They were narrowly self-centred in their interpretation of what was required to protect their interests, they were concerned to look after their own ease and comfort, to keep up appearances, and to look after their immediate dependants; beyond the park walls, figuratively, if not indifferent to wider issues of the social order in the countryside and how best to preserve it, they did not regard it as their business to make any special contribution. Those who could not be bothered much with the schools, churches, reading rooms, sick clubs, soup kitchens, drinking places, or recreations of the lower orders were the saving grace of the rural community. It was their indifference, quite as much as the inability of the methods of social control, if there was indeed such a deliberate effort at social management, to achieve their proposed ends, which preserved the capacity of the rural population for independent development. Liberty, after all, depends not only on eternal vigilance, but also on eternal sloth and inefficiency on the part of those with power and privilege.

II

Sloth, however, was not exactly what farmers and labourers felt to be the hallmark of the preservation of game, which was the most widespread and most rapidly growing country pursuit of the greatest number of landowners, the activity which more than any other made country life and the ownership of country estates gratifying, and the point at which landowners mobilized their maximum amount of directly coercive power and displayed most nakedly the legal and physical force which maintained the rights of the propertied over the propertyless in the countryside. A Scottish tenant farmer might 'call a gamekeeper's work doing nothing; the principal part of his business is tormenting the tenants. . . . I say that gamekeeping is an idle trade and an idle class of men go into it', but he meant not that gamekeepers were indolent but that they were interfering busybodies engaged in an unjustifiable, unproductive, and vexatious activity.[5] The systematic preservation of game, the employment of armies of keepers, the formation of special game departments in the managerial structure of large estates, the controlled and costly rearing of birds and the provision of special coverts for them to inhabit, the organization of large shooting parties, and the culminating attainment of grand *battues* where the hundreds or thousands of brace were carefully noted in the game record books, were essentially Victorian developments. As the earlier, more informal and less effective shooting of game that was wild-bred and not too thick on the ground developed into the formal Victorian shoot, with its improved shotguns, regular shooting attire, and increased numbers, landowners took increasing trouble to protect their stake in cash and in pleasure. The custodians of these investments multiplied, from about 8,000 at the beginning of Victoria's reign to over 17,000 at its end. In the rural districts there were, by 1911, more than twice as many gamekeepers as country policemen;[6] the popular impression, in any case, was that the rural police helped at public expense in the struggle to keep poachers away from private preserves, an impression which the 1862 Night Poaching Act did nothing to allay. It may well be that this Act, which gave the police powers to search on suspicion of poaching, was passed at the request of the

459

chief constables who were alarmed at the growing number of bloody affrays between poachers and keepers, and wanted firmer legal grounds on which the police could intervene to keep the peace by anticipating such conflicts;[7] that did not alter the fact that the police appeared to be assisting the keepers in putting down poaching, rather than engaging in the neutral task of preventing bloodshed and murder.

The ordinary countrymen's view was that of Joseph Arch: 'They object very much to being subjected at any time to be assailed by a police officer and searched; they do not like that idea of the law.'[8] The Act was looked on as blatantly discriminatory class legislation, since it was only the poor man on foot with bulging pockets who was liable to be searched, not the gentleman in his carriage; and it, and the whole parcel of game laws to which it was but a refinement, were regarded as draconian and unjust since wild animals ought not to be, and could not become, private property. Arch again expressed the general view: 'We labourers do not believe hares and rabbits belong to any individual, not any more than thrushes and blackbirds do.'[9] He was quite right in law: the offence in poaching was in trespassing on private land in pursuit of game, not in the mere taking of a wild animal that could not have a legal owner. Such niceties did not make the game laws any more acceptable. They were generally held in contempt by countrymen, who failed to see anything morally reprehensible about poaching, and who regarded poachers as heroes or resourceful and daring hunters who brought valuable and tasty food to meagre larders, not as villains, criminals, or sinners. Poachers themselves, apart from the professional gangs who lived by supplying the urban markets with illicit game, and which were thought to be particularly active and well-organized in the 1820s and 1860s, were the braver and more independent village men, who regarded themselves at one level as engaging in a battle of wits with the keepers, at another level as fighting a secret, just war against the tyrannical selfishness of the wealthy.[10] For once the radical politicians who denounced the game laws, from John Bright in 1845 to Joseph Chamberlain in 1885, were voicing a deeply felt grievance of genuine countrymen rather than expressing an urban radical's notion of what countrymen ought to be feeling.

There was no respect for the game laws, and gamekeepers were disliked and detested by farmers and labourers alike. Here was one way in which the landowners were doing what they could to unite the rest of the rural community against them. 'Gamekeepers are generally troublesome to farmers,' said a Norfolk farmer from one of the most highly preserved and most favoured sporting regions in the country, 'breaking down fences, leaving gates open, prowling about. They are generally men of bad character.' Clare Sewell Read, a Norfolk M.P., confirmed that 'gamekeepers are generally very much disliked by farmers'.[11] The interference by the keepers was one irritant; the interference by the hares, rabbits, and game birds themselves was another, breeding a long story of protests against crop damage and loss, which were reduced but not stilled by the Gladstonian 1881 Ground Game Act that gave tenant farmers the right to take hares and rabbits on their own holdings. If the evil repute and bad blood caused by game laws and gamekeepers are not to be doubted, however, the extent to which these infected the countryside is still worth examining. All regions, all climates, and all types of farmland and woodland were not equally suited to game or equally favoured by sportsmen. Grouse were partial only to the bare, uncultivated moors and fells of the northern uplands and the highland zones; they shared some of the bleaker and more remote parts of the kingdom with deer, for whose stalking men were already prepared to pay as much as £2,000 a week by the 1870s.[12] In these thinly populated and infertile parts there was little competition with agriculture and little contact with communities except for those who lived by gillying; there were vivid folk tales of brutal clearances of poor crofting families to make way for the deer, but the actual culprits were more often sheep. It was in the lowland areas that game and people came together, and here the partridge and pheasant needed ploughland and grain crops while hares and rabbits, though ubiquitous, thrived best on light and well-drained soils. The sporting map followed landowners' tastes as well as natural habitats, and hence the distribution of game preservation observed man-made as well as natural contours. It shows that preservation, and therefore the community's experience of game laws and keepers, varied widely from one part of the country to another.

The gamekeeping force, and hence presumably game preservation, reached its peak in the early 1900s, a fitting reflection of the opulent pursuit of amusement in the Edwardian countryside. The 60 per cent growth in the number of keepers since the 1860s is perhaps surprising, across the years of depression; but it suggests the switch from basic agricultural production towards the provision of leisure activities as the role of the land, and emphasizes the degree to which shooting rents supplemented or surpassed farm rents as sources of income from land in some areas. It is no surprise that, in 1911, predominantly rural and agricultural counties such as Hereford, Norfolk, Suffolk, Dorset, Shropshire, and Westmorland had twenty to thirty gamekeepers to every 10,000 inhabitants, while highly urbanized and industrialized counties like Middlesex, Lancashire, Durham, or the West Riding had only one or two keepers per 10,000 population, since this is simply a slightly eccentric way of measuring the difference between rural and urban communities.[13] It is of more significance that the heavily keepered counties also had six or seven times as many keepers per head of total population as did other almost equally agricultural counties such as Leicester, Cheshire, Essex or the East Riding, and over three times as many as deeply rural Cornwall, Devon, Lincoln and Bedford. Keepers, however, in so far as they were not merely private policemen, were more concerned with the population of game animals in their charge than with the size of the local human population, and a more functional measure of their presence is their relation to land area as the basic determinant of game population. On this scale Suffolk, at the top, with ten keepers per 10,000 acres of land in the county, had over five times the keeper density of Cornwall, at the bottom. The densely keepered areas, on this reckoning, were Norfolk, Suffolk, Hampshire, Hertford, Surrey, Sussex, Berkshire, Dorset, Kent, and Shropshire; the agricultural counties where keepers were comparatively sparse, less than half as common as in the strongly guarded counties, were Northampton,

461

Huntingdon, the East Riding, Devon, Leicester, Cumberland, Cambridge, Westmorland, Lincoln and Cornwall. A similar analysis can be made for the Welsh counties, where only Flint, Anglesey, and Denbigh had high scores on the Suffolk or Hereford level, and all the other counties, most noticeably Brecon, Merioneth, Carmarthen, and Cardigan, were thinly keepered on the Cornish model.

Both measures confirm the supremacy of Norfolk and Suffolk as shooting counties where there were three or four gamekeepers in every village, and they outnumbered the police by two or three to one; here the iron of the game laws and the bitterness of the keepers' war was likely to have entered most deeply into village life. The home counties, perhaps, required particularly strong protection to ward off marauding Londoners, and if they are set aside in a special category the other most popular preserving areas with high rates of contact with keepers were Hampshire, Hereford, Dorset, and Shropshire, closely followed by Sussex, and with a large group of middling counties headed by Buckingham and Oxford. Much of the best hunting country of the midland shires—Northampton, Leicester, Nottingham—had low keepering ratios, because foxes and pheasants were not compatible, and enthusiasm for the one tended to exclude the other.[14] Otherwise there was no special logic about the distribution of the under-keepered areas: there were some in the south west, in the east, in the west Midlands, the east Midlands, the north west, and the north east, in most cases rubbing shoulders with highly preserved counties; there was no particular correlation with the presence or absence of aristocratic or gentry estates. If, however, it is assumed that one gamekeeper could manage about a thousand acres with efficient care and protection of game, and perhaps twice that area with something short of perfection, then the figures mean that in more than half the counties of England and Wales, comprising nearly two-thirds of the countryside, at least half the fields and woods never knew the attentions of gamekeepers. It is a fair guess that some very large proportion, approaching half, of the rural population also never encountered gamekeepers or needed to take careful steps to avoid them.

There is some evidence that the regional contrasts, already apparent in the mid-Victorian years, became more marked in the later nineteenth century; in 1861 individual counties ranged 50 per cent above and below the national mean of keepers per 10,000 acres, while by 1911 the variance had grown to over 100 per cent. The widening differences were perhaps due to improved upper-class railway mobility that encouraged specialization on the best endowed and most favoured areas, perhaps to expansion of shooting in the counties most affected by falling grain prices, perhaps simply to the quirks of individual tastes. As a straw in the wind, Cheshire, a dairying county which maintained its agricultural prosperity, marked time in its appointment of keepers and dropped from the premier position in 1861, more closely watched even than Norfolk, to a middling position in 1911. It is likely, therefore, that what had been a general if somewhat thinly spread experience in the mid-Victorian years, became a much more localized and concentrated confrontation in the later nineteenth century. Perceptions of the inequity of the game laws became more vivid just at the time that practical encounters with their enforcement were becoming less typical.

III

The shooting gentry pursued the protection of their pleasures with no less zest than they devoted to the shooting itself, heedless of the social cost. That cost included the spread of animosity, encouragement of contempt for the law, and threats to public order; it also included the fostering of a popular poaching culture which lived on pub stories of daring feats, narrow escapes, and cunning ruses which outwitted gamekeepers, which embodied the local lore of the virtues of living independently and defying authority, and whose standards were those of the superiority of the rights of free men to take free, natural goods over the rights of private property.[15] The keenest shots, game preservers, and employers of keepers would have argued, no doubt, that their sport was such an integral part of landowning, and indeed constituted the chief benefit and reward from the possession of landed estates, that any hostility and alienation engendered by its full and proper enjoyment, although naturally misguided and regrettable, had to be accepted and countered just as any other anti-landlord tendencies were to be countered—by leadership, example, education, and Christian morality.

It is, nevertheless, one of the ironies of the countryside that the ardent game preservers, who had strong motives for residence on their estates and intimate knowledge of their locality which should have nourished close ties with the local community, in fact made a major contribution to creating frictions and inflaming passions. Hunting, that other sporting interest which brought landowners into the country, was generally held not to produce similar socially divisive effects, except among the ranks of the upper class themselves where foxhunter and game preserver were not infrequently at loggerheads. Great trouble and offence could be caused when either fox or pheasant was killed outside the ordained course of pleasurable pursuit, and preserving landlords who took stern measures to exclude the hunt from their properties and to destroy the foxes were likely to attract pungently expressed local disfavour. This conflict was never general, partly because there was to some extent a separation of hunting and shooting areas, and mainly because many sporting landowners both hunted and shot, either in succession on different days in the week or in succession in different stages in life, taking to shooting as they became too old and portly to continue riding to hounds. Where it did break out, however, the conflict could be decidedly sharp, rising to its peak in the early 1900s as the enormous Edwardian shooting parties mounted to a crescendo of slaughter and were bitterly blamed for a growing scarcity of foxes. The hunting community, with its effortless assumption of prior and superior rights, denied responsibility for causing these frictions which disrupted the solidarity of the landed classes and complicated, if they did not frustrate, the task of keeping rural society in order. Hunting literature, indeed, especially hunting fiction, gave a strong impression that there was a real hunting community, cutting across class lines, bringing together the rural classes, and acting as an important agent of social harmony. There is abundant evidence that many farmers regularly rode to hounds, from the wealthy Yarborough estate tenants who hunted with the Brocklesby in the late nineteenth century to the hundreds of Leicestershire farmers with the Quorn, and the Gloucestershire farmers who virtually controlled the running of the Vale of White Horse.[16] It was certainly not a gentry preserve or a male preserve—unlike shooting—but apart from local farmers, and large numbers of outsiders who flocked to the fashionable hunts, it is not clear that other social groups were much represented; country doctors and parsons maybe, but the hunting village blacksmith or carrier must have been a rarity, and other village workers, let alone farm labourers, were hardly in the hunt. If it is more than doubtful whether hunting was an all-class affair for rural society, its close dependence on a landlord–farmer axis was of considerable importance in bringing together those two groups which otherwise were socially distanced and liable to have some conflicting economic interests. Certainly some farmers were obliged by the terms of their tenancies to support the local hunt, by walking hound puppies and by allowing the hunt over their fields; and others showed their discontent at the considerable damage to fences and growing crops that a field of hundreds of horses could easily cause, by exercising their right to warn the hunt off their farms. These, however, were a minority; eased by the diplomacy and cash of hunt committees, and by masters of foxhounds who gave annual dinners to the farmers, paid some compensation for damages, and took trouble to cultivate friendly relations, hunting enjoyed the goodwill and support of the majority of farmers, without which it could not have existed. As for the majority of the local community, labourers may have derived some pleasure from the colourful spectacle of the meet, or a glimpse of a large field at full stretch, and relished the chance that persons of high degree might be levelled by falling into ditches, but at best they were bystanders with no place in the hunting network, and the goings on of the hunting folk did not affect them one way or the other.

In the eyes of the generality of landowners the function of their estates was to provide the income to support their life style; the function of the countryside was to provide good sport. If the sport was hunting, it did something to unite the upper reaches of rural society, bringing together landlords and tenants, and at least did nothing to antagonize the labourers. If it was shooting, on the other hand, it emphasized and exacerbated social divisions, irritating the tenant-farmers and imbuing the labourers, who felt the direct consequences of game preservation and game laws, with a sense of social injustice and a contempt for the law which the wealthy used to oppress the poor. In such a situation the rational and efficient behaviour for the landowners as a class would have been to make sure that in those regions where their own actions tended most to undermine social order and their own authority, counter-measures designed to neutralize such influences were most actively promoted. Direct strengthening of the power of the law by maintaining more rural police in the disturbed than in the quiet areas was one possibility. Such a course was indeed implicit in the advice of the chief constables of rural counties in 1859, whose figures of savage attacks on gamekeepers not surprisingly showed a clear correlation with the main game preserving counties.[17] It was not, however, followed

464

in practice. It was true that in 1861, when county police forces had not been long established and many were still in their first few years of feeling their way towards a desired size, the leading game and poaching county, Norfolk, had marginally more policemen per head of population than a hunting county like Leicestershire; but it was scarcely a significant difference that could suggest any deliberate reinforcement of coercive power.[18] In the next fifty years, as game preservation intensified and became more elaborate, the numbers of rural police were everywhere increased; but they did not increase as fast as total population, and in the great shooting counties police forces expanded markedly less than elsewhere. The result was that by 1911 policing ratios were practically identical in all the more agricultural counties, with only Cornwall, Rutland, and Shropshire apparently more law-abiding than the rest in so far as they had one third fewer policemen in relation to the population than the others. East Anglia functioned with exactly the same policing ratio as the great hunting shires, and indeed of the ten counties where gamekeepers were thickest on the ground only three—Hertfordshire, Kent, and Surrey—had a high police presence, twice that of the other seven, and that was accounted for by their large urban populations and proximity to London. There had clearly been no effort to match heavy concentrations of gamekeepers with heavy concentrations of police to contain the extra lawlessness engendered by strict preservation; rather, the reverse had happened, and the great shooting landowners, by multiplying the number of keepers they employed at least by two, had enabled their counties to economize on police, patrolling their covers with their own staff, perhaps consciously in order to avoid the unpopularity of being responsible for putting more policemen on the public rates.[19]

IV

Such figures might suggest that it was no more difficult to keep order in the areas of greatest exposure to the game war than anywhere else. Conceivably contemporary opinion exaggerated the popular hostility to the game laws and sympathy with the poachers, and there never was any particular problem in maintaining authority and landowner superiority in the affected areas, but this seems unlikely in the light of the clear-cut testimony. It is possible that the resentment was indeed widespread, but remained sullen rather than overt because of other pressures which were effective without there being any need for the display of extra physical force. Among such influences education took pride of place as the panacea prescribed by Victorians in authority when they sensed any whiff of social or moral decay or collapse in the populace, and was indeed frequently regarded as a more effective and enduring instrument of social order than troops, police, or magistrates. Support of village schools was one of the most typical activities of Victorian landowners, and the visit to the schoolroom, more often by the lady than the master of the big house, was the most common form of contact of the possessing classes with the generality of the lower orders outside the ranks of immediate employees and dependants, at least with the younger members of the general community. Support was typical, but not universal. It is not in doubt that before 1870, when popular education depended on the voluntary schools, these were two or three times more numerous, in relation to the population of school age, in the rural and agricultural than in the urban and industrial areas; this meant that rural communities subscribed more generously than urban ones to the building of schools. Which members of rural communities subscribed is, however, in some doubt; and while there were considerable variations in school provision among the predominantly agricultural counties themselves, it is more than doubtful whether these variations conformed to any scale of differing degrees of exposure to the risks of disaffection.

The history of education has been so preoccupied with questions of policy that the geography of schools has not been much studied. Kay-Shuttleworth's view on the extreme educational backwardness of East Anglia in the 1830s, where he found little except 'a lawless population of paupers, disbanded smugglers and poachers', may be only a small straw in the wind, since on his way to becoming the country's leading educational pundit he was biased towards noticing whatever proved the need for more schools; it does not look, however, as if the shooting squires were at this time aware of any particular call to concern themselves with educating the people.[20] A generation later the Newcastle Commission on Popular Education provided a more objective measure of the variations between counties in the support of voluntary schools, when in 1861 it published a table ranking the counties in order of the proportion of children on the books of their schools in relation to total population. This has been accepted 'as an index of the eagerness or reluctance with which local persons were prepared to subscribe to the building of the schools'.[21] After twenty-five years of considerable effort and achievement by the voluntary societies, during which the numbers and capacity of their schools had been increased four- or five-fold, this index recorded that the greatest eagerness had been shown by Wiltshire, Westmorland, Oxfordshire, and Rutland, and the most reluctance by Cornwall, Northumberland, Warwickshire, and Durham; the best performers were nearly three times more generous than the worst in finding funds for school building. The table does not distinguish between rural and urban areas, and it is arguable that the eduationally neglected counties were predominantly those with large industrial and urban populations: Lancashire, Yorkshire, Nottinghamshire, and Staffordshire did not appear far from the bottom of the league. On the other hand, decidedly rural and agricultural counties might be either very keen on schools, like Wiltshire and Westmorland, or definitely unenthusiastic, like Worcestershire and Devonshire; while the indifferent to mediocre performance of Norfolk, Suffolk, Hampshire, or Sussex suggests that the strong shooting interests of those counties had still seen no need to show any special interest in rural schools. They were indeed comfortably outclassed by the great hunting shires, all of which supported more schools. Hence, if there was any connection at all between the sport-based social characteristics and needs of a district, and the level of interest in and support for schools, it seems possible that the greater friendliness, neighbourliness, and comparative absence of social friction in the hunting shires, and indeed in counties not notable for any kind of sport, disposed the propertied classes to an active interest in the educational welfare of their communities, while the frictions and disaffections of the shooting counties, far from causing the landed gentry acute anxieties about the local moral order and inducing special zeal for carefully managed schools as a corrective, served to make them tight-fisted, suspicious, uncooperative, or even hostile towards the idea of helping ungrateful and disaffected people to better themselves.

In the final phase of voluntary activity, before rate-financed schools established effective control of elementary education, it is possible that landowners in some of the previously laggard areas were shamed or provoked into making good some of their earlier neglect and indifference. Leaving aside those cases where there was a stampede after 1870 to safeguard Anglican and paternalist interests by hastily founding new National Society schools within the few years' grace allowed by the Act, in order to ward off the threat that school boards would be set up to provide for local deficiencies of school places, there is some evidence of more sustained efforts. By the end of the 1880s the dust had more or less settled on the controversies over the establishment of school boards, and where none had been set up, either compulsorily or voluntarily, it is safe to assume that the voluntary schools were adequate in size and quality and were tolerably well supported by their communities. In 1889 school boards looked after the education of 62 per cent of the population of England, but there were extremely wide regional variations in their distribution: 95 per cent of the population of Middlesex came under school boards, and 80 per cent in Surrey and Warwickshire, but only 3 per cent in Rutland and 10 per cent in Dorset. Many of the counties which, by this standard, had the poorest record of support for voluntary schools merely confirmed the indifference that they had already demonstrated by 1861: thus Devon, Cornwall, Durham, Nottinghamshire, Yorkshire, and Staffordshire were at the bottom of the 1889 league just as they had been towards the bottom of the 1861 table. Similarly, Rutland and Dorset, Berkshire, Hertfordshire, Oxfordshire, and Wiltshire appear at the top of both tables. There were, however, some counties in which an apparently sharp change in attitude towards voluntary schools occurred between 1861 and 1889: there seems to have been a notable increase in the liberality with which schools were supported in Cheshire, Herefordshire, and Shropshire, that had transformed them from middling to poor performers in 1861 into front runners in 1889; and while Lancashire, Northumberland, and Worcestershire reached the middle of the order only in 1889, they had moved up from very lowly positions. On the other hand, support seems to have contracted severely in Gloucestershire, which dropped from ninth to thirtieth place, and to have dwindled significantly in Essex, Northamptonshire, Norfolk, and Westmorland, whose relative standings deteriorated markedly.[22]

The regional pattern of concern for education is an interesting one, not least for its failure to conform with the distribution of large or gentry estates, or with distinctions between pastoral and cereal areas, let alone with distinctions between hunting and shooting counties. Since it also shows, albeit tentatively, that it was possible both for counties which cared about schools and those which did not to manage with unusually small numbers of rural police, it suggests that education did not necessarily turn out the superior law-abiding citizenry it was intended to produce. It is, above all, an awkward pattern for any thesis which places landowner support at the centre of Anglican school expansion or regards an interest in the village school as a typical landowner activity. The implication that landowners as a group were erratic, unsystematic, and unreliable in their concern for local schools, however, accords well with the opinions of contemporary administrators, who saw the local parson as the key figure in initiating and sustaining the local school, and the local landowners as a set of potential but reluctant subscribers which the clergy had to struggle hard to mobilize. The conclusion of the assistant commissioner for the eastern counties, reporting to the Newcastle Commission on Popular Education, was that

> Farmers seldom feel any interest in the school, and seldom therefore subscribe to it. Landowners are often non-resident, and if they subscribe, do so to a very insufficient amount. Where landowners are resident and study the welfare of their tenants and labourers, they usually take an interest in the school and contribute liberally, if they do not wholly support it. But these cases are not frequent.

The assistant commissioner investigating a sample of parishes in the western agricultural counties found more than a third of the local landowners 'to whom the school in the parish from which they derive their income is a simple matter of unconcern'. The Newcastle *Report* itself summed up the situation in a passage which was sternly critical of the landowners:

> [The clergyman] is the man who most feels the mischief arising from want of education. . . . He begs from the landowners; if he fails to persuade them to take their fair share of the burden, he begs from his friends, and even from strangers; and at last submits most meritoriously, and most generously, to bear not only his own proportion of the expense, but also that which ought to be borne by others. It has been repeatedly noticed by the school inspectors, and it is our duty to state that as a class the landowners, especially those who are non-resident (though there are many honourable exceptions) do not do their duty in the support of popular education, and that they allow others, who are far less able to afford it, to bear the burden of their neglect.[23]

On this view the regional and chronological variations are to be explained largely in terms of the chance distribution of zealous, conscientious, and persuasive clergymen rather than in terms of differences between landowners in their perceptions of their self-interest or their ideas of their social responsibilities. The often passive role of landowners is a warning that the frequent references in family and estate papers to annual subscriptions of a few guineas to local schools are not to be taken as evidence of active involvement, but may more likely indicate no more than a token, and often perfunctory, compliance with the importunings of the local clergymen. The school managers, and of course the parson, would be well aware of which local landowners did subscribe and which did not, and the annual subscription was no doubt a small price to pay for securing freedom from vexatious calls, and a reputation for basic attention to a social duty, and as such served to smooth relations with that level of rural society. Those at the receiving end of education, however, the schoolchildren and their parents, are most unlikely to have known who the subscribers were, so that simple subscription offered no dividends of deference or obligation to the landowner, and provided him with no paternalist satisfaction. Active involvement, of a kind likely to be noticed by the villagers and to reinforce their attachment to the local gentry, required considerably more effort: the donation of a site, financing of the school building, or support of the teacher's salary were the material contributions likely to accompany a keen and continuing interest in a school and to bring a patron into direct and impressionable contact with the children. Many landowners did indeed contribute on this scale, like Lord Shaftesbury, who within three months of inheriting the family estate in Dorset had launched three schools where before there were none, and ended by meeting the salaries of six or seven school masters and mistresses; less pious peers did no less, like the Duke of Bedford, Lord Pembroke in Wiltshire, or Lord Cholmondeley in Norfolk. The example, however, was far from widespread. A sample of seven recent volumes of the *Victoria County History* mentions 118 National Society schools; 68 of these apparently had no particular patron worthy of mention, while of those which were substantially supported by individuals only 21, or 17 per cent of the total, had patrons from the landowning classes.[24] This is probably a reasonable measure of the extent of serious, as distinct from superficial, landowner contact with the education of rural labourers.

V

As with schools, so perhaps with churches, closely linked as they were as the centres of authority and social discipline in village life. Unfortunately there are no sources which permit a ready assessment of the extent of landowners' activities in church building, extension, and restoration, let alone of their involvement in the life of the church and the conduct of its parishioners. There were some, like Lord Tollemache at Helmingham in Suffolk, who insisted that all the farm workers attend church every Sunday; and others like Sir Tatton Sykes who rebuilt or restored twenty churches in the parishes near his seat of Sledmere in the East Riding.[25] It is not likely, however, that such individuals were typical of their class, which by inclination would regard such matters as the parson's business, to attend to as best he could. If concern with succouring and supervising the main agencies which were held to mould the morals and behaviour of the rural labourers was a minority pursuit for landowners, it is possible that concern for their material welfare was more widespread. Next to their wages, which were directly controlled by farmers, not landowners (except for household servants and estate workers), and were effectively determined by the market, housing was the labourers' chief concern. The condition of their home profoundly affected the welfare or misery of a labourer's family; many social observers believed that it was also a decisive influence on their morals. Rural overcrowding was commonly held to encourage immodesty, licentiousness, promiscuity, and incest; a typical view was that 'in the villages where the cottages are most crowded there are the greatest number of illegitimate children'.[26] While overcrowding was also thought to cause intemperance, by driving men to the beer-shops, the drive for cottage improvement was no doubt more strongly nourished by the desire to eradicate incest and promiscuity, an object to be attained by providing enough rooms to separate the sleeping arrangements of the sexes. Success in such endeavours was probably never very great, since the incest taboo seems to have been as firmly held by the labouring as by other classes, and despite the prurient shock with which country parsons and doctors claimed to have observed incest it is unlikely ever to have been anything but exceptional; while there are no grounds for supposing that rural fornication fell out of favour.

Even if the desired effects on sexual behaviour may not have been realized, cottages were none the less built. Among a certain group of landowners discussion of cottage improvements and the merits of two- or three-bedroom designs, and the exchange of restrained complaints about the meagre financial returns on cottage building as an investment, became as absorbing as the talk of record bags or record runs among other groups. Many individuals, from Lord Shaftesbury in Dorset—who in spite of his initial confession on inheriting the estate that

> surely I am the most perplexed of men, I have passed my life in rating others for allowing rotten houses and immoral, unhealthy dwellings; and now I come into an estate rife with abominations! Why, there are things here to make one's flesh creep; and I have not a farthing to set them right,

in the end managed to find the money to build many cottages[27]—to the Duke of Northumberland in his county, from the Earl of Leicester in Norfolk to Lord Dartmouth in Staffordshire, acquired considerable reputations in the middle years of the century as builders of model cottages. Some, like the Earl of Leicester, went further, and as well as building cottages, let them direct to the labourers instead of following the normal system of letting cottages along with farms to tenant farmers, who might then use their power to threaten eviction from tied cottages to intimidate their workers; the earl's arrangement turned cottage-owning to paternalist account by interposing the landowner as the labourer's protector in this sector of the conflict between farmer and labourer, although it may not have done much to help agricultural efficiency. Individual instances, however, are an unsatisfactory foundation for any generalization; if it is accepted that, by 1914, landowners as a group had built some 22,000 cottages for farm workers, cottage-building is revealed decidedly as a minority pursuit.[28] Several individuals are known to have built two hundred or more cottages on their estates in the period of greatest activity, between 1850 and 1880, so that the total may have represented the work of no more than one or two hundred landowners. In any case, even in relation to an agricultural workforce which had shrunk by about one third between 1851 and 1911, these cottages cannot have contributed as much as 5 per cent of its housing; it was a rare and untypical labourer's family that experienced the joys of living in a model cottage, or whose home harboured reminders of landowner influence.

With landowner attention to basic living conditions confined to such a limited scale it is hardly likely that their provision of such frills in the way of village amenities as reading rooms, village halls, or playing fields was more lavish or widespread. Some individual landowners did indeed provide some or all of these things as part of their concept of social duty and leadership, although the impression conveyed by country house literature is that gentry-sponsored sport for the locals was confined to an annual cricket match between the big house eleven and the servants and labourers, played on a pitch in the park, until in the early twentieth century the idea of more permanent and specialized playing fields began, especially under the influence of football, to be imported into the countryside from the towns.[29] An even more casual impression is that the great majority of villages went without any public meeting places until the crop of memorial halls began to appear after 1918. It may be that the less expensive and less capital-intensive forms of helping the local community—running a village clothing club, distributing blankets and coal, opening a soup kitchen in winter, subscribing to a local benevolent or friendly society—were more widely practised by landowners. Such help for the needy and encouragement to the thrifty, whatever the explicit, conscious motive for giving it, no doubt helped to establish the character, influence, and authority of the donor and thus to preserve his position at the head of the social hierarchy in his country; one might expect it to be given above all to the villages which stood directly outside the park gates, living in the shadow of a big house.

VI

It might seem, indeed, as if all the evidence of landowners' involvement in providing the material equipment of village life—schools, churches, cottages, and clubs—pointed towards the conclusion that their horizons of social responsibility and spheres of active social leadership and control were limited to the villages and parishes that they held in sole ownership. Such an explanation would dovetail neatly with the strong mid-century concern over the distinction between open and close parishes and the differences in their states of misery or well-being. Open parishes were those with no dominant landowner, in which property ownership was diffuse and sites for cottages could be readily acquired; they were overcrowded, overpopulated, poorly housed, heavily burdened with poor rates, and the source of much of the labour, which commuted daily on foot, for working the farms of the close parishes. These, by contrast, were in single ownership, or at most in the hands of two or three owners; the numbers of cottages were carefully controlled and restricted in order to keep population below the labour needs of the parish and thus ensure that poor rates were kept low. It would not be unreasonable to expect that close parishes were the ones to receive close attention. The object of close parishes was to keep down expenditure on the poor, however, and this could be achieved by simple restriction of numbers without any need for the restricted number of cottages to be better than those elsewhere, or for the inhabitants to be better looked after. It could be argued, indeed, that from the point of view of a landowner concerned only with the essential requirements of keeping social order and preserving deference the powers of property were so complete and unchallengeable in close parishes by virtue of their monopolization, that there was less need than in other places for deploying the more subtle instruments of control through benevolence. Hypotheses aside, the available figures do not support the idea of an association between close parishes and paternalism. In the country as a whole close parishes amounted to perhaps 20 per cent of the total in rural areas at the middle of the century, a proportion much in excess of those which saw any cottage building by landowners. The regional variations in 'closeness', moreover, which range from high points of 33 to 43 per cent of all townships being close in Norfolk, Leicestershire, Rutland, Lincolnshire, and the East Riding, to low points of 6 per cent in Essex, Cambridgeshire, and Hertfordshire, with much of the midland shires and west country in the middle of this range, do not correspond at all with the variations in the support of village schools, unless they hint vaguely at an inverse correlation.[30] There were too many close parishes, in the wrong places, for these to have been necessarily the places where village life was most dominated, regulated, nursed, and cosseted by a powerful landowner.

That there were many villages in which there was much doffing of caps, either because people did not dare risk giving offence by doing otherwise or because they wished to show appreciation of favours and good works received, is not in doubt. If the distribution of good works, embodied in churches, schools, cottages, clothing clubs, free coal, soup kitchens, and, towards the end of the century, patronage of healthy recreations and the occasional cottage hospital, was not determined by a random scatter of individual landowners and their wives who happened to have lively social consciences, it may well have depended on the residential habits of landowners and the extent to which particular big houses were identified with immediately dependent villages. A map of rural communities which were particularly under the eye, or thumb, of a landowner patron might well, therefore, be very similar to a map of estate villages, defined as those which, although not necessarily custom-built in uniform style, adorned and complemented the big house and housed estate workers, pensioned dependants, and some of the outdoor servants as well as the more typical village population of farm labourers and village workers and tradesmen. The map would have many large blank areas, for all the general evidence indicates that paternalism was restricted and localized in its appearances, and above all that it was not systematically deployed in those places and situations where the traditional social order and respect for the law were most threatened by social stresses and strains. It is possible to conclude either that the benefits and comforts of social services provided by landowners were reserved for a privileged minority in the countryside, or that only a minority were unlucky enough to be subjected to the constraints of social discipline and control imposed from above; either that the majority of landowners neglected their social responsibilities towards the majority of the people living on their estates, because they were indifferent, lazy, or self-centred, or that the majority declined to abuse the power of property by interfering in other people's lives. Either way, for most country folk landowners were remote figures who left them to fend for themselves, living their own lives and fighting their own battles with farmers and other employers. Pockets of sheltered, protected, and regimented rural communities studded a landscape populated by much more independent, self-reliant, and exposed villages; which set of communities were more contented, or more resentful of their lot, is an open question.

Notes

1 E. P. Thompson, 1965, ch. 7; Green, 1913.
2 Arch, 1898, 55.
3 Dunbabin, 1974, 14.
4 Howitt, 1838, I, 286., quoted in Horn, 1976b, 5.
5 BPP 1873 XIII, Q. 3028–30.
6 1911 Census, England and Wales, occupation tables, rural districts.
7 BPP 1862 XLV.
8 BPP 1873 XIII, Q. 8067.
9 Arch, 1898, 159.
10 The chief constable thought there were 300 men in Hertfordshire who maintained themselves for several months each year by commercial poaching: BPP 1873 XIII, Q. 240.
11 BPP 1873 XIII, Q. 1616–27, 6653.
12 *Ibid.*, Q. 6637.
13 Statistical information is from the occupation tables of the 1861 and 1911 censuses.
14 Itzkowitz, 1977, 146–50.
15 Sources as far apart as Engels, 1950, 266, and the chief constables in Memorial, BPP 1862 XLV 2, agree, approvingly and disapprovingly, that poachers were generally regarded as 'village heroes'. See also Samuel, 1975a, 207–27.
16 *Victoria County History: Lincolnshire* I (1906), 494; Itzkowitz, 1977, 172–3.
17 BPP 1862 XLV.
18 The figures were 19 police per 10,000 inhabitants in Norfolk, 15 in Leicestershire.
19 The normal ratio in 1911 was 11–12 police per 10,000 inhabitants in the agricultural counties; in Cornwall, Rutland and Shropshire it was 7–8, and in Hertfordshire, Kent and Surrey 19–21.
20 Hurt, 1971, 22.
21 Hurt, 1968, 6.

22 BPP 1889 LIX, 6–7.

23 BPP I 1861 XXI, II 157, 74; I 78.

24 *Victoria County History: Essex VI; Gloucestershire XI; Middlesex V; Oxfordshire VIII, IX, X; Wiltshire X.* A complete count of the National schools mentioned in these volumes shows that the sites were provided, or the costs of building largely met, by

Members of landed aristocracy or gentry	21
Wealthy non-landowners	15
Local clergy	10
Oxford colleges, and bishops	4
No particular individuals	68
Total	118

25 Evans, 1970, 123–4; Pevsner, 1972, 43.

26 Quoted in Burnett, 1978, 45.

27 Hodder, 1887, 449.

28 Whetham, 1978, 48.

29 Girouard, 1978, 271, 285.

30 Holderness, 1972b, especially 135.

34   Country Sports

Raymond Carr

Country sports were dependent for their development on a series of interlocking variables: forms of land tenure; techniques of farming; changes in transport facilities; technical innovations in sportsmen's instruments—both animal and inanimate. They also reflected, and were an index of changes in, income distribution and social mobility. Some sports were socially divisive—shooting for instance. Some were generally popular as creating the sense of a coherent rural community, as was hunting—with some startling exceptions. Some were socially neutral, as was fishing. Some—horse-racing, cock-fighting, pugilism—were regarded by the respectable as degrading and vicious; others—rowing and cricket—as manly exercises. All were regarded as typically British. When Queen Victoria died Britain considered itself, and was considered by others, as the greatest sporting nation in the world.

I

The simplest elements to isolate are technical changes in farming methods and the effects of the 'railway revolution', as sporting writers referred to the mid-century development of the railway system. Technical innovations revolutionized shooting, whereas there were few technical advances in hunting. The railways changed the face of the hunting field; they had a less dramatic effect on shooting.

Shooting changed completely in the Victorian period as a consequence of successive improvements in guns; it is characteristic of the mentality of sportsmen that each of these improvements was fiercely resisted by the old school, accustomed to the old guns. After 1815 even as obvious an improvement as the percussion cap to replace the flintlock was criticized because it sometimes failed. By the 1860s the superiority of the breech loader over the sometimes dangerous and certainly slower-firing muzzle loader was evident; it was resisted because it threatened to change the nature of the sport. In early nineteenth-century prints the sportsman is pictured with a friend shooting over pointers at birds flying *away*, a relatively easy shot; rapid-firing guns (and the increased killing power of the choke bore after 1874) made it necessary for 'sport' to make birds more difficult to hit and led to *battues* in which pheasants were driven *towards* the guns. Old-fashioned sportsmen criticized *battues* as little better than massacres and as un-English. In November 1867, with an unwilling Emperor of Austria as his guest, Napoleon III, in violet velvet with precious stones as buttons, used 250 beaters to kill 3,829 head of game. If English gentlemen did not indulge in such 'burlesques' they did begin to keep game books and look on the number of birds killed as an index of the sport enjoyed.

Changes in the way England was farmed—reflected in the landscape itself—lay at the root of the changed patterns in hunting and shooting. The primacy of the midland shires as a fox-hunter's paradise—the 'eye of hunting England' as the hunting journalist Nimrod (Charles Apperley, 1779–1843) called it—was advanced by the enclosure movement and better drainage. The new hedges created the jumps that made shire hunting a unique experience; better-drained pastures created splendid scent-carrying turf that sent bitches screaming over the grass and enabled a field to gallop up to them, and sometimes, to the horror of successive masters of the Quorn, over them. 'In proportion as the agriculture of the country is improved, the speed of the chase is increased.'[1] Throughout the century the supply of good grass to gallop over depended on the relative profitability of arable farming and grazing. The post-war depression in 1815 increased pasture; so did the agricultural decline of the 1880s. What was bad for farmers was good for fox-hunters.

Later another change, the use of wire, and especially barbed wire, as a cheap method of fencing, was regarded by hunting men as a major disaster in that it could bring down a horse. In 1862 the Duke of Rutland stated bluntly that 'unless wire fencing was done away with, fox hunting must cease in Leicestershire'.[2] Since wire was cheap farmers wanted to use it, and the outrage of fox-hunters threatened to ruin the 'harmony' between them and the farmers. In the end, as so often in the history of fox-hunting, harmony was saved by hard cash: the farmers were paid to take down wire in the hunting season.

High farming and enclosure changed the pattern of shooting. The old, thick, pre-enclosure hedges held game that could be flushed out by spaniels, as did the stubble of corn fields where pointers were used, before the advent of the mechanical reaper. This encouraged, if it did not cause, hand-rearing of game and intensive preservation.

'This trebly accursed revolution of railroads', argued Delmé Radcliffe, would end fox-hunting. It would turn rural England into 'one vast gridiron'. It would drag the fox-hunting squire to London—and it was a consistent argument of fox-hunters that only a resident gentry saved England from a 1789 or 1848. In fact fox-hunters like

Surtees became railway enthusiasts; railways brought new, rich subscribers, expanding the hunting field socially and geographically; and they took hounds and horses to distant meets.

II

The rural sport *par excellence* was fox-hunting. With some exaggeration the novelist Anthony Trollope—himself a brave hunter, since he was shortsighted and could never afford good horses—called it *the* national sport.[3] This claim was only credible given the absence of rivals: cricket and golf were still geographically limited, and the great spectator sports and club activities of the twentieth century—except, perhaps, for rowing—were still in their infancy. Fox-hunting, on the other hand, had become by 1860 more than a private diversion; it was 'a highly organized, extremely influential public institution . . . with a significance out of all proportion to its role as a mere sport'.[4]

The fox-hunter's claim that his sport was 'national' was based not merely on its geographical ubiquity—all England except near the great industrial towns was hunted. The ultimate justification of fox-hunting in the eyes of its supporters was that it was 'democratic', that it involved *all* social classes, that it was a Platonic image of a supposedly harmonious rural society, an institution that bound together farmer and landlord while excluding the common enemy of both—the agricultural labourer, consistently portrayed in hunting literature as a brutish clodhopper who merely interfered with sport.

Hunting on horseback with hounds was, in its origins, an exclusive royal and aristocratic pursuit and the quarry was the deer. With the shortage of deer in the seventeenth and eighteenth centuries the fox (hitherto a despised vermin and the quarry of village hunts whose activities persisted in remoter regions to distress early nineteenth-century masters) became the prime quarry. The hare was a popular rival. It was the great aristocratic families—the Spencers, Somersets, Fitzwilliams, Pelhams, Manners—who financed and organized the 'smart' packs of foxhounds of the later eighteenth century. It was a fashionable midland squire, Meynell, who revolutionized the technique of fox-hunting during his mastership of the Quorn (1753–1800) and established Leicestershire in the eyes of the sportsmen as the 'Vale of Cashmere'. But beside these magnates and rich landowners modest squires all over England were turning from hare-hunting to fox-hunting in the early years of the nineteenth century; and though the old generation of enthusiasts believed that hare-hunting was more technically exacting, their sons preferred the faster, more exciting sport. At the bottom end of the social scale there remained local farmers' packs and the scratch packs near the large towns. Surrey fox-hunting allowed London merchants to get back to the city in order to catch the evening post. For early Victorian fox-hunting was not even exclusively rural: it entered into the life of market towns, and the stockingers of Leicester still came out for a day with the

Quorn. The artist George Morland (who died of drink in 1804) lost all his sitters to a local meet. 'Last Monday week almost everyone in Margate was drunk by reason of the Freemasons' meet and fox hunt.'

When Queen Victoria came to the throne fox-hunting therefore embraced a varied and wide social spectrum, from the Duke of Wellington to George Morland's Margate inebriates and John Peel (d. 1854), who kept his pack on an income of £400 a year. It is characteristic of the snobbery so evident in *Punch* that her reign showed a process of social contraction at the lower end of the scale and inflation in its middle ranges. Though scratch packs persisted in the provinces, the tone of fox-hunting as a whole was set by the smart midland packs. Mr Jorrocks, the city grocer who, as a master of foxhounds, was not above peddling tea to his field, called himself a 'Post Office Directory man'. Very few packs by 1850 would have taken on such a master. R. S. Surtees (1803–64), the greatest of hunting novelists, was an incurable romantic describing a rapidly vanishing scene; the young blades who people the novels of Whyte Melville (thrown and killed stone-dead, in 1878) are socially respectable, with little of the old-fashioned countryman's knowledge of the ways of hounds and foxes. They are out, by 'jealous riding', to show off their expensive horses. They take tea with vicars' daughters.

The early Victorian hunting field still exhibited in the morals and life style of masters like Osbaldeston (1787–1866) and Jack Masters (1777–1849) the social promiscuity and rough manners of Regency England. Masters was a compulsive womanizer; Osbaldeston lost his fortune gambling. Victorian respectability came with the most professional of all early nineteenth-century masters, Assheton Smith (master of the Tedworth, 1826–58). He was a regular church-goer (though he held up the congregation by talking with his huntsman in the church porch), a classical scholar, and an astute businessman who administered a vast fortune founded on Welsh slates supplied to the new industrial towns.

Field sports, at least from the sixteenth century, had been an arena of social mobility. To take over the local pack, put on a red coat, provide drink and food for a lawn meet, was to become socially acceptable in a rural society of which the local master of foxhounds was a dominant figure. In Surtees's greatest novel, *Mr Sponge's Sporting Tour*, Mr Puffington, the son of a starch manufacturer, takes on a pack of hounds 'because he thought it would give him consequence'. Already in the eighteenth century ironmasters and cotton-spinners had bought landed estates for sporting and social purposes.[5] In the mid-nineteenth century the arrival of the 'purse proud *parvenu*' distressed conservatives and led to an unfortunate outburst of anti-Semitism. But by the 1860s *British Sports and Pastimes* talks of sport—above all of hunting—as a 'most serious influence on the lives of Englishmen of the upper *and middle classes*'. It was part of the process that so distressed Cobden in 1863; it led 'manufacturers and merchants . . . to prostrate themselves at the feet of feudalism'.

This advance was facilitated by the most fundamental change in the economics of fox-hunting. In the 1830s to maintain a midland pack in style cost between £4,000 and £5,000, when a peer's average income was £10,000.[6] By the 1860s, and even more so after the agricultural depression in the 1880s, only the richest of magnates could continue to supply free hunting for their neighbours. A contribution from the field was inevitable. With the advent of the subscription pack, if what Trollope called 'feudal grandeur' vanished, the hunting field was open to all who could subscribe. Combined with the 'railway revolution' this meant an expansion of the field both numerically and socially. Sir Robert Foster, Member of Parliament for the City of London, arrived at Paddington to hunt with the Beaufort: hacking back to the local station he amused himself by reciting the third chapter of Hallam's *Middle Ages.*

This expansion of the field tested the central alliance which supported fox-hunting: the alliance of farmers and fox-hunters. Fox-hunting meant licence for fields of galloping horses to crash across land they did not own, a licence freely granted to known neighbours but which was less easily given to large, 400-strong fields of 'strangers'. Since the legal right to cross other people's property was never established by fox-hunters—their claims to do so were dismissed in the Capel case of 1808[7]—the freely given permission of the occupiers was vital. When the bankrupt exiles in Dieppe and Boulogne set up a fox-hunt, the local peasantry called out the gendarmerie. That English farmers as a class never sought to challenge fox-hunting is one of the strangest features of rural life.

Fox-hunters were sometimes warned off by shooting landlords, and very occasionally challenged by individual farmers. Many tenant farmers were bound in their leases to allow hunting, many more were wary of annoying a landlord who might let him off lightly in a bad year. But the evidence is overwhelming that farmers either actively supported hunting—Cobbett had earlier noticed a deplorable propensity in farmers to take up hunting themselves—or accepted it as part of the unchallengeable hegemony of the landed gentry. Fox-hunting was not merely a symbol of that hegemony; it was consciously used as a form of political patronage, as George Osbaldeston found out to his cost when he criticized an innkeeper out with the Duke of Beaufort—the brewer was an important voter. Conscientious masters, like the Dorset squire Farquharson, spent a great deal of their time and energy fostering good relations with farmers, presiding over endless farmers' dinners and patronizing agricultural shows. They usually succeeded. It was where such assiduous cultivation was impossible, or where intensive farming made hunting particularly damaging to crops, that fox-hunters were cursed, as when they were pursued with pitchforks in Harrow.

The alliance of fox-hunters and farmers resisted both the propaganda of urban radicals and, more surprisingly, the strains of the agricultural depression of the 1870s and 1880s. Nevertheless, it survived in an altered form as the depression eroded the— always idealized—image of a harmonious rural society. The supposed community of interests between landowners and farmers was under increasing attack from radicals aiming at 'the utter abolition of the present landed aristocracy'.[8] With falling rents, landlords found it harder and harder to bear alone the costs of a hunt. They were forced either to cut costs or accept a subscription; one of the severest shocks to the hunting community came when Lord Yarborough—whose family had maintained the

Brocklesby hunt since the eighteenth century—was forced to sell his dog pack in 1895, keeping only the bitches. And even the Duke of Rutland cut back to four days a week.

If landlords were feeling the pinch so were the farmers, and falling prices made them less willing to accept the damage inflicted on their crops and fences by large fields, and on their poultry by preserved foxes. Just as magnates were forced to accept subscription, so farmers demanded heavy compensation for damages. The old alliance was saved by cash—wire and poultry funds rose dramatically. On these conditions farmers still tolerated fox-hunting; but they now demanded a say in its management. In 1878 the Quorn farmers acted in one of the recurring disputes over the right to hunt a country; by 1887 they were on the hunt committee that selected the master—and this in the smartest hunt in the country.

Thus the fox-hunting society was changing. Subscription became *compulsory*. The idea of a sport open to all was, in the words of the editor of the *Field*, 'a pleasant fiction'. It was open to money, and with money came a new influx of moneyed upstarts—the financial saviours of late Victorian hunting. Farmers no longer accepted fox-hunting as being in the unchallengeable order of things; they had in many areas, though by no means all, to be paid indirectly for preserving foxes and refraining from actions for trespass and damages. 'Almost at the end of Victoria's reign, hunting society was taking on the connotations of "Victorian" that we associate with business and industrialization.'[9] Yet there can be no doubt that hunting remained not merely a central feature of rural society, but for those outside it who wished to be accepted in it an activity to be supported. As Professor Thompson argues, as long as the horse and carriage remained symbols of social standing, so the landed aristocracy retained its predominant place.[10] A magnate master like the Duke of Beaufort was still a great figure in his country; and there were still toadies and snobs like Mr Jawleyford with social pretensions, ready to flatter a red coat in the hopes of a smart marriage for their daughters.

There can be little doubt that the fox-hunter's claim that his sport was 'democratic' was even less well-founded in 1901 than it was in 1837. But fox-hunters were never at a loss to find new social merits in what they could never look on as a mere amusement. To its defenders, the hunting field became an instrument in the formation of an imperial class. In 1899 the historian of the Belvoir claimed that on 'sharing the sport of his superiors the young middle-class Englishman began to acquire the virtues and good qualities of a governing race' by combining his 'sturdy common sense' with 'aristocratic boldness', thus filling out a class that could rule 'an immense dependency of mixed races'. Fox-hunting, by 'the grafting of aristocratic virtues on a democratic polity', was thus the secret of the 'peculiar strength of English character and power of rule'.[11]

III

There is a sense in which racing spanned the widest social spectrum of all sports.

Newmarket had been made famous by the Stuarts; it was the seat of the ruling oligarchy of the Jockey Club; yet like every other racecourse, Newmarket attracted crowds of all classes. Many of the Victorian owners—particularly in the later years of the reign when a good stallion cost £12,000—were great patricians. The Duke of Westminster owned Bend Dor who sired Ormonde; the Duke of Portland the faultless St Simon, sire of Persimmon, who won the Derby for the Prince of Wales in 1893; and yet Eclipse, the greatest eighteenth-century horse, was bought by an Irish adventurer who had once been the 'legs' of a sedan chair. The punter who had lost his all could feel in the same boat as that inveterate loser, Lord Glasgow; the more fortunate could share some of the elation of Henry Chaplin who won £115,000 on the Derby of 1857 from Lord Hastings—who had just run off with his fiancée.

The racing community was not snobbish—on the contrary, it was the familiarity between well-born and 'vulgar' which was regarded by the snobs and prigs of Victorian England as the great social vice of the sport. It did, indeed, see some curious and unsavoury examples of social mobility. John Gully was the son of a bankrupt Bristol butcher: prize-fighter and publican, he became a prosperous bookmaker, ending up as M.P. for Pontefract in 1832 and an owner with three Derby winners to his credit. But he remained what he had always been—a crook—and in 1854 he was warned off the course at Epsom.

Racing not only united a curious variety of social classes, it was the only sport that united country and town. In the early years of the reign a host of small race meetings still took place all over the country—much disapproved of by Surtees as shoddy affairs run by landlords and bookies. But the great racecourses were mostly in or near towns (Doncaster, York, Chester, Aintree). Indeed, many nineteenth-century municipal corporations established racecourses in the hope of attracting trade: Epsom was established, as was Cheltenham, to improve the trade of the spa. Most of these municipal ventures collapsed; but the great race meetings—particularly in the north—brought farmers and squires to the town where, at parties and balls, they mixed with the citizens.

Apart from during the Interregnum, racing had developed continuously since the days of James I under royal patronage. George IV was a keen racegoer and owner; William IV considered patronage of racing a duty, until hit in the eye at Ascot by a gingernut. Queen Victoria went to the Derby only once, and abandoned Royal Ascot after the Prince Consort's death. The eighteenth century had established the thoroughbred horse, the three great classic races, the Jockey Club dominated by the humourless, obsessed Sir Charles Bunbury, *Weatherby's Racing Calendar* (1722) and the *Stud Book* (1796), and the professional jockey. Nevertheless, when Queen Victoria came to the throne the sport was discredited. It was, in the words of its most recent historian, 'at the lowest moral ebb of its history'.[12]

The reason for this discredit was evident to all—gambling. This surrounded racing with petty crime: 'crimped' matches fixed by the owners, pulling (checking) horses (even the great George Osbaldeston confessed to this), breaking into stables and feeding horses with lead shot or opium. In the 1820s Mr Thornhill, a Yorkshire squire and member of the Jockey Club, got Sam Chiffney to win races only by offering him more to win than the bookmakers offered him to lose. Such practices persisted even amongst the most respected owners.

But it is typical of Victorian attitudes that society was less repelled by gambling-inspired crime than by the effects of gambling on the class structure. Young aristocrats would fall into the hands of common 'legs' and money-lenders, as Osbaldeston's autobiography and John Mytton's death as a discredited bankrupt prove. Gambling attracted a crowd of undesirables to racecourses: the throng of tipsters, card-sellers (called *spivés*, the origin of 'spiv'), gipsies, acrobats, made Epsom 'disgusting' to Disraeli.

The racing world attempted to reform itself. Lord George Bentinck, himself a great 'plunger', attacked the betting fraternity with the hatred of familiarity. In 1844 he exposed the 'Running Rein' scandal, the most notorious fixed Derby; he made Goodwood an ordered affair in contrast to the 'obscene Bohemianism' of Epsom. Later Admiral Rous cleaned up handicapping and improved starting; but though he detested heavy betting, he refused to join Sir Joseph Hawley and *The Times* in a crusade against betting as such. It was, he saw, the life-blood of racing. Without it, the sport would become the profitless private concern of a few aristocratic *aficionados*.

The onslaught of outraged morality on flat racing was as nothing compared with the attack on the more truly rural sport of steeplechasing which had developed out of riding matches between friends across country. The organization of steeplechases by publicans with aristocratic backing disgusted Nimrod as cruel to horses and unfit for women to watch; above all, it entailed undesirable contact between the nobility, whom Nimrod loved, and the 'vulgar', whom he hated as only a successful social climber can. 'The most *cocktail* pursuit', he called it, 'ever entered into by English gentlemen.' The *Liverpool Courier* came out against Aintree as 'wanton torture'.[13] Again it was the 'barefaced swindling' of the gambling world surrounding steeplechasing that almost killed it. However, by the 1870s the National Hunt Committee began its fight against crooked practices, and in 1885 the Heythrop organized the point-to-point, later to be a pillar of hunt finance and a means of winning local support—it was still a rough affair, and the saddle and bridle of a fallen horse were stolen by the crowd.[14]

IV

Those who shot could never even pretend, as fox-hunters pretended, that their chosen recreation contributed to some ideal of rural harmony. It was, by late Victorian times, deeply divisive. It not merely divided rich and poor, landlords and tenant-farmers: it divided the sporting community itself with a bitter war between fox-hunters and game preservers. Even before the mass shoots of the 1880s and the introduction of the breech loader, shooting was unpopular. The laws that restricted the shooting of game to certain income groups and forbade the public sale of game—the absurdities which encouraged poaching and covert sale on a huge scale to supply the new rich of London with a game course at dinner—had been savagely attacked by Sydney Smith. But even after the repeal of the laws the terms of the farmer's lease still usually ensured that the shooting of game was confined to the landlord.

This quasi-monopoly, as it applied to hares and rabbits, was the most resented feature in the rural hegemony of English landowners, and an irritating source of friction between landlords and tenant-farmers (though there were other and more serious conflicts—compensation for improvement, for instance). Rabbits—preserved in warrens in enormous numbers—and hares did a great deal of damage to crops and even to bank hedges. This grievance was not removed till the Ground Game Act of 1881. It is a curious proof of how ingrained and enduring are traditions of aristocratic privilege that, as a boy on a farm, I still believed we must not shoot hares, and indeed I was once beaten for so doing.

As we have seen, the driving of large numbers of game—pheasants and partridges—*over* guns, the 'much vituperated system of *battue* shooting',[15] was deplored as a mere 'massacre' by conservatives bred on walking up game with dogs. By the end of Victoria's reign the country house shooting weekend, to become an institution in Edwardian England, was already well established. Huge bags became a necessity and a source of pride. At Holkham, in 1790, 3,000 birds were shot in a year; by 1880 the same number were shot in a single day. Payne-Gallwey considered 1,000 birds a day normal for a good shoot; Lord Walsingham quoted the game book of a Norfolk estate: in 1821, 39 pheasants; in 1875, 5,069.[16]

Preservation made landlords much more particular about any rights of the general public to cross their land, disturbing 'their' game, even taking the occasional pot-shot. By closing up old rights of way landowners were 'on the eve of losing the sympathy of a very important class'; outraged countrymen would join 'vestrymen in black satin waistcoats and black cloth boots who slobber over their soup', i.e. the urban radicals, in their crusade against 'feudalism'.[17] Nothing revealed more clearly the tensions between shooting landlords and the rural community than poaching. While few countrymen sympathized with the town gangs who fought pitched battles with keepers and policemen, the individual poacher became something of a folk hero. Such a poacher was James Hawkes. His journal reveals him as an intelligent man, opposed to drink, an organizer of bicycling clubs, a radical in politics and a supporter of Bradlaugh. He saw poaching, which was his passion, as a legitimate means of feeding the poor and as a protest against 'the Class'.[18] He clearly enjoyed the sympathy and respect of his neighbours who took his view that birds were a gift of God not the property of the landlord. When they were involved in heavy expenses in preserving and hand-rearing—it was estimated that each preserved pheasant cost £1—landlords took the opposite view. Birds they reared were their property, poaching was robbery with violence; this was particularly the case with night poaching which was severely punished under the act of 1844. On the big shoots of East Anglia, and near Yorkshire mining villages, a minor guerrilla war was waged.

483

The complications of the Game Laws made the gamekeeper's task a difficult one. 'The number and intricate arrangement of the Statutes at present in force make it very difficult', ran a manual first published in 1889, 'for any one, not a practical lawyer, to obtain such a knowledge of their varied provisions as to ensure that the right thing shall be done at the right time.' Some of these complications were the result of the ingenuity of the poachers themselves. Since killing game on land was illegal, poachers trained their dogs to drive game onto the public highway: thus killing game on the public highway had to be made an offence (7 & 8 Victoria, cap 29), but the powers of arrest on the public highway remained obscure.[19] That these laws were enforced in rural districts by magistrates in whose interests they had been drawn up made them seem even more intolerable. Town magistrates simply refused to transport men for night poaching.

In the later years of the reign landlords were encouraged by royal example. The Prince of Wales bought Sandringham in 1863 and turned the estate into one of the finest shoots in Europe. The prince rode roughshod over his tenants, driving one of them, Mrs Cresswell, who wrote a bitter attack on his 'sport', to emigrate to Texas in desperation at the Sandringham agent's indifference to farming profits.[20] Queen Victoria was disturbed. She asked the prince to stop his excesses 'and to do a little away with the *exclusive* character of shooting'. Here the queen, as she so often did, put her finger on the real issue: shooting was a minority sport. Its only conceivable social benefit was the employment of keepers and of villagers as beaters. Their wages were not handsome: even in the 1920s I was paid sixpence a day as a beater. One of my beater friends, who amused us by digging shot out of his arm with a penknife, was given £1 by the landlord as compensation.

Shooting divided not merely rich and poor—it divided the sporting establishment. Game preservers did not welcome the local hunt disturbing their birds. To a fox-hunter vulpicide was a crime; to a gamekeeper concerned to provide a bag for his master and his shooting tenants, the fox was a vermin which devoured expensive birds. Coverts were drawn blank or found replete with mangy 'bag' foxes after all the wild foxes had been poisoned. The war between the two sports became bitter. Foxes were disappearing at such a rate in shooting counties that a well-informed journalist could argue that 'hunting has become [by 1908] little more than a farce'.[21] In the end a solution was found by paying gamekeepers to preserve foxes; but it was often an uneasy compromise enforced, as that inveterate pheasant-slaughterer, Lord Walsingham, admitted, 'because of the amusement [fox-hunting] afforded *all* classes of society'.

It was in Scotland that shooting was at its most exclusive. Grouse-shooting (birds were driven after 1870) was a rich man's sport at £1 a brace and bags of 300. Deerstalking was 'a millionaire's sport', though physically extremely strenuous; shooting stags in a first-class forest might cost nearly £100 a day.[22] Both had been made more easily accessible by the railway revolution. 'On one day you may be lounging along the hot pavements of Pall Mall . . . the very next afternoon you may be in the heart of the Highlands.'[23]

Hunting, shooting, and racing were all in their different ways contentious: all, for instance, were attacked by Evangelicals as wicked, and by radicals as relics of feudalism. All enjoyed upper-class patronage. Fishing was never aristocratic, but there was a division between coarse fishing and fly fishing. Coarse fishing became more popular with cheap railways fares and more organized after the establishment of angling clubs with an annual subscription of 10s. 6d. Fly fishing became steadily more expensive, both in terms of tackle and rents, as it became, like shooting, preserved. The technical revolution came with F. M. Halford's *Dry Fly Fishing* in 1889. The very rich went to Scotland to practise their art. It was expensive—£5 per salmon caught in the 1890s when a season's rent might be £1,500. More modest fishermen could get their fishing at hotels at £1 a day all found.[24]

V

How had the social composition of field sports, particularly the hunting field, changed in Victoria's reign? It had both contracted and expanded.

One of the first recorded fox-hunts started from Preston; by 1900 there was no hunting in industrial Lancashire. The same process of urbanization had eaten up good hunting country round London. This meant that the occasional middle-class city fox-hunters—Engels had been such a one—vanished. The 'purse proud *parvenus*' were buying up the manor houses and had become residents. The fox-hunting businessman was becoming a rarity, though Mr Brassey, son of the railway contractor, was to keep the Heythrop in great style. The stayers were the rich: banking families like the Drummonds, the Barclays—for a long while masters of the Puckeridge in Hertfordshire—and the Rothschilds. The invasion of the rich and the expansion of subscription certainly tended to drive out the less affluent from the *smart* packs, but in Devon and parts of the north old traditions persisted of hunts composed of gentry, farmers, solicitors, and corn merchants. Everywhere a great magnate—such as the eighth and ninth dukes of Beaufort—was the natural master if he was willing to serve; but in the 1870s Moreton Frewen sensed the changes at Melton Mowbray, capital of hunting England: 'I arrived to find no oligarchy; but vast numbers of rich, well-dressed, absolutely idle people who constituted the society of the day.'

Army officers—particularly cavalry officers—hunted and were given long leaves so to do; the local garrison was a valued support, however much the jealous riding of young officers—and also of young undergraduates—distressed masters. Hunting parsons were a less steady support. Their numbers were always exaggerated by sporting journalists and fox-hunters engaged in proving the respectability of their sport. As the clergy became more professional and were less often recruited from the landed gentry, so the supply of hunting parsons dried up as incomes declined. Moreover the ecclesiastical climate had turned against fox-hunting: Bishop Phillpotts of Exeter waged an unsuccessful campaign against west country hunting parsons in a diocese where the Reverend Jack Russell (a guest at Sandringham, and on one occasion ready to hack seventy miles to a Salisbury meet) rather than the bishop set the tone; but elsewhere, as Trollope sadly admitted, 'he [the hunting parson] is making himself to stink in the nostrils of his bishop, and is becoming a stumbling block and a rock of offence to his brethren'.[25] Charles Kingsley gave up hunting as 'not a suitable occupation for a parson and anyway I am too proud to ride unless I am as well mounted as the rest'; this latter condition he could not fulfil on his stipend. When the Bramshill hunt servants turned up at his funeral they stayed discreetly outside the churchyard.[26] By 1900 the hunting parson was a rarity.

He was replaced in hunting literature and on the hunting field by the woman fox-hunter. The objections of conservatives were based on the moral hazards of aiding a lady who fell off, yet the long skirts that preserved decorum were very dangerous in jumping country. The improved side-saddle and new designs in skirts solved the conflict between morals and safety. By the late 1860s women feature in all hunting literature, and it is in order to become respectable that Trollope's Lady Eustace takes up the sport. If some of the women fox-hunters were high-class tarts like Skittles, when so eminent a personage as the Empress of Austria hunted regularly with the Pytchley the hunting woman was royally sanctified. It must be painful to proponents of women's liberation that it was in field sports that women achieved equality with men. This was less true of shooting. Ladies were essential ingredients of the country house shooting weekend; but they were less welcome in 'the actual shooting party'.[27]

VI

I have dealt in detail only with hunting and shooting, the field sports *par excellence*. Coursing and otter-hunting were popular in many parts of the country. Stag-hunting was recovering once more in the west after its near collapse after 1825 when the last English staghounds were sold to a German buyer. Nor have I dealt with those sports which were practised in the country but which did not involve either the breeding of animals, as with racing, or killing of animals, as in the case of fox-hunting or shooting. Cricket began as a rural sport and was spreading out from its old homes in Kent and Hampshire. It united country gentlemen like Osbaldeston and Assheton Smith and professionals who were not gentlemen; but its Mecca was, after all, London. Rowing was popular in a way that is hard to imagine today. Osbaldeston tried his hand at it, as he did at everything else from billiards to walking races. The day of the Regency all-rounder was vanishing and sport was becoming professionalized. Nevertheless, the hunting, shooting, and fishing countryman, the sporting squire, has come down to us as an enduring image of the Victorian age.

Notes

1 Egan, 1836, 197.
2 *Field*, 7 November 1863.
3 Trollope, 1868, 71.
4 Itzkowitz, 1977, 1.
5 E. P. Thompson 1965, 218.
6 Carr, 1976, 116, 124.
7 Bovill, 1962, ch. 4.
8 Carr, 1976, 149 ff.
9 Itzkowitz, 1977, 175.
10 F. M. L. Thompson, 1963, 1.
11 Dale, 1899, 40.
12 Longrigg, 1972, 115.
13 Seth-Smith, 1969, 22–64; Blew, 1901, 1–70.
14 Hutchinson, 1935, 94.
15 *New Book of Sports*, 1885, 35.
16 Longrigg, 1977, 250–1.
17 Gale, 1885, 139, 142.
18 Christian, 1961, 20.
19 Porter, 1907, 30–1.
20 Chenevix-Trench, 1967, 173.
21 Richardson, 1908, 26–50.
22 Grimble, 1886, 58.
23 *New Book of Sports*, 1885, 22.
24 Aflalo, 1899, 75.
25 Boyd, 1934, 75–6.
26 Chitty, 1974, 163, 297.
27 *New Book of Sports*, 1885, 35.

V   Labouring Life

35   The Workfolk

W.A.Armstrong

I

The stages by which the medieval English peasantry disappeared, and the impact of successive phases of enclosure, continue to be debated. However, it is clear that the classic tripartite division of rural society (landlords, tenant-farmers, landless labourers) had already made its appearance by the early eighteenth century. To the extent that it could not be met by creating new holdings on hitherto uncultivated land or by an unthinkable restructuring of land tenure, the ensuing growth of the rural population after about 1740 brought about an inexorable increase in the ratio of labouring men to farmers and landlords. This outcome has been observed in a number of European countries as well as in England and Wales. As was certainly the case in the Scandinavian countries, population growth was primarily induced by falling death rates, a consequence of a distinct abatement in the incidence of epidemic disease, and, in some parishes, a noticeable improvement in the survival of infants.[1] In the early nineteenth century land drainage schemes were another factor deemed to have exerted a favourable influence, for example at Wisbech, Dunmow, Newhaven, Ongar, and in east Kent where the marshy land bordering the Isle of Thanet was effectively drained.[2] Thus, by the mid-nineteenth century low annual rates of mortality were a matter of common observation: 19 per 1,000 at risk (Cranbrook, Pateley Bridge, Romney Marsh); 18 (Farnham, Liskeard); 17 (New Forest, Bideford, Hendon); 16 (Builth, Holsworthy); and even 15 (Glendale).[3] Although these figures relate to rural districts as a whole, farm labourers had shared in the favourable trend.

According to statistics collected by the Manchester Unity of Oddfellows, only carpenters among twenty-five occupational categories had a higher expectation of life than labourers, and at twenty the farm labourer could anticipate 45.3 further years, at thirty 30.7; at forty, 29.9; at fifty, 22.2; at sixty, 15.8.[4] These advantages extended to their offspring. Although women's work in the fields evidently had a tendency to increase infant mortality, the long-run trend was unmistakable. By 1911, when the national infant mortality rate was 125 per 1,000 live births, the level in families of agricultural labourers stood at 97, compared with dock labourers (172), carters and carriers (147), bargees (161), and bricklayers' labourers (139).[5] Of course, this is not to suggest that there was no preventable wastage of life among them (comparable figures for the offspring of solicitors and clergymen were 41 and 48 respectively), but such levels supported very considerable rates of natural increase when their comparatively high rates of fertility are taken into account.

There was a widespread impression that the usual age at marriage for both labourers and their brides was falling in the late eighteenth and early nineteenth centuries, associated with the decline in indoor service and, in particular, with the nefarious influence of the Old Poor Law, which was believed to encourage improvident unions and reckless breeding. These suppositions, which persisted well after 1834, often depended upon highly untypical illustrations. For example, a contributor to the *Cornhill Magazine* in 1864 invited his readers to picture the labourer 'some fine morning, before he is two-and-twenty, on his way from church, with his bride, who is only seventeen'.[6] However, there is remarkably little evidence to support the idea of a change in their usual age at marriage, and in point of fact a much more plausible argument is at hand to suggest a higher level of rural fertility. From the 1861 census (which gives details of proportions ever-married, convertible to mean marriage ages), Anderson has inferred that in agricultural registration districts under 15 per cent 'traditional' (i.e. where labourers were abundant and correspondingly less of the labour force consisted of farmers, their relatives, and servants), the mean age at marriage was 26.6 (males) and 25.6 (females). Conversely, in districts more than 45 per cent 'traditional', they were 28.4 and 27.0 respectively, indicating differences in marriage ages of nearly two years (for males) and seventeen months (females) respectively. A structural shift involving only 20 per cent of the labour force thus had the capacity to raise potential marital fertility by some 6 per cent.[7] What probably occurred between, say, 1750 and 1860 was a relative increase in the number of those who at all times had tended to marry comparatively early. It will be noticed that far from invoking a shift in marriage habits, the argument assumes a degree of inertia in behavioural patterns. Moreover, it would appear that this extended to the labourers' reproductive characteristics, for during the second half of the nineteenth century they were comparatively slow to reduce marital fertility rates. Flora Thompson offers some interesting comments on the moral precepts which influenced procreation. On the one hand it was reckoned unseemly for grandmothers to bear children ('when the young 'uns begin 'tis time for the old 'uns to finish'). Yet marriage subsequent to conception was 'a common happening at the time and little thought of', and the control of births within marriage seems to have been frowned on in village circles. An admission of recourse to coitus interruptus met with the comment, 'Did you ever! Fancy begrudging a little child a bit o' food, the nasty greedy selfish hussy.'[8] At all events, according to evidence gathered in 1911, completed fertility per hundred wives of agricultural labourers, standardized for marriage age, was 7 per cent above the all-class average for marriages taking place before 1851, and while the all-class average moved down by 21 per cent when the marriages of 1881–6 were compared, that of farm labourers was reduced by only 16 per cent, their fertility now standing 14 per cent above the all-class average,[9] so that in a sense, relative to the rest of society, it was actually increasing.

With a sizeable gap between fertility and mortality, rapid rates of natural increase were apparent both before and during the Victorian period. Between 1750 and 1831 the population of sixteen 'agricultural' counties rose by 1.75 millions (88 per cent), notwithstanding a net loss of 0.75 millions by migration. In the Shropshire village of Moreton Say, where the population doubled between 1680 and 1800, the number of labourers quadrupled: at Ash (Kent), which also experienced a doubling of population between 1705 and 1842, the number of holdings did not keep pace, in fact they declined by a quarter.[10] Save in the exceptional circumstances of the French Wars of 1793–1815, the forces of natural increase constantly threatened to swell the number of labourers faster than new employment opportunities could be created, and the danger was still very much in evidence in Victoria's day. In the words of Dr Hunt, this was an 'uncalled-for increase' which imposed strains on all rural economies,[11] most obviously in the south where the alternatives were fewer. The implications of demographic increase in any case, were serious for the labourers' standard of life; it does not take much imagination to see that had there been no migratory outlets the outcome would have been economically and socially disastrous.

II

By comparing the educated guesses of Gregory King for 1695 with information from the 1831 census, Clapham reached the plausible conclusion that the ratio of labourers to all occupiers had moved from about 1.75:1 to 2.75:1 over the intervening years—or 5.5:1 in relation to occupiers known to be employers.[12] Corresponding figures for 1851, the point at which the agricultural labour force reached its recorded zenith, are 3:1 and 5:1 respectively.[13] There was, of course, a good deal of regional variation reflecting prevailing patterns of farming and land-holding, so that in Wales, where 72 per cent of all holdings were below 100 acres, the percentage of farmers with more than two labourers was only 17, and outdoor agricultural labourers accounted for but 36 per cent of all males engaged in agriculture. By contrast, in south east England where 22 per cent of holdings were over 500 acres, 59 per cent had more than two labourers, who accounted for 82 per cent of all males in agriculture. At the national level, the 1851 census enumerated nearly a quarter of a million farmers and graziers

(226,000 males, 23,000 females) as well as 112,000 male and 269,000 female relatives including farmers' wives. Their hired employees numbered 1,125,000 males and youths (chiefly outdoor labourers but including 102,000 described as servants) and 144,000 females, mostly indoor servants who numbered 99,000. After 1851 the number of employees began to fall.

Table 35.1   *Employees in agriculture in England and Wales, 1851–1911**

Thousands

	1851	1861	1871	1881	1891	1901	1911
Males	1,124.5	1,114.0	939.6	850.6	776.5	637.5	674.4
Females	143.5	90.6	58.1	40.4	24.2	12.2	13.6
Total	1,268.0	1,204.6	997.7	891.0	800.7	649.7	688.0
% change since previous census:							
(i) males	–	−9.3	−15.7	−9.5	−8.7	−17.9	+5.8
(ii) females	–	−36.9	−35.9	−29.8	−40.1	−49.6	+11.5
Ratio of employees to farmers and graziers	5.08	4.82	4.00	3.97	3.58	2.89	3.00

*Derived from Taylor, 1955, 36–8. *N.B.* the table includes farm servants but seeks to exclude such categories as estate managers, gardeners, agricultural and forestry pupils, machine proprietors and attendants, woodmen, dealers, land proprietors, etc., as well as farmers' relatives. A few retired persons were included among the occupied before 1881.

Although there appears to have been a slight reversal of established trends during the Edwardian period, the pattern is otherwise consistent. There was a declining labour force in relation to farmers, whose numbers sank by only 10 per cent down to 1901, and thereafter rose by 2 per cent. This contraction was especially marked with respect to females, whose participation had hitherto been encouraged by the increasing neatness of agriculture (affording more hoeing and weeding); by the erosion of alternative opportunities in activities such as hand-spinning, and, perhaps was prompted by the more stringent conditions of relief after the Poor Law Amendment Act of 1834.

So far as women were confined to mainly indoor service, including such tasks as firelighting, cleaning utensils, preparing meals, milking cows, and making butter, there could be no objection to female employment. However, their systematic deployment on outdoor work presented a society of increasing moral rectitude with a dilemma, noticed especially at two points. One was localized, namely the situation of the 'bondagers' of Northumberland, where the hinds were often required to provide an extra female labourer for farm work. These women, sometimes although not invariably female relatives, excited admiration for their versatility and strength, and stimulated as well a good deal of concern about their moral welfare and apparently feudal status. A more widespread problem was the employment of women and children in public gangs, particularly in the eastern counties. Although there was no evidence of unusual ill-health among them, the system was roundly condemned in the 1843 inquiry on women and children in agriculture on account of the loss of educational opportunities for children, 'impudent' behaviour among the women, and the unbridled power it gave to gang-masters frequently described as 'low' and 'hard'. In 1867, following further inquiries by the Children's Employment Commission, a new Act sought to prohibit the employment of children under eight and gangs of mixed sex, and to license gang-masters. This did not apply to the private gangs employed by farmers which were in any case more numerous, and indeed, some of the twenty-two public gangs said to exist in Lincolnshire towns became private by the simple expedient of the farmer paying their wages directly.[14] But the employment of juveniles came to be further curtailed with the Agricultural Children Act (1873) and the Education Act of 1876.

Factors other than legislation were primarily responsible for an increasing reluctance on the part of women to engage in field work, in gangs or otherwise. Those encountered by F. G. Heath in 1874, stumbling along the road between Dorchester and Milborne in heavy boots 'with a sodden and sulky expression of weariness', were becoming less and less representative.[15] In the late 1860s Farmer Rollinson of Igburgh in Norfolk had been unable to get a woman worker 'in the last three years', whilst at Felthorpe able-bodied women preferred to walk three miles to the paper mill at Taverham, and at Salhouse it was remarked that the women 'did not care to come out' as their husbands' wages improved. Likewise in the Westhampnett Union in Sussex female labour, 'once largely used', was now rarely employed outside haytime and harvest, and at Slinfold there was scarcely one tenth of the employment of female field labour characteristic of twenty years before. By the 1880s it had become largely a memory at Lark Rise in Oxfordshire.[16] Meanwhile, bondagers were disappearing as the image of the institution became increasingly unpopular and the hinds voiced the grievance that they had to keep the woman for a year but were paid only for the days when she actually worked. By the 1890s this, too, had almost vanished, at any rate from the Glendale Union investigated by Wilson Fox.[17] Even female farm service was in headlong decline. It is possible that the figure of 99,000 female farm servants of 1851 exaggerated their numbers by including a good many who were primarily domestic servants, but there can be no doubt about the trend, for their numbers were reduced to 24,000 in 1871, and by 1891 they were no longer separately distinguished within the agricultural category.

In one respect, the declining role of women in agriculture was part of a more general trend to decasualization. This is not a process upon which the census statistics in Table 35.1 can throw much light, partly because the returns must be presumed to show a man's main occupation, although not necessarily his only one. In practice, a variegated pattern of employment was facilitated by the prevalence of piece rates and short—frequently weekly—engagements. Moreover, since they were invariably taken in late March or early April, the censuses did not reflect either the size or the complexity of the labour force at peak seasons when the farmer's outlay on labour might well double or more.[18] To some extent these abnormal requirements were met by a redistribution of labour within the agricultural sector itself. Collins has identified one category of movement from grass and woodland pasture to arable areas, for example from the Vale of Gloucester and the cheese districts of north Wiltshire to the southern chalklands; from the Yorkshire dales to the East Riding; from the pastoral districts of Devon and Somerset to the Isle of Wight. Another category aimed to exploit the different timings and sequences of work between hill and vale, light and heavy land, and different farming systems, with a view to taking two or more harvests in a season. Yet a third category, and quantitatively the most significant, was between the 'small-farm subsistence and large-farm capitalist sectors of British agriculture'.[19] In the west Midlands this had formerly come chiefly from the hill counties of Wales, and in northern England entailed a flow of crofter folk from the counties of Argyll, Perth, and Ross and Cromarty, but by the Victorian period Ireland was a much more important source. The number of recorded immigrant 'harvesters' peaked in 1846–8 at the time of the Famine, and thereafter tended to decline, with a tendency for the Irish to fall back on those areas where wages were highest, such as Yorkshire, Lincolnshire and the fen country.[20]

Traditionally, rural domestic industries such as hand-weaving had been another important source of seasonal labour, and through much of the Victorian period the polyglot armies of casual workers in towns, including many women, remained so, as Samuel has shown.[21] In the long run, and particularly after 1870, the importance of these 'wandering tribes' declined, for a number of reasons. These were in part technological, occasioned by increased use of the scythe and fagging hook in place of the sickle, and later the adoption of reaping machines which tended to lower the earning capacity of part-timers who were increasingly confined to the subordinate tasks of gathering and binding. Other factors included the greater regularity of employment in towns at wage-levels which came to be higher than those which could be earned in the harvest field, and the gradual divorcing of an increasingly street-bred urban population from rural contacts.

However, the process of decasualization was far from complete by the end of the century. In the Monmouth Union in 1893 many of the labourers were reckoned to rely for nine months in the year on other work, such as quarrying and mining, and in 1913 the Land Enquiry Committee guessed that some 100,000 farm workers (about one tenth of the total) could fairly be described as casuals.[22] This figure did not include those who continued to venture into the countryside to engage in market gardening, hop-picking, and fruit-picking, activities which were expanding their labour requirements through the Great Depression period as the arable acreage contracted. For those who in the 1890s worked in such disagreeable metropolitan industries as fur-pulling, match-making and white lead manufacture, the attractions of hopping in Kent were obvious, and this particular seasonal influx remained in being until after the Second World War. But in agriculture proper there was no doubt about the trend. Agricultural commentators had long realized the value of the farmer's 'constant men' and advocated long engagements for specialist workers such as ploughmen.[23] Even in Wiltshire in the 1840s, where the overall situation of the agricultural labourer was poor, farmers would provide ten to twenty perches of land, ploughed and manured, together with a cottage and a good garden at 30–50s. rent per annum.[24] It is fair to assume that the easing by migration of the rural labour surplus would have had the effect of gradually increasing the regularity of employment of those who remained on the land, thereby increasing the farmer's reliance on his regular staff. In a sense, Wales offered the extreme case. Here the social distinctions between masters and men were very much less marked than in England and outdoor labourers were very hard to come by. In a primarily pastoral region requiring constant supervision for livestock, indoor service became the increasingly dominant form of hired labour in the later nineteenth century.[25]

III

The labour surplus apparent in southern England during the early Victorian period seems to have favoured a tendency on the part of farmers 'to pay low wages in order to maximise employment for the men with poor-law settlements in the parish because the economic alternative of paying low wages for a small marginal product was unremunerative expenditure on poor relief'.[26] Against such a background cash wages showed no significant sign of advance before the middle of the century when the national average, according to Caird, was 9s. 6d. — no higher than in 1824. Thereafter it moved to 11s. 6d. in 1860–1; 12s. 5d. in 1867–71; 13s. 9d. in 1879–81; 13s. 4d. in 1892–3, and 14s. 5d. in 1898.[27] Mechanization seems to have had little impact on wages except in as far as it served to benefit a small number of operatives, such as the sixty 'formerly ordinary but intelligent farm labourers' employed by the Northumberland Steam Cultivating Company, whose wages had risen, in consequence, from 15s. a week to 20s. or 23s.[28] Nor did the organization of labour have a lasting impact. It is true that between 1871 and 1873 advances of 2–3s. a week were frequently achieved without industrial action, for example on the farms of Lord Braybrook at Audley End and Viscount Dillon at Ditchley in Oxfordshire, whilst in an essay on *The Dorsetshire Labourer* Thomas Hardy noted an average increase of some 3s. in this notably backward county.[29] But wages rose by at least as much in northern England, where there were very few trade unionists, and also in Wales, where it was said in 1892 that there was no trade unionism and nothing in the nature of a strike had ever been known.[30] Moreover, the waning agricultural unions proved powerless to resist effectively the loss of at least part of these increases as employers, beset by falling prices, retaliated in the later 1870s and 1880s. Rather, the long-term improvement was primarily due to changing conditions of demand and supply. Against a background of 'improved cultivation, more general and thorough management of root-crops, the extension of sheep farming, and winter feeding of stock' in the 1850s and 1860s, migration began to deplete the number of workers on offer so that by 1871 Dent considered over-supply to have become unusual.[31] As it gained further momentum migration frequently brought about a situation where the supply of labour was reckoned hardly equal to demand, as at Bryngwyn near Hereford where the counter-attraction of industrial employment in south Wales was keenly felt.[32]

However, nothing could be more fallacious than inferring earnings exclusively from the cash wages so far considered. Perquisites and allowances in kind played a large, if slowly diminishing part in the labourer's gross income. Notwithstanding the near-universal condemnation of the practice of supplying alcoholic beverages to field workers in the *Reports of the Special Assistant Poor Law Commissioners* (1843), beer continued to 'appear in the accounts of every farmer as an addition to his labour bill' in East Anglia,[33] and the practice remained very common in the southern, western, and south Midland counties. It was made illegal with the passage of the 1887 Truck Act, but continued nevertheless, as Rider Haggard was informed in the neighbourhood of Bridgewater in 1900.[34] Drink apart, the 'privileges' noted in 1867 in Devon and Dorset included the provision of a potato patch and cheap fuel or wheat although, as Hasbach points out, no farmer provided all together;[35] whilst in the 1893 Labour Commission there is evidence of the survival of various payments in kind.

If perquisites, and along with them extra harvest earnings, are reckoned as additional to cash wages, other factors worked in the opposite direction as potential deductions. One was simply loss of time in bad weather, although there was considerable variation of practice. From Wiltshire in 1893, it was reported that many farmers tried to keep their men on, wet or dry, in order to have a sufficient supply in the busy season. On the other hand, as Spencer observed after driving through the Essex villages of Latchingdon and Steeple on a wet day, 'most of the male occupants of cottages appeared to be at home or in the public house'.[36] Probably, as Clifford contended, the larger farmers were more ready in wet weather to pay their weekly men at any rate, if not those engaged in task-work.[37] The most comprehensive evidence on the subject, collected by the Land Enquiry Committee in 1913, suggested that time was lost by inclement weather in 47 per cent of parishes, ranging from 19 per cent in the north to 68 per cent in the south Midlands and eastern counties.[38] Loss of work through illness was another obvious way in which wages could melt away, and injury another, for sadly, accidents could give rise to atrocious conduct on the part of employers. In illustration Canon Girdlestone pointed to the case of an unfortunate carter who having saved a valuable team and waggon when they bolted, at the expense of having his ribs crushed, received from his ungrateful master neither wages, a visit, nor as much as a quart of milk for his children.[39]

So far as such factors could be taken into systematic account, Wilson Fox concluded that the earnings of ordinary labourers stood in a ratio of 119:100 to current weekly wages, although the variation was vast, ranging from 148 (Pewsey) to 106 (Uttoxeter and Wetherby).[40] Undoubtedly, as the Land Enquiry Committee maintained, labourers' earnings (as distinct from cash wages) were by far the more important figures,[41] and, whilst the earlier wage material does not lend itself to comparison, they appear to have moved on the lines indicated in Table 35.2.

498

Table 35.2   *Agricultural labourers' earnings by region**

	1867–70	1898	1907
London area and home counties	16s. 6d.	18s. 5d.	18s. 6½d.
South west	12s. 5d.	15s. 7d.	16s. 10d.
Rural south east	14s. 4½d.	15s. 9d.	16s. 5d.
South Wales	12s. 7½d.	17s. 0½d.	18s. 2d.
Rural Wales and Herefordshire	13s. 0d.	16s. 1¼d.	17s. 8d.
Midlands	14s. 1d.	17s. 10d.	18s. 4½d.
Lincolnshire, Rutland, Yorkshire (E. and N.R.)	17s. 1d.	18s. 0d.	18s. 10d.
Lancashire, Cheshire, Yorkshire (W.R.)	17s. 1d.	18s. 8d.	19s. 7d.
Cumberland and Westmorland	18s. 6d.	18s. 9d.	19s. 2d.
Northumberland and Durham	18s. 9d.	20s. 5½d.	21s. 5½d.
England and Wales, average of the regions	13s. 9d.	16s. 0d.	17s. 11d.

*Based on Hunt, 1973, 62–4. The unweighted average relates to fifty-four English and Welsh counties.

To what extent did such earnings support a rising standard of life? Prior to 1870 it is probable that any improvements were slight, and contingent upon a greater regularity of employment than had been obtainable in the 1830s and 1840s, coupled with an increasing solicitude for the welfare of their shrinking labour force on the part of more enlightened landlords and employers.[42] But with wages failing to fall commensurately with prices in the years that followed, there was a more noticeable advance. The falling cost of necessities was reflected in many ways. In 1893 Chapman noticed that on clothes lines good linen appeared instead of rags. The cottages contained a better standard of furniture, and every young man over sixteen carried a watch. Butchers' carts called in the villages at least once a week, and not the least significant sign of progress was the appearance of lamps fuelled by cheap paraffin putting an end to the old habit of going to bed (or the public house) as early as seven or eight o'clock. At Chatteris a great many labourers took a weekly newspaper and patronized seaside trips, whilst there was a noticeable increase in the consumption of tobacco.[43] Although such comparisons were by no means entirely novel, in districts where small units prevailed, such as the Isle of Axholme, in Cumberland and in Wales, the situation of the labourers was often favourably contrasted with that of the farmer himself.[44]

These impressions of a rising standard of comfort have to be qualified in several important respects. One critical factor, as Rowntree was so effectively to demonstrate in his study of York, was the family life cycle. Given the most favourable auspices (i.e. where there were adult children living at home) it was pointed out that gross family income could compare with that of a city clerk or a poor curate;[45] but as Rowntree's own excursion into rural sociology made clear, the presence of a large brood of younger children was a very significant factor in rural poverty,[46] and, as we have seen, the fertility of farm labourers was definitely on the high side. Secondly, even if we disregard significant local disparities at the district or parish level, there were well-marked regional variations in earnings, as is apparent from Table 35.2. From at least the 1780s wages in the north of England had tended to pull away from those in the south. In 1850 Caird suggested that the difference was of the order of 37 per cent, and confidently ascribed this to 'the proximity of manufacturing and mining enterprise'.[47] There were differences of opinion among contemporaries about subsequent trends, as well as the importance to be attached to 'indulgencies' as a countervailing factor. In fact, Hunt's researches suggest that the percentage (of the British average wage) by which the maximum regional wage exceeded the minimum fell from 44 in 1867–70 to 28 in 1907. The important point to note is the persistence of variations, and his striking conclusion that 'wage differentials at any one time were as great as the overall improvement in wages between 1850 and 1914'.[48] Nor did the employment of women and children offset these differences, even when it ran at its height in the first half of the Victorian period. Hunt concludes:

> Four shillings is probably a generous estimate of the average gross earnings of wives and children in the 1850's, and this was no more, and in many cases less, than the margin between farm labourers' wages in the north and south . . . [and] whatever residual compensations the rural south may have enjoyed at the beginning of the period were not enduring.[49]

IV

With the southern labourer in mind, Hunt has argued elsewhere that 'sectors of the English agricultural labour force were living at a standard which, whilst adequate to sustain life, fell short of the level needed to ensure maximum labour efficiency', and that low wages were a consequence as well as a cause of low productivity.[50] This state of affairs was mitigated only slowly after 1870 as agricultural wages rose and regional variations became less marked. It is true, as his critics have pointed out, that as well as the varying quality of land, the relative amount of capital per worker would tell on labour productivity, and that his argument depends heavily on the citation of mainly impressionistic comments.[51] Yet it is striking how consistently the grain of this evidence runs in the same direction, that is, if one compares adversely the quality of labour in the south and east with that obtainable in Scotland, the north of England, and the north Midlands. In cases where southern labourers were transferred to the north it was often observed that they found difficulty in staying the pace. Thus in 1855 George Grey had attracted some two hundred southern labourers to dig drains in Northumberland by the prospect of earning 20–25s. a week by the piece. Within a short time only ten remained, and they never succeeded in making more than 15s. 'There was not a man among the whole importation that had legs and shoulders to compare with our lads of seventeen years of age.'[52] Caird, Clifford, Culley, Read, and Brodrick were but a few of the experts convinced of such disparities in labour efficiency, and Wilson Fox in 1906 was following a well-established tradition in ascribing them to the cumulative effects of 'generations of bad feeding' in the south.[53]

Poor nutrition, presumably, should be reflected in an above-average rate of sickness among farm workers, and there are conflicting impressions in the literature. On the one hand, Flora Thompson's recollections of Lark Rise in the 1880s are favourable: the doctor was rarely seen there and the general state of health was excellent owing to the 'open-air life and abundance of coarse but wholesome food'. At the other extreme we have Canon Girdlestone's view that the labourers of north Devon in the 1860s did not live, they merely 'didn't die'.[54] As we have seen, the rates of mortality prevailing among farm labourers were low by contemporary standards. Yet the Yorkshire doctor, Charles Thackrah, had emphasized in the 1830s that they were 'far less robust in figure than we would expect from the nature of their employ', and a few years later the published statistics of the Manchester Unity showed that although farm labourers enjoyed outstanding longevity, nevertheless they experienced 'an aggregate amount of sickness of 6.2 per cent more than the whole of the rural districts'. At age twenty the average was 4 days, 2 hours sickness; at age thirty, 6 days, 5 hours; at forty, 8 days, 2 hours; at fifty, nearly 14 days, at sixty, nearly 27 days.[55]

The relationship between age and sickness revealed in these figures of Ratcliffe takes on further significance when the age structure of the agricultural labour force is examined, for as a result of age-selective migration it had come to be characterized by a comparatively high proportion of very young workers and an excess of the elderly, with a great dearth of men who who were at once fully experienced and still in the prime of life, say, between twenty-five and forty-four. Notwithstanding comments like that from Zeal (Devon)—'our young men have all gone, only old people and cripples left'[56] W. C. Little contended that a comparison of the census returns for 1871 and 1891 gave no support to the prevailing impression of an ageing labour force; likewise the Registrar General was of the same opinion and succeeded in misleading Hasbach entirely.[57] In fact, a lateral rather than an historical comparison was more appropriate since the ageing process had been going on for many years. Such an approach reveals that in 1891 elderly workers (i.e. those aged fifty-five and over) were approximately three times as numerous, as a proportion, in the farm labour force than among railway employees or coal miners. A more broadly-based comparison is made in Table 35.3.

Youths loomed large as a proportion only because of the shortage of men in their twenties and thirties, and by this time even they were sometimes hard to come by. Thus in south west Wales farmers had become reliant in part on the importation of lads from English reformatories, ragged schools, and industrial schools.[58] An Easingwold farmer remarked that they were 'quick in getting hold of machinery and interested in it, and in that respect better than the older men'; but, he added, they did not care to learn 'the old-fashioned arts'.[59] These were increasingly the province of the elderly, and the situation produced mixed effects. Often enough, and especially if they worked heavy land, men were 'very much bent' by their fifties.[60] Yet it was

Table 35.3 *Age composition of the male labour force aged 10 and upwards, England and Wales, 1891**

		Percentage aged				
	under 20	*20–24*	*25–34*	*35–44*	*45–54*	over 55
A. Agricultural labourers, farm servants, shepherds	28.0	11.9	16.8	12.7	11.9	18.6
B Remainder of male occupied population	19.8	13.9	23.6	18.1	12.9	11.7
C % by which A exceeds B	+41.4	−14.3	−28.8	−29.8	−7.7	+58.9

*Based on BPP 1893–4 CVI [C. 7058]. *1891 Census, England and Wales. Ages, etc., Abstract.* Table 5, pp. x–xxv.

claimed in the 1870s, 'go where you will, you find old servants retained . . . sometimes receiving full wages, sometimes treated as "three-quarters", or "half" men, but hardly ever earning the wages paid them'. One of Clifford's Suffolk correspondents remarked: 'Neither I nor any decent farmer would turn a man off simply because he was old.'[61] From the employer's point of view sentimental considerations would often coincide with his interest in handling the lighter work of the farm cheaply, if with only modest efficiency. Taking this into account, Charles Booth remarked that 'in one way or another, effective working life is ten years longer in the country than in the town, or . . . is as seventy to sixty', and in a study of 262 rural parishes he found that 55 per cent of persons aged sixty-five and over could exist by their own earnings or means.[62]

Matters of the kind so far discussed do not exhaust the list of factors detrimental to labour efficiency. A very lengthy walk to work might result in labourers resting the moment the master's back was turned, as Farmer Norgate of Sprowston (Norfolk) complained in 1867.[63] Moreover, for many years the condition of the labourer, especially in the south, bred what Jefferies described as 'an oriental absence of aspiration'.[64] A Suffolk farmer recalled that when he asked labourers who had finished their stint of piece work by 1 p.m. to continue, the response was, 'No, master, we don't want no more money. We've as much as we care about! We'd rather go home and smoke a pipe.' Likewise in the west country the reluctance of labourers to forgo their cider allowances in order to secure a higher wage was much remarked upon in the 1860s and 1870s, and indicatively a meeting of eight men (with a total of fifty-two children) at Newent agreed, with one exception, that they preferred their cider allowance to 1s. 6d. extra wages, its cash equivalent.[65] It may be that the ensuing years saw a greater responsiveness to cash incentives but the process has yet to be traced in detail.

Many of these features served to encourage a stereotyped image of the farm labourers' bearing and address. According to Flora Thompson they detested nothing as much as being hurried,[66] and their sedate pace appears to have communicated itself to the young. Youths who, unlike their urban counterparts, had not been trained 'to appreciate the value of time' were criticized in characteristic terms by a speaker at the Framlingham Farmer's Club in 1867; if asked to fetch a rake a boy would 'open his mouth, turn his eyes on you and wheel on his heels with the precipitate motion of a Polar Bear'.[67] An article in the *Girls' Own Paper* in 1885 described the country lads of Dorset moving 'as though they have a heavy weight tied to each leg, so that it can only be moved by a heave of the whole body in the opposite direction'.[68] Such witticisms were heard more frequently with the passage of time: society as a whole, perhaps particularly the working classes, were prone to judge their own social and economic progress, albeit unconsciously, by the extent that they distanced themselves from the farm labourer's style and standard of life. There was point in their doing so. For notwithstanding a perceptible improvement in the agricultural labourer's condition during the Victorian era, it was pointed out in 1913 that in only five northern counties did his income reach the level necessary to avoid primary poverty;[69] and also—it would seem correctly—that he received a much smaller proportion of the wealth he helped to create than did his urban counterpart.[70]

Notes

1   See, for example, Chambers, 1972, 97–106; Tranter, 1973, 90–3; Martin, 1976, 33–8.
2   Flinn, 1965, 151–2.
3   Greenhow, 1858, 162–4.
4   Ratcliffe, 1850, 50. No doubt these farm labourers able to afford membership of the Manchester Unity were better off than the average, but this would also apply to other occupations to some extent. The data appear to cover upwards of 17,000 rural labourers.
5   BPP 1912–13, XII [CD. 6578] xli, xliii, 73–87.
6   Anon., *Cornhill Magazine*, 1864, 179.
7   Anderson, 1976, 65, 76.
8   Flora Thompson, 1954, 112, 142, 143.
9   Innes, 1938, 47.
10 Deane and Cole, 1962, 108; R. Jones, 1968, 9–10; information on Ash from Mrs A. E. Newman.
11 Hunt, 1973, 237.
12 Clapham, I, 1930, 113–14.
13 These and the following statistics are drawn from BPP 1852–3 XXXVIII pts I and II. Census 1851, population tables, pt II, vols I and II. See especially pp. lxxviii–lxxxi, clxxv, cclxxxii.
14 BPP 1867–8 XVII. Appendix, Pt I, 77.
15 Heath, 1874, 35.
16 BPP 1867–8 XVII. Appendix, pt I, 9, and pt II, 31, 36, 61, 77; Flora Thompson, 1954, 49.
17 Dunbabin, 1974, 155; BPP 1893–4 XXXV [C. 6894–III] 104.

18 For examples see Morgan, 1975, 39–40.
19 Collins, 1976, 43–5.
20 *Ibid.*, 50–1.
21 Samuel, 1972; Samuel 1975b, 3–5.
22 BPP 1893–4 XXV [C. 6894–IV] 66; Land Enquiry Committee, 1913, I, 4.
23 See, for example, Wilson, 1851, III, 874.
24 Little, 1845, 177.
25 Howell, 1978, 93–4.
26 Digby, 1975, 79; Morton, 1868, 76.
27 Orwin and Felton, 1931, 233.
28 Dent, 1871, 348.
29 Horn, 1976b, 132; Orwin and Whetham, 1964, 234.
30 Hasbach, 1966, 284; BPP 1893–4 XXXVI [C. 6894—XIV] 48.
31 Dent, 1871, 346–7; E. L. Jones, 1964, 328–9.
32 BPP 1893–4 XXXV [C. 6894—IV) 84.
33 Clifford, 1875b, 117.
34 Horn, 1976b, 124.
35 Hasbach, 1966, 337, 411.
36 BPP 1893–4 XXXV [C. 6894—V] 8, 76.
37 Clifford, 1875b, 121.
38 Land Enquiry Committee, 1913, I, 21.
39 Heath, 1874, 165.
40 BPP 1893–4 XXXVII [C. 6894—XXV] 84.
41 Land Enquiry Committee, 1913, I, 4.
42 E. L. Jones, 1964, 331.
43 BPP 1893–4 XXXV [C. 6894—II] 45, 57, 83.
44 See, for example, BPP 1893–4 XXXVI [C. 6894—XIV] 172; Howell, 1978, 93; Dent, 1871, 361–3.
45 BPP 1893–4 XXXVII [C. 6894—XXV] 87.
46 Rowntree and Kendall, 1913, 33–4.
47 Caird, 1852, 511.
48 Hunt, 1973, 1, 58.
49 *Ibid.*, 121.
50 Hunt, 1967, 286.
51 Metcalf, 1969, 118; David, 1970, 504–5.
52 BPP 1867–8 XVII, Appendix, pt I, 138.
53 Aronson, 1914, 63, quoting evidence to the Select Committee on the Housing of the Working Classes Amendment Bill, 1906.
54 Flora Thompson, 1954, 3, 141; Heath, 1874, 71.
55 Thackrah, 1832, 14; Ratcliffe, 1850, 50, 116.
56 BPP 1893–4 XXXV [C. 6894—II] 92.
57 BPP 1893–4 XXXVII [C. 6894—XXV] 33; Hasbach, 1966, 341.
58 BPP 1893–4 XXXVI [C. 6894—XIV] 9.
59 BPP 1893–4 XXXV [C. 6894—VI] 68.
60 Heath, 1893, 224, quoting Dr Batt of Witney.
61 Clifford, 1875b, 120.

62 Booth, 1894, 321, 339. *N.B.* his figures exclude those in union workhouses.

63 BPP 1867–8 XVII, Appendix, pt, II, 29.

64 Jefferies, 1880, II, 78.

65 Clifford, 1875b, 106; Heath, 1874, 88; BPP 1867–8 XVII. Appendix, pt II, 133–4.

66 Flora Thompson, 1954, 46.

67 BPP 1867–8 XVII. Appendix, pt I, 14.

68 Kerr, 1968, 117.

69 Rowntree and Kendall, 1913, 31. Note, however, that they compared earnings in 1907 with prices current in 1912.

70 Aronson, 1914, 73. The statistics in Deane and Cole, 1962, 152, 166, confirm this impression. Thus in 1901 the share of wages and salaries in the total income generated in the agriculture, forestry, and fishing sector stood at 38.8 per cent against 48.1 in mining, manufacturing, and building, and 46.5 per cent in trade and transport.

36   In the Sweat of thy Face: The Labourer and Work

Alun Howkins

I think that the Tiller of the soil is the highest and oldest workman of all. No one can do without him and the product of his hands. The Gold miner cannot eat his gold, nor the Coal miner his coal, nor the Iron miner his Iron. All and every one is dependent upon the soil. He is the Father of all Workers.[1]

I

The farm workforce of the nineteenth century was far from being an undifferentiated mass of John Hodges. Although the national census of 1901 was the first to acknowledge the major divisions they certainly pre-date it, while even the divisions of 1901—shepherds, horsemen, cowmen and labourers—conceal the gradations of skill and prestige attached to these different jobs. On occasion these bland descriptions can be seriously misleading. Joseph Arch, for instance, was a champion thatcher and hedger and ditcher. At these crafts he earned enough to buy his own house and find employment throughout the south Midlands, although a known 'troublemaker'. Yet he would appear in the census as a labourer.[2] Similarly, oral evidence reveals an enormous variety of jobs and job descriptions. The father of one man I interviewed was by turns a labourer, thatcher and quarry man, while another was a builder's labourer, farm labourer, poacher, marl digger and fish hawker.[3] It would be sheer chance which of these jobs he was following on census day.

Further, there were regional distinctions. These produced a variety of localized categories of worker as a direct result of different types and patterns of farming. In Aberdeenshire the continued survival of the croft system, where married labourers held a small piece of land, created a peculiar intermediate stratum of labourer-farmers.[4] In south west Wales up to the 1900s the men of the farms went to the coalfield in the winter months, returning in the summer to help pay off the families' labour debts.[5] In large areas of Northumberland and Durham the bondager system, whereby a labourer had to provide a woman worker (the bondager) to work with him, created another local category.[6]

Even beyond these local categories there were variations, meaningless perhaps to the outsider, but important in the village community. In the south east, for example, it was usual for the horseman to be the 'superior' workman and, therefore, the older. When a boy went on a farm he went to 'learn a trade' which would stand him in good stead and increase his earning power as he grew older. Elsewhere, though, the situation was quite different. In Aberdeenshire, Cardiganshire and the East Riding of Yorkshire, among other areas, the process was reversed.[7] Here, because of the living-in system and hiring by the year, the young men looked after the horses and the older, usually married workers, did the less skilled work. As David Jenkins has written of south west Wales,

> A farm servant (*gwas*) was quite distinct from a farm labourer (*gweither*). Farm servants were unmarried and generally young men who were engaged to work with horses and lived in at the farm while labourers were usually married men who lived in their own houses. The general labouring work of the farm such as hedging, ditching and drainage was specifically the work of the farm labourer. . . . The care of cattle . . . was for men the work of the lowest standing and accepted only as a last resort when nothing else was available.[8]

However, through all the regions basic divisions remained. As Wilson Fox wrote in 1905:

> On farms of a sufficient size to admit of definite spheres of occupation being allotted, the work is organised, as far as possible under a system of sub-divided labour. With the exception of stewards, bailiffs, and foremen, the most responsible positions are those of the men in charge of the animals, and these are speaking generally, a higher paid class of farm servant than the 'ordinary labourer' and are usually on longer terms of engagement.[9]

In addition we can observe divisions within these categories. Firstly, within the category of men employed with animals it is important to divide them by the kind of animals they were working with. Secondly, it is necessary to divide the 'ordinary labourer' category into regular and casual. And, lastly, it is essential to note that the situation throughout the nineteenth century was not a static one.

The skills involved in farm work were many and various. Wilson Fox's division between those who worked with animals and those who did not seems to have been the primary one, yet quite how the division came about is difficult to determine. In most cases there seems to have been very little on-the-job training; as Jack Leeder said about the old horsemen he worked with, 'They weren't too good at [teaching] . . . you had to find out for yourself. They used to say, "Find out for yourself and you'll know how to do it."'[10] In many cases boys seem to have learnt from their fathers. A boy would go to work with his father from an early age to 'help out'. Arthur Amis, for instance, who was the cowman son of a cowman, did this,[11] as did Bert Hazell, whose father was a horseman.[12] Even this, though, could not guarantee that a boy would become a horseman or a cowman. There was always competition for jobs, and the individual's temperament was very important, particularly with horses. As Jack Leeder said, many boys were simply 'scared' of horses and had no control.[13]

The father–son situation, however, was almost universal in labourers' skills. A man who could thatch a rick, for instance, inevitably taught his son. Charles Leveridge started with his father when he was eleven years old: 'We used to have to go to pull the straw, before we left school, that was where I learnt my thatching.'[14] One suspects that this informal training in basic skills, and there were many, went right down the scale of farm work since all those interviewed spent a good deal of time, before and after school, in the holidays and playing truant, in the fields with their fathers.

II

The Victorian labourer, unless he or she was casually employed, was hired by the year. In most of north eastern Scotland, Northumberland, Durham, Cumberland, Westmorland, Yorkshire, north Lancashire and north Lincolnshire 'all classes' of workers were still hired and paid by the year in 1900.[15] In north Cambridgeshire and south Lincolnshire men hired by the year were mostly horsemen and shepherds. A similar situation existed in parts of the Midlands: mainly in Derbyshire, Shropshire, Staffordshire, Warwickshire, Leicestershire, Worcestershire, Oxfordshire, Berkshire and Buckinghamshire. By 1900, however, even the yearly hiring of 'skilled' men went on 'to a much smaller extent than formerly'.[16] In the south west the system 'was rapidly dying out', though it still continued in some parts of Monmouthshire and Herefordshire, and to a lesser extent in Hampshire, Dorset, Wiltshire and Gloucestershire.[17]

Where men were hired by the year, they were engaged at a hiring fair ('feein' fair' in Scotland; 'sittings' in Yorkshire; 'mop' or 'statty' in the south). Here the worker stood in the streets on the day of the fair with a badge of calling in the lapel of the coat. Indoor and semi-indoor female servants were also hired by the year. A description of Bridlington hirings in 1895 catches much of the flavour of the fairs:

Everyone tried to look smart; it is only right to say that. Many of the girls
were brightly dressed, and only their speech betrayed them; but the lads
still cling to the past in their sartorial get-up, which includes gaudy silk
neckties and pearlies. . . . The waggoner has a bit of fancifully twisted cord in
his cap, a bright flower . . . in his buttonhole, and his jacket not buttoned.
. . . The proper fastening is two or three inches of brass chain, the better to
display a capacious chest. Feathers on some of the bowler hats are
suggestive of the fold yards, while the occasional flashes of bright colour in
the feminine head-gear are suggestive of primitive Arcadia rather than the
latest Paris fashions.[18]

Men and women hired in this way worked for a fixed wage plus board and lodging.
This was the dominant pre-industrial pattern, though it had been gradually
disappearing since the mid-eighteenth century, especially in the economically most
advanced wheat-growing areas of the south and east. As early as 1804 Arthur Young
noted that the custom of living and feeding in the farmhouse was vanishing, while in
Suffolk by 1813 he noted that 'the great mass of work in this county is done by the *piece*'
[*sic*][19] which was the antithesis of yearly hiring. Where the system did continue the
men usually lived in 'bothies', separate rooms over the stables, and the women in the
house. On the smaller farms both sexes lived in the farmhouse itself.

The transitional form of employment between living-in and weekly labour was
hiring by the year, when a man lived off the farm but actually received his money
weekly or fortnightly. This usually applied to men who worked with animals. In 1905
Wilson Fox noted that shepherds were almost inevitably employed by the year, as
were stockmen, since 'it might put employers at great inconvenience if their shepherds
or stockmen left them at short notice'.[20] This kind of contract was often extended to
horsemen. The overwhelming weight of oral evidence suggests that horsemen (in
Norfolk team-men) were employed by the year, and this is borne out by prosecutions
under the Employer and Workmen's Act. Men employed to look after animals were
graded. Each farm had a head horseman (in Norfolk head team-man, in the north head
carter), who was the most skilled.[21] Similar grades existed for stockmen (in the south
east, cowmen) but not for shepherds, except on very large farms, as the shepherd
usually worked alone with his page (boy).[22] This group of labourers was often housed
in tied housing near the farm—the only substantial nineteenth-century group, other
than those on estate villages, to live under this system.

Finally there were those groups hired by the week. Even here there was a sense that
the contract of employment ran for a year. Wages books from Norfolk farms show
that by the 1870s there was a regular core workforce of labourers, employed all the
year round in many cases,[23] though often laid off in wet weather. This retention of the
notional year's contract was related to the domestic economy of the labourer,
especially the necessity of paying the rent once a year (usually at Michaelmas). In
addition to these more or less regular workers there were those who were truly
casual. The work of E. J. T. Collins and David Morgan has shown how the economic

and organizational changes in agriculture in the early years of the nineteenth century created an enormous seasonal demand for casual workers. In the late 1860s this could mean a temporary increase in the workforce of 30–100 per cent.[24] Until the mid-1870s this extra workforce came largely from travelling and migrant workers. The Irish, the Scots, town-dwellers, gipsies, all once tramped the roads, following the same routes year after year. In some areas these migrants formed bands of skilled men and women who would travel from one farm to another taking harvests in turn. Such were the men of Blaxall in Suffolk described by George Ewart Evans, the travelling harvesters of Leafield in Oxfordshire or, in a different context, the travelling sheep-shearing gangs of Sussex.[25] As well as those who travelled, there were local workers who could be drawn upon for casual work. Crucial among these, until the mid-1870s again, were women and children. The practice of using the wives and children of labourers was at its most developed under the gang system. This was a system of subcontracting work to a gang-master, who then provided labour for particular tasks; it was widely used in Norfolk, Suffolk, Cambridgeshire and north Lincolnshire between the mid-1820s and the 1870s.[26]

In the course of the nineteenth century all these regional variations in hiring, work and classification were in a state of flux. In the south and east the dominant trend was away from a regular living-in workforce employed by the year towards a casual workforce living away from the farm, with a reduced number of regular, and usually skilled, workers. Thus at the end of the 1840s there seem to have been in Norfolk three casual to every two regular workers.[27] After the late-nineteenth-century depression the pattern seems to have been reversed. As early as the 1860s there were complaints of labour shortage as rural depopulation bit and the supply of Irish casuals dried up after the Famine.[28] This really began to show at the end of the 1890s. By 1900 all observers were agreed that there was a serious labour shortage in rural areas, leading to much more regular employment. As Wilson Fox wrote in 1905: 'Generally speaking, since about the year 1896, ordinary farm labourers have been regularly employed. During this period farmers in all parts of the country have complained a scarcity of labour.'[29] The most eloquent testimony to this change is that by 1920 there were nationally five regular workers to every casual one.

The reasons for this are not far to seek. By the 1890s there had been a century-long drain on the over-populated rural areas, and even by the early 1870s some signs of crisis were apparent. However, the depression, coupled with some mechanization, softened the blow, and it was only with recovery in the 1890s that the full extent of the loss was clear. Additionally, in the south at least, women and children had been withdrawn effectively from regular involvement in the workforce by the gangs legislation of 1867 and the Education Acts. In the north the situation was different. The farms were smaller and had always competed with industry in terms of wages. This meant that a regular workforce, living-in, had been set as the pattern early in the nineteenth century: it was simply not possible to casualize the labourer when all could earn high regular wages nearby. Thus young men living-in, together with married men living out, but in regular work, was the northern pattern.

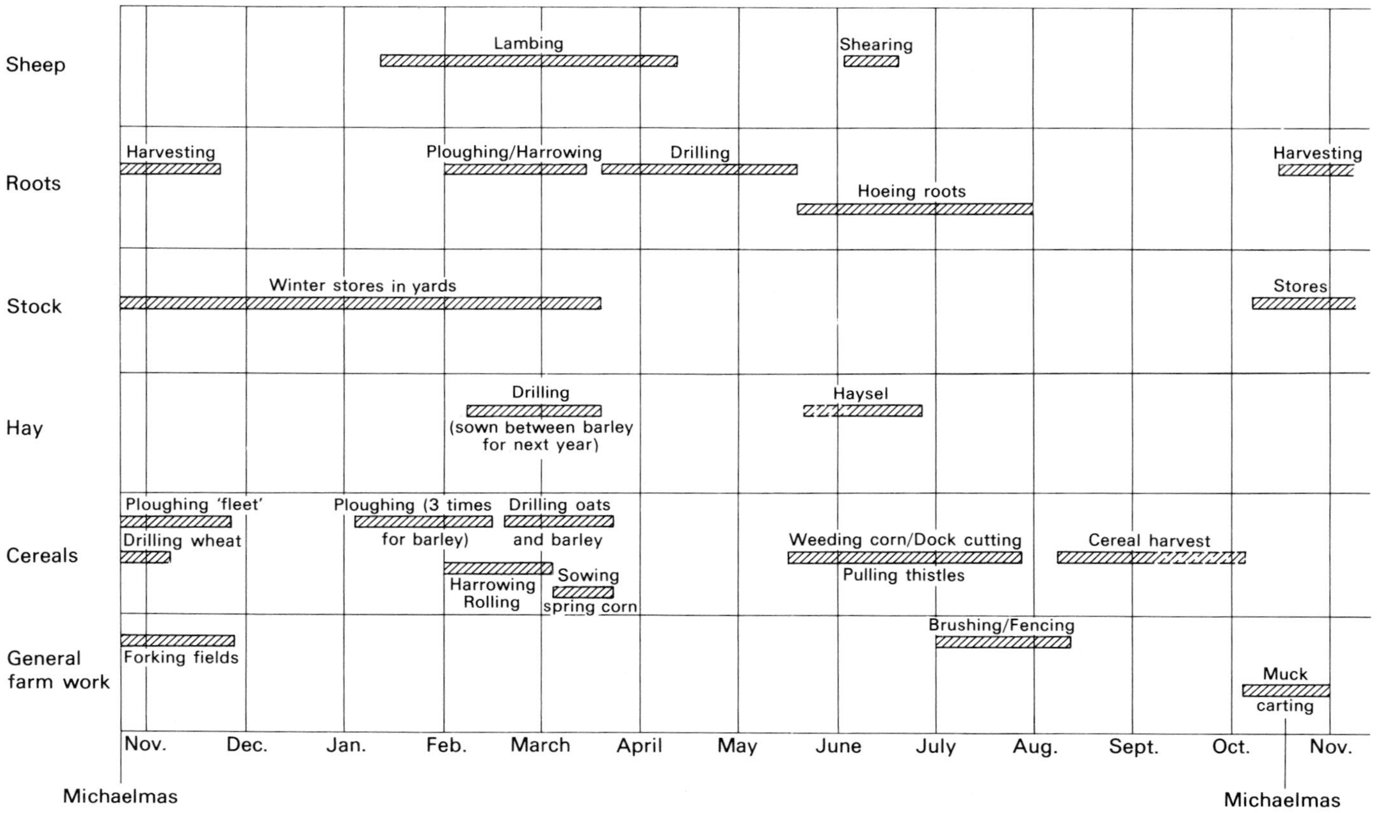

Figure 36.1 The seasonal cycle of farmwork, Norfolk 1900–20 — based on a four-course shift: hay/wheat/roots/oats

III

The actual work done by the farm worker varied according to skill and, crucially, season. This is best shown, in the first instance, diagrammatically. Figure 36.1 is based on the farming year in Norfolk at the turn of the nineteenth century, but with very little modification it could stand for the cereal-growing areas of the country for most of the century. The non-cereal modifications to this figure will be considered briefly at the end of this chapter.

The working year began and ended at Michaelmas or old Michaelmas. This was the end of harvest when the rent was paid and men changed jobs. As the daughter of a Norfolk team-man told me:

> In those days you see, farm workmen [at] Michaelmas, that was the 11th October in the country [old Michaelmas day], if they wanted another place they left the one they had and moved to another one . . . well then if they wanted to move again they just packed up and moved again. . . .[30]

Another respondent said the roads were 'thick' with 'dicky carts' at Michaelmas.[31] Even here there was considerable regional variation. Michaelmas or old Michaelmas seems to have been the predominant time of year for moving in the arable areas, but elsewhere, especially in the north and Scotland, old May Day, Martinmas or Whitsun were favoured.[32]

The horseman who came on the farm in the autumn faced a short period of intensive work, provided the weather was not hard:

> You'd start after harvest . . . what we called 'scaling', that's ploughing very fleet, which really cuts all the stubble and the weeds, harrow it . . . so it all pulls out, walk behind and lift the harrows . . . and of course that then all had to be shook about by hand, by fork, and then ploughed in.[33]

For the labourer, apart from forking behind the fleet ploughing, and muck carting, the main work of the winter was the root harvest. Early in the autumn the work, though hard, was pleasant enough:

> The method employed was this: you grasped the leaves of the mangold with the left hand. . . . You pulled the mangold out of the ground, swung it upwards, and at the right moment slipped your knife blade through the leaves where they joined the root. Then, if you had judged it correctly, the mangold flew into the cart and you were left with the leaves in your hand. You dropped them, and stooped to pull another. The whole process took the labourer one second.[34]

As the winter came on the process was less pleasant. Once the frost came the mangolds froze in the ground and getting them out became backbreaking work in which a misplaced swing of the knife could take a thumb or finger off. Along with the potato harvest, the root harvest in mid-winter was the most disliked of farm work. If the weather held, ploughing fleet was followed quickly by ploughing for wheat and barley: 'they'd start and plough, plough as much as they could before Christmas'.[35] Ploughing for barley was a much longer process: 'they used to plough three times for barley . . . that was a big job, with all horses, and of course you couldn't rush'.[36]

Ploughing was the most skilled work of the most skilled men—the team-men or horsemen.[37] Under horse culture even a relatively small farm of 100–150 acres employed two or three team-men. A man who started work on a farm near Wyndham in Norfolk in 1919 talked about the organization of this side of the farm:

> You had five horsemen, five adults and a boy . . . [and] we all had six horse each, and then there would be another two or three looked after by someone else. They would be sub-divided so that we would run ten plough teams.[38]

The teams were rigidly organized. At the top was the head team-man: he was the most skilled, was paid more, and occasionally received a free cottage. He acted as a kind of foreman, 'keeping time and setting men off to work'.[39] This relationship was symbolized by the order of going out in the morning:

> When we were working in the plough teams [the head team-man] would take the lead, and nobody would dare to leave the yard until he'd got onto his horse and he'd got in front. He'd be followed by the second team-man and then subsequently down the line.[40]

Once in the fields he usually 'cut the field out'. Every forty yards across the field ('a forty-yard rig') the head team-man would cut one furrow, then turn it back. He was then followed by a less skilled man with a three-horse and double-furrow plough, who took his line from him. When the gap between the rigs narrowed the head team-man would finish the work.[41]

The skill required of a team-man was considerable and was surrounded by mystique. Even in the 1820s there were old horseman who believed in and practised magic, mainly connected with the bones of the 'running toad'.[42] The younger generation were more sceptical. Jack Leeder, who started work in 1915, knew about the 'toad's bone' but 'didn't believe in it'. Nevertheless he did know recipes for making horses eat, making their coats shine and dealing with cuts.[43] Team-men were very close about this kind of knowledge. All those I talked to, even the young ones, were extremely wary. Few learnt from their fathers: Jack Leeder's grandfather was 'a great horseman . . . but most of the things that he knew died with him'.[44]

To return to the yearly cycle. As winter set in farm work gradually came to a stop. Starting at the bottom men were laid off, although this practice was dying out by the 1900s. Nevertheless, the *Labour Gazette* regularly noted that numbers of labourers were out of work in Norfolk parishes.[45] Team-men and cowmen were seldom laid off in winter—their skills were too valuable:

> some of the labourers was laid off, but see that's where you got the benefit of it if you was team-man or yardman you got your full time in. But if you got a

lot of bad weather, labouring chaps, they used to send them home.[46]

The period of laying off depended crucially on the state of the weather. In a really bad winter, for instance that of 1911–12, men could still be out of work at the end of March, having suffered three or even four months of unemployment. However, in most years farm work started up again soon after Christmas. Ploughing continued and drilling of spring wheat started as soon as possible. There was also threshing, although this was most usually done by travelling gangs hired by the threshing contractor. The men who worked the threshing tackle were a separate breed, men who for various reasons could not get or did not want a regular job. It was often the resort of a man dismissed for trade union activity, like Billy Dixon, who was sacked after leading a strike in a wood yard. He spent a year as 'second corn' on Bullimore's 'chining' crew from Bacton.[47] Another group who went threshing were fishermen. The enginemen often had experience of steam engines from the drifters, and many crew men 'did a couple of days threshing' in January and February when there was no fishing.[48] Threshing also provided work for the few true casuals as well as frozen-out farm workers.

In the middle of March, as the weather improved and the days grew longer, the workforce went on to summer time. The date of the change and the actual hours varied considerably. In Paston men went on to fifty-four hours on 1 March and wages went up by a shilling a week.[49] In Trunch they went on to sixty hours on 21 March for an extra shilling. Labourers worked all round the clock but team-men usually went two journeys, six in the morning until eleven, and one-thirty until six-thirty. The single journey was six until four.[50]

Also by March drilling was under way. This again was highly skilled work. If a man's ability could be judged by a straight furrow it could just as well be judged by the rows of green shoots as the corn came up. On a Sunday it was a favourite pastime of team-men and labourers alike to walk around the parish and those nearby, gaining 'traveller' status and thus able to drink, but also examining the ploughing of their peers. A phrase like 'it looks as though a lot of bloody old chicken have been in there' could easily lead to a fight in a strange pub.[51] Drilling was usually done with a three-horse team, harnessed in a row, and led by a boy to get the accuracy needed.[52] Drilling followed a strict pattern. In many areas wheat went in in October if the weather was fair, though this was by no means universal. Then in February the rest of the wheat went in, then oats, then barley; in April, May or even June the roots were drilled.

Between the end of drilling and the beginning of haysel (hay harvest) there was a period of slack:

> By the time you got your turnips and mangolds in there'd be quite a spell then, that'd be perhaps the slackest time on the farm. Then you'd do repairs and weeding of corn. There was a lot of dock digging them days and cutting thistles.[53]

At this time women and children appeared in the fields, weeding and picking stones. Stone-picking was paid by the piece—a penny a bushel[54]—as was weeding. As the roots came up they were thinned and hoed. This was done by the piece, usually by men working in gangs, the price negotiated by the head labourer, still called the 'lord' in some areas.[55]

At the beginning of June, again depending on the weather, haysel began. The hay crop was vital to the horse economy, and because of weather its gathering was fraught with some of the tensions which were so much a part of the later cereal harvest. For much of the century hay was cut by scythe, but by the 1900s mechanical mowers were becoming common. The haysel was perhaps the hardest of all harvests. Once the hay was cut it lay in the fields to dry, as the stacking of green hay could easily lead to spontaneous combustion. While in the fields the hay had to be turned by hand every couple of days, then raked into cocks and eventually loaded and stacked. There was seldom any extra payment for haysel and the men very rarely worked in gangs or by the piece. All this produces very different memories of haysel than the pictures evoked by the idyllic writings of many contemporaries. To the labourer the turning, raking, cocking and loading in the heat of June, without the compensation of the extra money earned at harvest, was drudgery.[56]

Between haysel and cereal harvest there was another slight lull. In this hedges were cut, weeding of corn continued, and the fields were brushed. This was the laying of thorn bushes across the cut fields to stop poachers long-netting rabbits on them.[57] Then in mid-August cereal harvest began. As the corn yellowed the men would begin harvest bargaining. With the head team-man speaking for the horsemen, and the lord for the labourers, the rate for harvest was fixed on each farm. All watched their neighbours, as the first to agree usually set the price for the whole area, and even within a county there would be considerable variation.[58] When the price was fixed the men 'had a day hanging their scythes' at the blacksmiths. This involved sharpening and getting them set at the right angle in the shaft. Hanging was usually accompanied by drinking, with part of the cost borne by the farmer.[59]

The following day harvest began. Through the nineteenth century changes in technology can be observed—the change from the sickle to the bagging hook and scythe, and from the scythe to some form of mechanical reaper. Until well into the second half of the century the scythe predominated. Working in gangs of about twenty, the men cut in staggered line across the standing corn, taking their timing from the lord who stood at the head of the line: they stopped as he stopped and started as he started. Behind them a row of women scooped the corn into armfuls (sheaves or shooves) and tied them with bands of straw. In the stifling summer heat it was backbreaking work, but had a dignity and power about it that fixed this part of the labourers' work in the minds of those who saw it in its final years. One old man who had helped take the harvest with a scythe said: 'They were men in them days real men . . . they seemed more happy at work, they were continually whistling and singing. That's something I'm glad I've been able to be mixed up with, those old times. . . .'[60]

By the mid-1890s the sight of a gang of mowers strung out across a field was becoming rare. Although a man still 'mowed round the edges' to clear a path for the mechanical reaper, the gang was gone. In its place the windmill-like blades of the sail reaper, and then the less poetic drum of blades of the reaper-binder, cut their way through the corn.

In the weeks of the cereal harvest the men battled against the weather. While it held they worked fifteen or sixteen hours a day. Rain would not only ruin the crop but crucially delay work. Since harvest was paid by the piece this could be disastrous. As one labourer said: 'The season ruled all, if you got a wet time you'd be about eight weeks, and your harvest [wage] was five pounds . . . and they were in debt [and] they'd drawn all their money . . . before they'd got half the corn in. . . .'[61] But harvest did not end with the cutting of the corn. It was shooved, and when dry carted and stacked. Stacking was a skilled job. Wrong stacking or stacking too early could lead to rotting or burning. Crucially, it had to be thatched. Sometimes this was done by the head team-man, if he had the skill, more commonly by a local thatcher.[62]

When harvest ended there was a period of respite. The farmers would often go to sales while the men took their traditional harvest holiday. In the middle of the century, and up to the 1900s in some areas, they would 'cry largesse', visiting the market town and collecting pence from the tradesmen who dealt with their masters.[63] Later it was a trip by train to the county town or the sea to buy boots and clothes with the harvest earnings.[64] In some areas it was the start of the fair season. By the 1870s labourers flocked in their thousands by excursion train to fairs like Saint Giles in Oxford.[65] And then, after a brief glimpse of pleasure, the yearly round began again with moving place, ploughing fleet and the bitter cold of the root harvest.

IV

In sheep country, like Sussex, the pattern of seasonal work centred round the flock and took on a different rhythm, though few farms produced sheep alone and so the basic pattern of cereal production was still present. In the autumn in Hampshire sheep were turned out on to the stubble or folded with rape and turnips; in Sussex they went out on the downs.[66] Lambing, the shepherd's harvest, was between January and March, depending on the area and the mildness of the weather. During this time the shepherd lived out in the fields in a wheeled shepherd's hut, alone, except for his pages, for weeks on end. After lambing the shepherd had a period of ease: 'as a general rule, save for lambing and other busy times, a shepherd reckoned to finish his actual laborious work by dinner time. After that he studied your sheep.'[67] Dipping and shearing were in June: 'June was one of the busiest months in the sheep farmer's year. It brought none of the anxieties of lambing time, but in terms of sheer hard work, it stood out from all the other.'[68] A. G. Street summed it up well when he wrote:

> [Then] you will require swedes and kale for the flock. So your ploughs and harrows must follow them in May, June, and July as they feed on the rye, winter barley, and vetches, and then sow swedes and kale for winter. And so it went on, year after year, one continual hopeless striving to feed the